Management
Powertools

Pierre Mattheÿ

Harry Onsman

Management Powertools

A guide to 20 of the most
powerful management tools and
techniques ever invented

The **McGraw·Hill** Companies

Sydney New York San Francisco Auckland
Bangkok Bogotá Caracas Hong Kong
Kuala Lumpur Lisbon London Madrid
Mexico City Milan New Delhi San Juan
Seoul Singapore Taipei Toronto

Professional

Text © 2004 Harry Onsman
Illustrations and design © 2004 McGraw-Hill Australia Pty Ltd
Additional owners of copyright are named in on-page credits.

National Library of Australia Cataloguing-in-Publication data:

Onsman, Harry

Management powertools.
Includes index.

ISBN 0 074 71345 0.

1.Management. I. Title.

658

Published in Australia by
McGraw-Hill Australia Pty Ltd
Level 2, 82 Waterloo Road, North Ryde NSW 2113
Acquisitions Editor: Javier Dopico
Production Editor: Sybil Kesteven
Editor: Sharon Nevile
Permissions editor: Jill Roebuck
Proofreader: Penny Galloway
Indexer: Diane Harriman
Designer (cover and interior): Jan Schmoeger/Designpoint
Illustrator: Alan Laver
Cover images: gettyimages, Jan Schmoeger/Designpoint
Typeset in 10/12 pt Stone Serif by Jan Schmoeger/Designpoint
Printed on 70 gsm bulky woodfree by Pantech Limited, Hong Kong.

Contents

About the author

Harry Onsman is a management consultant and writer. His previous books are *The uncertain art of management* (McGraw-Hill, 2002) and *Taking control of training* (ABC Books, 1989). He has written extensively for management publications such as *Business Review Weekly, Management Today* and *AFR Boss* magazine.

He is the Managing Director of The Management Tools Company, publisher of 'The Tool Kit for Managers'. This unique management information service provides subscribers with access to the latest management tools and techniques. Drawing on the very best research material published around the world, this service delivers powerful new management tools directly to subscribers via email.

The service provides:

- a new management tool or technique based on the latest research, delivered each week by email
- access to a searchable database of hundreds of management tools
- access to archives of summaries of important management articles.

The service can be found at www.tkfm.com

Preface

Management is an art, not a science. It involves a great deal of uncertainty, ambiguity and guesswork. But over time this art form has developed a range of tools that can be deployed to guide and smooth the work of management practitioners. These tools are known and proven approaches to management issues and they will generate sound results. I call them *management powertools*. Many of these powertools still require a degree of judgment and at times a strong intuitive element to make them work to maximum effect. But they are the true 'tools of the trade' for management.

If management has seen any real development over the last quarter of a century, it has been the codification of some of these better-known techniques and tools to the point where they are (or should be) a standard part of any manager's toolbox. In that same timeframe, the theory of management has not made much progress. It may well be that we will never develop theory of the type that is useful in driving progress in the sciences. Maybe that standard is simply not relevant to the practice of management. In any case, I suspect that it is a debate that is not very relevant to managers as they go about their daily routines.

What truly matters in management is the dissemination of good ideas. In this book, I have tried to describe some of the best tools and techniques that have emerged in the field of management in recent years. Some of these have been developed by researchers and academics; others have simply evolved through use over time by practitioners. Some are associated with particular individuals; others are the result of a collaborative effort. All of them make life easier for managers.

Of course, for every classic tool, there are dozens of versions to be found in industry. Those great disseminators of management ideas—management consultants—not only drive the dispersal of ideas but they also modify, improve, re-invent and trademark those same ideas. The differences between the various versions rarely matter, except to those with a pecuniary interest in brand issues. If you prefer an alternative version, then use that one. If you have not previously used the tools described in this book, then the versions offered here at least have stood the test of time in my own consulting practice.

The versions in this book are the most generic I could find. But regardless of the version, what matters is that the tools and the ideas behind them are being used, because doing so will help to create more productive organisations. The particular selection included in this book is entirely my own choice. Other tools and techniques could have been included and some may argue should have been included. I like these ones for their impact and effectiveness.

For each tool, I have tried to explain a little of its background and development over time. The tool itself is then described in some detail. I also provide some personal commentary about the tool—this section affords me the opportunity to state my reservations and hesitations. Next, I provide some advice to the user on how to apply the tool. Finally, each chapter closes with some suggestions for further reading.

I have tried to include as much research evidence as I could find for the effectiveness of each tool. In some cases, that evidence is a little thin on the ground; in other cases, there is a rich research base on which to draw. The research often shows that what is accepted wisdom in management circles is not always backed by empirical research, and is sometimes contradicted by them. Most importantly, managers should beware of the prescription sellers—those with a commercial interest in advocating one approach or another. Snake oil is snake oil, no matter if the seller is an MBA-carrying certified consultant or a retired senior executive now treading the boards on the speaker circuit.

Management powertools can simplify the life of any manager. As an occupation, management no longer has quite the same reputation that it had a generation or two ago. Bitingly incisive Dilbert cartoons, near-daily business scandals and unflattering television programs have done little to create a positive image for management. Yet we are still reliant on managers to keep the business world going. For all us of involved in the task of management, we may as well use the best tools we can find to be as effective as possible.

HARRY ONSMAN
July 2003

Acknowledgments

In addition to all the researchers I have credited with specific references, there are a host of ideas in this book that I have accumulated over the years from sources now long forgotten. To all of those involved, my thanks and a promise to provide credit where it is due if the opportunity presents itself in the future.

It is inevitable that there is some overlap between management books, including the ones I have written. Specifically, a few ideas discussed in this book have also been discussed in *The uncertain art of management*. My thanks to the co-publishers, the Australian Institute of Management and McGraw-Hill, for tolerating any overlap.

Most of the chapters in this book have benefited from being read and reviewed by various colleagues and friends. They made many suggestions that have improved the book. Any remaining faults are purely my own responsibility.

My thanks to:

Peter Armstrong, Rob Barnett, Geoff Bird, Miriam Bass (double thank-you), Peter Chandler, Wal Chandler, John Crofts, Geoff Fitzpatrick, Graeme Holmes, John Kerr (double thankyou), Colin Pidd, Martin Schembri, Peter Robertson and Mark Whelan, as well as the teams at OnQ Business Systems and ACI-Glass Packaging.

Editing a book full of opinions and assertions is never an easy task, and my very special thanks are due to Robyn Coy who slaved away at improving the rough manuscripts I sent her and improved them immensely with her suggestions. Also thanks to Javier Dopico and his team at McGraw-Hill.

Finally, thanks to Nikki for tolerating the time it took to write this book when I should have been finishing the renovations on our house. I now have no excuse left but to return to the other kind of powertool.

Managing the organisation

CHAPTER 1

Strategic intent
Vision, mission and values statements

Organisations exist to do something—but what? As simple as that question sounds, it has preoccupied senior management ever since early capitalism spawned managerial capitalism. At a very general level, most managers know what their organisation is supposed to do: make profits; serve members; educate children; and so on. But at a more specific level, the purpose of an organisation can be less clear-cut. In recent years, this uncertainty has led to a call to define more clearly the purpose of an organisation—a need that can be summarised under the broad heading of 'strategic intent'.

But what is the best way to determine strategic intent? Probably the best known and most used tools are vision, mission and values statements. Although these statements are no longer as fashionable as they were 10 or 20 years ago, most organisations still seek to clarify their basic 'purpose in life'. The 2001 Bain & Co survey of business leaders rated 'vision and mission statement' as the second most commonly used tool by organisations around the world.[1]

Vision, mission and values statements form part of a hierarchy of tools for determining strategic intent. Some writers describe this hierarchy as:

1. a broad *vision* of what the organisation wants to be
2. a more specific *mission* and set of *values*
3. specific goals
4. specific objectives.[2]

The idea is that each step in the hierarchy addresses a specific need for the organisation; each level informs the level below it and supports the level above it.

Mission statements were the first attempt to sum up *what an organisation is in business for*. They have been around since military graduates started to join commercial organisations in key roles after World War Two, bringing military terminology with them. Descriptions of various kinds emerged that tried to capture the essence of the organisation (its mission), presumably from a desire to bring some clarity to the task of explaining what an organisation was all about.

Vision statements followed in the 1980s, arising from new ways of looking at leadership that emerged at about that time. The thought was that leadership at the top was a key element for corporate success, and part of leadership involved the leader having a vision of where he or she would take the organisation.[3] The vision statement was different from the more descriptive mission statement. It was shorter, pithier and aspirational, and intended to be uplifting or worthy.

At about the same time, managers were urged to examine the 'culture' of their organisations. Typically this was part of 'the search for excellence' (which was, of course, the title of the highly influential and best-selling business book by Peters and Waterman, published in 1982[4]). It seemed that culture would make the difference between excellence and mediocrity. And culture was based on the *shared values* of those within the organisation. *Values statements* were an attempt to mould those shared values and steer them in a desired direction.

All of these statements share the characteristic that they are an effort by management to create *alignment*. (Alignment is about creating a situation where everyone sings from the same songbook. The theory is that this will help create unity of purpose and effort. It works for choirs so maybe it will work for organisations.) With that application in mind, these statements remain practical and useful tools that will help direct and focus organisational effort.

Background

There is considerable confusion about the exact difference between a vision statement and a mission statement, and the connection of either to a values statement. This is understandable since these terms refer to fairly similar concepts. Furthermore, it was never intended that the concepts would be defined in specific, technical ways. This linguistic and conceptual confusion stands in the way of a clear understanding of the purpose of these tools, and it certainly encourages pedantic discussions about which is the best to use at any one time. All of this is exacerbated when even more descriptions and terms, such as 'purpose statements' and 'statements of principle', are introduced into the debate.

Essentially, it doesn't matter what we call these things. What matters is whether they work or not. In fact, some of the better examples of the genre are not called by these traditional descriptions. 'The HP Way' (Hewlett-Packard) and the 'Johnson Credo' (Johnson & Johnson) are frequently cited as classic examples of statements that do have meaning and value, and yet they have their own unique tags.

However, it does help to keep in mind some broad differences between mission and vision. For example, the Disney Company's mission is 'to make people happy'; its vision is 'to become the leading entertainment company in the world'. The first is about what the company is there to do; the second is about what the company hopes to become.

By reviewing the different mission and vision statements of many organisations[5], it becomes apparent that the key elements of a mission statement are:

- It describes an organisation's long-term *intentions* (as opposed to shorter term statements about strategy or action).
- It tries to capture something about the *unique way* in which the organisation will *realise* its intentions.
- It specifies a *scope of operations* in terms of what the organisations does (products/services) and who it delivers these to (customers).

Sometimes, these and other elements are used to structure the mission statement. For example, one structure is:

1. a statement of purpose—why the organisation exists
2. a statement of principles—what the organisation believes in
3. a statement of behaviours—what is expected from people
4. a statement of strategy—how the organisation will succeed in the marketplace.[6]

Another popular structure for a mission statement is based on the answers to four questions:

1. *What* functions will the organisation perform?
2. *For whom* does it perform these functions?
3. *How* does it fulfill these functions?
4. *Why* does it exist? [7]

This 'what/for whom/how/why' framework has an appealing simplicity that hides some complex issues. For example, by asking the 'what' question often enough, people in organisations sometimes realise that the business they thought they were in was not the business they are actually in. An illustration of this is provided by former Avis CEO, Robert Townsend, in his book *Up the organisation*, where he describes how he realised that the Avis car rental company's primary business was not car rental, but rather producing second-hand cars.[8] This realisation led to significant changes in how the company operated, such as opening its own used-car sales division and buying low-maintenance new cars.

Clearly, mission statements can become quite lengthy, and this was possibly the motivation for the emergence of vision statements. The second structure above hints at the vision statement in its fourth point: Why does the organisation exist?

Vision statements are closely linked to visionary leadership and what Henry Mintzberg has described as the 'Entrepreneurial School of Strategic Planning'.[9] The outstanding characteristic of a vision statement is that it aims to be *inspirational*. Warren Bennis suggested that: 'if it is really a vision, you'll never forget it'.[10] So, the vision statement shouldn't be a long and wordy description (which possibly rules out many of the statements that are frequently seen in company foyers!).

My personal favourite is a vision statement that immediately makes everyone realise which company it comes from and what that company aims to do: 'Beat Coke!' I doubt if any other corporate statement conveys so much in just two words. Its power is such that it is unnecessary to explain that the statement comes from Pepsi.

There are many other examples in business literature that demonstrate the power of an inspiring vision. In many cases, they are linked to the stories of great business founders and business builders. Time and again, we can observe examples of a simple idea made powerful by the inspirational qualities of the leader advocating the idea. Organisations—even business empires—are built in this way. But what all these cases have in common is that they are dependent on a single individual. Such *visionary leadership* cannot be mandated, purchased by means of an MBA or (in many cases at least) sustained after the founder has gone.

Some organisations do not actually need vision or mission statements because their uniting vision is so obvious that a formal statement is not required. Often, these are volunteer organisations. That is, organisations where the employees join because they really want to work there. Many examples can be found in the not-for-profit sector (the Red Cross; Oxfam; Amnesty International), but the concept of 'volunteer' goes beyond the 'doing good works' type of organisation. Some for-profit organisations are staffed by people who have such a strong *shared vision* and ethic that formal statements are not necessary. Organisations such as Virgin and Southwest Airlines seem to have both visionary leaders and a truly shared vision. Typically, the shared vision within these organisations is strongly supported by, and sometimes founded on, *shared values*.

Traditionally, shared values have been treated as part of organisational culture (a set of principles that are understood by all and that guide the behaviour of the people in an organisation). Sometimes, these values have been formalised and exist in written form. The resulting *values statement* can have a powerful impact in aligning people behind common standards of behaviour. Possibly the first values statement was the Bible's ten commandments. In fact, many values statements actually follow that 'commandment' format in describing what is and what is not acceptable behaviour.

Once managers began to realise that culture was a major organisa-tional force, the next step was obvious. Managers wanted to change the culture to align it more closely with the organisation's strategic objectives. Values statements developed as a tool for changing culture. By stating the preferred way of working espoused by the organisation, managers hoped that this would become the actual way of working.

Reality turned out to be a bit harder. Most values statements languished as ideals that lived out their life only in a frame hanging in the office foyer. Such framed statements were often mandated by the CEO, presumably in the misguided hope that a simple announcement would actually change their organisational world.

Nevertheless, a statement about what the organisation aspires to in terms of how it does what it does can play a useful role. For example, it can provide a final reference point for what constitutes acceptable ways of working, or provide guidance for various corporate policies. Values statements need not be confined to the corporate foyer.

The tools

Mission statement

The 'what/for whom/how' framework is one practical approach in developing a mission statement. It provides a three-step guide for what needs to be covered. (The fourth step of 'why' seems to belong more properly to the vision statement.) It works best if it is cast in the future tense and uses inclusive language; that is, each component should start with 'We will...' or some derivative of that.

Statements about what the organisation will *be* or will *become* ('We will become the number one choice supplier in our chosen market segments') are best left to the vision statement. Similarly, statements about how the people in the organisation will work together ('We will achieve this by using teamwork in all aspects of our work') should be left to the values statement.

What?

What functions will the organisation perform? This is about defining what customer needs the organisation is attempting to meet. Note that this is not the same as simply listing the services or products that the organisation is delivering. The difference can be critical in limiting the perspective of the organisation. 'Making packaging materials' is very different from 'Delivering packaging solutions'.

However, it is possible to make the statement too broad. A former CEO of United Airlines lost his job when he tried to take the airline into the car rental and hotel business. He failed to convince others that the expansion of 'airline industry' into 'transport and hospitality industry' was workable. Usually, a solid debate within the organisation can establish the right frame. Over time, it should be tested for relevance. For example, for centuries it would have been adequate for libraries to have mission statements referring to books. Today, such references would seem inadequate and the words in the mission statement would be about 'providing access to information'. In an era of lessening dependence on oil, oil companies may see the need to reinvent themselves as 'energy companies'; however, they may push the focus too far if they think of themselves as 'resources companies'.

For whom?

For whom does the organisation perform these functions? This involves defining the customers of the organisation. This is always a segment of a market, as no organisations can truly service a global market (although someone may have forgotten to tell Bill Gates this). There are many ways to segment a market: by demographics, psychographics, geography and a host of others, including multiple factors. But unless the segment provides a clear focus on who is being serviced, then it becomes almost impossible to define their needs (see 'What?' on page 7).

How?

How does it fulfil these functions? What are the methods that will be used to meet the needs of the selected customer segment? This describes the substance of the service or the products that are being delivered. It may involve matters of strategy (for example, lowest-cost producer or most innovative products or highest quality); service delivery (for example, Internet-based delivery or shopfront retail); technology or expertise (for example, glass container manufacturer or legal services firm); or many other distinctions. As long as it clarifies how customer needs are being met, and the people within the organisation understand what that is, then it will work.

The risk is that the 'how' becomes a marketing slogan. Marketing slogans are for external use, a way to communicate with customers. Mission statements are for internal consumption, a way to engage employees and other stakeholders. Applying marketing techniques (especially marketing hype) to the mission statement usually creates a statement that is instantly dismissed by the employees as just that: hype.

Vision statement

In many ways, vision statements answer the fourth mission statement question ('why?') because they relate to the reason the organisation exists. At the same time, they are intended to convey what the organisation *aspires to be*. If that goal seems worthwhile to others, it may then inspire them and motivate them to contribute to achieving the goal.

In *Built to last*, Collins and Porras argue that the vision (along with the values) should be the unchangeable part of the organisation; its core essence that must be preserved for the organisation to continue to exist.[11] They suggest that the vision has two parts:

1. the *core ideology*, combining core values with a core purpose (the reason why the organisation exists)
2. an *envisioned future*, combining a broad long-term goal with a vivid description of what it will be like when that goal is achieved.

Collins and Porras argue that, for this approach to be successful, *the vision must be a lasting goal*. It must be something that cannot be realised in 100 years, or may never be realised. This enduring characteristic is what gives the vision its power—strategies come and go but the vision endures. They also argue that *the vision must be worthwhile*. It must be sufficiently important to make people want to contribute to bringing it about. That means that, typically, it is less about 'becoming the most profitable company in the packaging industry' and more about 'saving the planet'. This type of powerful vision cannot be invented; it can only be discovered within the organisation.

Values statement

Values statements are closely linked to vision statements (and also to mission statements for that matter) but differ by placing a specific focus on behaviour. *A value is a belief in action*. It can only be deduced by observing people's behaviour; it is the behaviour that demonstrates the values.

This creates a risk for some organisations. As they seek to espouse certain values in the form of an explicit statement, it becomes easy for employees to compare what is espoused with what is actually acted out. If managers in an organisation with an espoused value such as 'support each other' actually engage in behaviour that contradicts that value, then employees will quickly draw their own conclusions about the 'real' values that are in place. This is likely to lead to a decline in trust and an increase in cynicism.

In creating values statements, then, organisations must take great care. These statements cannot be aspirational (like a vision statement); instead, they must be thoroughly realistic. It is also best to consider the implications of adopting this management tool. For example, a CEO may have to state publicly that management does not always adhere to the espoused values and that when this happens, employees should remind management of the gap.

Whenever an organisational issue revolves around behaviour, it is dangerous to rely only on your own assessment, because what we think we do and what we actually do are typically quite different things. The challenge here is usually summed up as 'walking the talk'.[12]

Assuming that organisations and managers are up to handling this challenge, there is no doubt that a vibrant values statement can help to resolve otherwise complex issues in many ways. Values statements can help by:

- guiding management's thinking on courses of action
- defining acceptable standards of behaviour
- creating commonly used rules for how people and teams work
- resolving conflict between people and between functions
- creating closer links with customers and suppliers
- making the organisation a desirable place to work.

An illustration of a values statement in action occurred in 1982, with the poisoned Tylenol scare (pharmaceutical giant Johnson & Johnson faced a blackmail threat that involved placing poisoned packets of the analgesic on supermarket shelves). When the threat became known, Johnson & Johnson managers took immediate action to withdraw from sale and destroy 31 million capsules. This was entirely driven by the espoused value of Johnson & Johnson that 'customers come first'. Hiding the threat because of the potential impact on profits was not even considered as an option by management.

On a similar note, the Australian airline Qantas will delay a plane's departure for even the smallest safety concern. Usually such delays are explained to passengers, most of whom are very aware that at Qantas 'safety comes first'. Certainly, the staff act out that value. Given the airline's exceptional profitability and exceptional safety record, it has turned out not to harm business in any way and has possibly boosted it.

There is little practical guidance on how to write or structure a values statement. Tom Kenny suggests that the process of writing a values statement involves moving:

- from implicit to explicit statements
- from vague and abstract to specific and concrete
- from not agreed to agreed
- from not shared to shared
- from subjective and biased to objective and standardised
- from talked-about to acted-upon.[13]

Each one of these steps addresses a critical flaw in most value statements. Kenny's rules-of-thumb clarify what an organisation needs to do to turn its values statement into something that actually benefits the organisation.

But is a given value a core or true value? One test is to ask: 'If the organisation were to be penalised for holding this value, would we still keep it?' If the answer is 'no', then it is not a true value of the organisation. Sometimes organisations are afraid to leave out a value in case it looks 'wrong' to do so. Collins and Porras provide an interesting list of organisations and the values they do *not* subscribe to:

- Sony: customer service
- Disney: respect for the individual
- Wal-Mart: quality
- Hewlett-Packard: market responsiveness
- Nordstrom: teamwork.[14]

The point here is that although organisations might aspire to a wide range of practices and principles, its list of true, core values is likely to be very short. Not every conceivable value can be core!

Observations

These days, most people don't get too excited about vision, mission and values statements—they are seen as 'part of the furniture'. However, they remain useful tools, especially in situations of significant organisational change. They can provide the bedrock that reassures people in the organisation that they still know what the organisation is all about.

Possibly, the visionary leadership approach is best suited to start-up organisations where a high degree of enthusiasm and 'volunteerism' is needed. Such organisations have yet to develop routine and prescribed ways of working. For such organisations, the vision can provide the unifying force.

The following criticisms have been made of visionary leadership. They have been summed up as the 'heart attack' problem—if the leader dies, so does the vision:

- Forming a vision is not a useful response when the future is unknowable.
- Visions can create such a narrow focus that managers miss what is really happening in their industry.
- Visionary leadership is untenable, in that it places too heavy a burden on a few people (maybe one person) and absolves all others from responsibility for direction setting.[15]

For more mature organisations, it seems that a more appropriate approach may be to think in terms of building a *shared vision*. Although this may not be as exciting as visionary-based leadership, it can still have a significant impact. Unfortunately, it is much harder to create a shared vision (you have to involve people, and you have to get agreement and buy-in) but it can help pull organisations together in a way that few other mechanisms can.

Evidence is now starting to emerge that vision and mission statements do impact on organisational performance, including financial performance, providing that the process of developing these statements is done well.[16] What remains a bit of a mystery is just *how* they impact on people in organisations. Where does their power come from? One suggestion by Eugen Tarnow is that vision and mission statements work by triggering the mechanism that is called 'social categorisation'.[17] This mechanism helps the formation of groups by enabling the group to coalesce around a common thing. In one famous experiment, simply giving a group of small boys a bright orange jersey to wear—setting them apart from all others—was enough to induce a sense of team spirit that led to improved sports performance! Similarly, a mission statement channels the forces of group formation towards a common objective.

Based on the logic of social categorisation, vision and mission statements are most effective if they:

- suggest action towards a distant goal
- only vaguely identify the action
- use inclusive language and descriptions that help create a group.

Using this approach, Tarnow has rewritten a number of actual statements from organisations in a format based on social categorisation principles. 'Lead in providing applications to the construction industry around the world' becomes 'We provide the world's builders'. And 'Be the recognised leader in national security space system engineering' becomes 'We secure space'.

In any case, it seems that the process of constructing any of the three types of statements can be more important than the resulting words. In the words of John Mullane:

> The usefulness of [such statements] is found in the development and implementation processes, not the final product. Managers who understand this will look for benefits of ... statements that indirectly affect the bottom line, rather than focusing on the tangible value of a mission. ... Managers should not ask what their mission statement is doing for them, but what they can do to properly use this very valuable strategic tool.[18]

User's guide

Typically, the development of vision, mission and values statements is a collective task. Often it is the management team that undertakes this task, but that is not always the case. In fact, the development of these statements is actually the first opportunity to build support for them by involving a larger group drawn from all levels of the organisation.

Given that it is likely to be a group process, it usually works better if someone is appointed to act in the role of facilitator. Because the group will be discussing contentious issues and deeply felt matters, it is critical that someone steps away from the content of that discussion to ensure that the discussion itself is productive. An external facilitator can also be used for the same reason.

Instructions

How to develop a mission statement[19]

1. *Decide on the people who should be involved in developing the mission statement.*

   Typically, this will be the senior management team, but it may well include people from other parts of the organisation.

2. *Ask the group to describe the purpose of the organisation.*
   - Capture some of the responses on a whiteboard or a flipchart.
   - Make sure input is obtained from all participants.
   - Review what has been suggested and discuss the issues that arise from the various descriptions.

3. *When the first round is complete, ask: 'Why is this important?' or 'Why does this matter?'*
   - Repeat the question until people start to talk about the things that *really* matter. Make sure their observations are recorded.

4. *Ask the group to reflect on their recorded observations.*
   - Help point out similarities and connections. Edit out repeats, redundancies and overlaps, with their agreement. Rephrase the words to remove ambiguity and uncertainty.
   - Try to reach consensus even if this is only 'working agreement' to enable the group to progress.

5. *Ask the group: 'What would be lost if this organisation ceased to exist?'*
   - Add more layers of detail to their recorded observations based on the meaning of their contribution. Sometimes this will overlap with the core values of the organisation. Re-write as necessary.
   - Arrange to have the final material made available to all those involved and re-convene the group some days or weeks later to finalise the words.

How to develop a vision statement

Follow a similar procedure as that for the mission statement. Remind participants of the differences between the two without getting into arguments about precise definitions. The vision statement will be shorter than the mission statement and is therefore a bit harder to write. Make sure it is inclusive; tolerate vagueness about the actions involved (it helps); and make the ultimate goal distant and difficult to achieve.

How to develop a values statement

Again, use a similar procedure as that for the mission statement, but in addition try to focus on the core values that are *currently* being acted on within the organisation. Find examples that describe what is and what is not tolerated by the organisation. Get people to tell stories about what has happened in the past about others' behaviour.

One of the risks that managers run with this part of the process is that some heartfelt stuff will come out in these discussions. You need to decide how you will deal with widely varying opinions on the values that the organisation actually lives out. It can be confronting, especially if your organisation is based on values that many people in it find repulsive! Be prepared to deal with such issues. One way is to make the values statement a little more aspirational; that is, admit that there are shortcomings and that the development of a values statement is an important opportunity to focus on getting things right.

If all this is to work well, it is important to get the right people into the group that works on the values statement. The participants need to be those who can best articulate the essence of the organisation.

Further reading

A number of recent articles elaborate on the debate about how best to articulate the strategic intent of an organisation. The most interesting ones in my view are:

- A Brache & M Freedman, 'Is our vision any good?', *Journal of Business Strategy*, vol. 20, issue 2, 1999, pp. 10–13.
- J Porras & C Collins, 'Building your company's vision', *Harvard Business Review*, Sept–Oct 1996, pp. 65–77.
- M Raynor, 'That vision thing: do we need it?', *Long Range Planning*, June 1998, pp. 368–76.

Notes

1. See the Bain & Co web site at http://www.bain.com/bainweb/expertise/overview.asp: 70% of respondents used this tool, second only to strategic planning (77%). These figures are identical to those of the 1999 survey.
2. A Miller & G Dress, *Strategic management*, McGraw-Hill, New York, 1996.
3. It has been suggested that Bennis and Nanus first raised the idea of vision statements, as opposed to mission statements. See W Bennis & B Nanus, *Leaders: The strategies for taking charge*, Harper & Row, New York, 1985.
4. T Peters & R Waterman, *In search of excellence*, Harper & Row, New York, 1984.
5. For example, see G Hooley, A Cox & A Adams, 'Our five year mission', *Journal of Marketing Management*, vol. 8, no. 1, 1992, pp. 35–48.

6. This is loosely based on A Campbell, M. Devine & D Young, 'A sense of mission', *The Economist Books*, Hutchinson, London, 1990.
7. The version presented here is based on L Goodstein, T Nolan & W Pfeiffer, *Applied strategic planning*, Pfeiffer & Co, San Diego, 1992.
8. R Townsend, *Up the organisation*, Fawcett Books, New York, 1984.
9. H Mintzberg, *Safari strategy*, The Free Press, New York, 1998.
10. W Bennis, op. cit.
11. J Collins & J Porras, *Built to last*, Random House, London, 1998.
12. For a more theoretical approach to the same issue, see C Argyris, *Organisational learning II*, Addison-Wesley, Reading, 1996; especially the material on theory-in-use and theory-in-action.
13. T Kenny, 'From vision to reality through values', *Management Development Review*, vol. 7, no. 3, 1994, pp. 17–20.
14. J Collins & J Porras, op. cit., p. 222.
15. R Stacey, *Managing chaos: Dynamic business strategies in an unpredictable world*, Kogan-Paul, London, 1992.
16. For example, see C Bart et al., 'A model of the impact of mission statements on firm performance', *Management Decision*, vol. 39, no. 1, 2001, pp. 19–35.
17. E Tarnow, 'A recipe for mission and vision statements', *Journal of Marketing Practice*, vol. 3, no. 3, 1997, pp. 184–9.
18. J Mullane, 'The mission statement is a strategic tool when used properly', *Management Decision*, vol. 40, no. 5, 2002, pp. 448–55.
19. Based in part on K Denton, 'Mission statements miss the point', *Leadership & Organisation Development Journal*, vol. 22, no. 7, 2001, pp. 309–14.

CHAPTER 2

Strategic positioning
Porter's Five Forces analysis and Generic Strategies

Strategy is what we turn to when making it up as we go along doesn't work any longer.[1] In the early days of the life cycle of an organisation, 'ad hoc' management of the direction of the company often works well. But when an organisation develops and matures (along with the industry in which it competes), better ways of steering the organisation are needed. This is the job of strategy.

All this now seems obvious, but it has only been so since Michael Porter came along to make it obvious. Porter wrote the book on strategy and has been the strategy supremo ever since. His rigorous analysis of strategic concepts turned a battlefield analogy into a management tool. Although some of his concepts may be argued about, most of his techniques have stood the test of time. They deliver results.

Background

Most managers talk about strategy. Just about everyone involved in business knows it is important to 'get your strategy right'. All of which sometimes makes us forget that strategy is a relatively recent arrival on the business stage, basically lifted in its entirety from that other great field of conflict, the battleground. For example, as late as the 1960s great writers on management, such as Alfred P Sloan (the man who created General Motors), could write on management without addressing the topic of strategy in any great detail.[2]

Michael Porter is generally and rightly credited with bringing the subject of strategy into fashion. He made strategy an indispensable topic for managers and his name has become synonymous with the field of strategic management. Michael Porter is a professor at Harvard University Business School and the author of 16 books and over 60 articles, most of them on strategy. His key book, *Competitive strategy: Techniques for analyzing industries and competitors*[3], was published in 1980 and its companion, *Competitive advantage: Creating and sustaining superior performance*[4], in 1985. The third book in the ground-breaking trilogy appeared in 1990, *The competitive advantage of nations.*[5]

Although the books are largely about developing a theory of strategy, this is definitely a case where there is nothing as practical as a good theory. The reason for this is that senior managers routinely make decisions that will determine the future of their organisations. Make a wrong strategic call and your organisation will be in trouble. At stake is supremacy in the marketplace, although for most organisations survival will do. Picking the right or wrong strategy will make or break the careers of even the most senior and respected figures in industry. CEOs do not get fired for having the wrong interpersonal skills; they get fired for getting the strategy wrong.

In the twenty-first century, Michael Porter's theories dominate the strategy-making processes used by most companies around the world. No other person amongst the array of consultants and academics has had such influence on how managers run their businesses. Porter's Five Forces model and the application of his Generic Strategies have become the standard way for senior managers to choose the markets in which they want to compete and decide what to offer the customers in those markets. The robustness and simplicity of the Five Forces model explains much of its popularity. Both models are truly classic management tools.

The Five Forces model is a tool for analysing an organisation's industry structure. The model is based on the critical insight that:

> Corporate strategy should meet the opportunities and threats that exist in the external environment.

Porter identified five competitive forces that shape every industry and every market. These are usually described as:

1. bargaining power of suppliers
2. bargaining power of customers
3. threat of new entrants
4. threat of substitutes
5. competitive rivalry between existing players.

These forces determine the intensity of competition and hence the profitability and, therefore, the attractiveness of a particular industry. The objective of corporate strategy should be to deal with these competitive forces in a way that improves the position of the organisation. So, Five Forces analysis can help an organisation decide how to respond to particular characteristics of its industry.

The Generic Strategies model is the second of Porter's industry modelling tools, dealing specifically with the position of an organisation relative to its competitors. It is about ensuring that, in any given industry, an organisation is more profitable than its competitors. It is *not* about selecting profitable industries, as it is quite possible for an organisation to compete in a structurally low-profit industry and yet make handsome profits year after year.

Porter argues that the key to such success is to have a 'sustainable competitive advantage'. By now, this phrase has entered the language of business but, unfortunately, it is often misunderstood. In Porter's model this phrase means specifically an advantage gained in relation to *cost of operations* or through *product differentiation*. These relate back to the Five Forces model in that both derive from how well an organisation manages the five competitive forces compared with its competitors.

Porter then adds one more element to the mix—the scope of the activities in which an organisation is engaged. By focusing either on a broad customer base or a much narrower segment of that market, organisations can create *strategic focus*.

Bringing these different ideas together, Porter offers three generic strategies for gaining competitive advantage:

- cost leadership
- product/service differentiation
- narrow market focus (of which there are two variants: cost focus or differentiation focus).

Porter argues that these three are the only strategy options that organisations have for achieving above-average profit performance. Although the actions taken to implement these three generic strategies will vary from industry to industry, they are the only options open to pursue competitive advantage. This suggests that strategy is about choosing one route over another, and that it as much about saying 'no' to some actions as it is about saying 'yes' to others.

The tools

Five Forces model

Porter provides a handy overview of the model for the five competitive forces in Figure 2.1: Elements of industry structure.

Each competitive force has a given strength in any industry at any one time. The elements that determine that strength are listed in the figure. By considering each of these elements, it is possible to calculate a relative strength for that force. In the first cut, an organisation might

---

Figure 2.1 (opposite) Elements of industry structure
Source: Reproduced with permission of The Free Press, a division of Simon & Schuster Adult Publishing Group, from *Competitive advantage: Creating and sustaining superior performance* by Michael E Porter. Copyright 1985, 1998 by Michael E Porter. All rights reserved

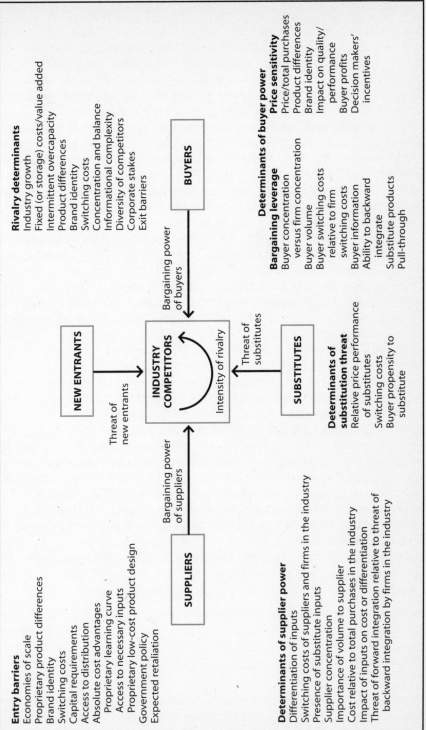

Entry barriers
Economies of scale
Proprietary product differences
Brand identity
Switching costs
Capital requirements
Access to distribution
Absolute cost advantages
  Proprietary learning curve
  Access to necessary inputs
  Proprietary low-cost product design
Government policy
Expected retaliation

Rivalry determinants
Industry growth
Fixed (or storage) costs/value added
Intermittent overcapacity
Product differences
Brand identity
Switching costs
Concentration and balance
Informational complexity
Diversity of competitors
Corporate stakes
Exit barriers

Determinants of buyer power

Bargaining leverage
Buyer concentration
  versus firm concentration
Buyer volume
Buyer switching costs
  relative to firm
  switching costs
Buyer information
Ability to backward
  integrate
Substitute products
Pull-through

Price sensitivity
Price/total purchases
Product differences
Brand identity
Impact on quality/
  performance
Buyer profits
Decision makers'
  incentives

Determinants of supplier power
Differentiation of inputs
Switching costs of suppliers and firms in the industry
Presence of substitute inputs
Supplier concentration
Importance of volume to supplier
Cost relative to total purchases in the industry
Impact of inputs on cost or differentiation
Threat of forward integration relative to threat of
  backward integration by firms in the industry

**Determinants of
substitution threat**
Relative price performance
of substitutes
Switching costs
Buyer propensity to
substitute

NEW ENTRANTS

SUPPLIERS

INDUSTRY
COMPETITORS

BUYERS

SUBSTITUTES

Bargaining power
of buyers

Threat of
new entrants

Intensity of rivalry

Bargaining power
of suppliers

Threat of
substitutes

use a ranking of High, Medium or Low. Subsequent and more data-driven judgments might use a more discriminating scale. Alternatively (often as part of an annual review of the industry), a simple rating of 'increasing' or 'decreasing' could be used. (It should be noted, however, that it is possible to over-analyse an industry by spending too much time simply to discover fine distinctions. Keep it simple!)

The *supplier* and *buyer* forces combine to represent the bargaining power of the various suppliers and buyers in an industry. They are vital to the profitability of an industry because they represent cost inputs at one end and profit margins at the other. For example, an industry in which input costs are high (because suppliers are able to charge high prices) and profit margins are low (because buyers negotiate low prices) is likely to be a low-profitability industry.

The *new entrants* and *substitutes* are the threats that face an industry. They affect not just profitability but the viability of the industry. For example, if new entrants can enter the industry relatively easily because there are low barriers to entry then this will affect profitability (new entrants often sacrifice profit margins to gain market share). Likewise, if substitutes are easily available and are better or lower priced products, then the long-term viability of the industry is threatened. In such situations, existing operators tend to sacrifice margins in order to dissuade buyers from switching to the substitute products.

The *internal rivalry* of an industry (competitive rivalry between existing players, sometimes referred to as the level of competition) will also determine profitability. In an industry where rivalry is low, there is little pressure on organisations to provide better prices to their customers. This creates the temptation for organisations to band together to maintain prices. Many countries have legislation and enforcement mechanisms that make it illegal to collude in order to keep prices high. Yet price fixing scandals are never far from the headlines and, on a global scale, there are many instances of price maintenance. The Organisation of Petroleum Exporting Countries (OPEC) is one prominent example of a cartel that keeps oil prices high.

By adding all of the five forces together, it is possible to judge whether any given industry is inherently profitable. For example, an industry is likely to be very profitable if it has the following characteristics:

- many small and non-critical suppliers
- many buyers
- no threats of substitution
- high barriers to entry
- low rivalry.

One example of this is the pharmaceutical industry. Its raw materials (chemicals) are cheap and plentiful; buyers are counted in the millions, if not billions; patents and trademarks can keep a drug exclusive; and to develop alternatives takes a large amount of investment. Of course, rivalry is high, as a few large operators chase this very lucrative market. You can only be an exclusive supplier until your competitors bring out an alternative. But the gains involved are usually so great (think Viagra!) that it is worth the initial investment.

On the other hand, an industry is likely to be low-profit if it has the following characteristics:

- only a few large and powerful suppliers who keep prices high
- only a few large and powerful buyers who buy at low prices
- many alternatives to the product
- almost no barriers to entry
- intense competition within the industry amongst many operators.

An example of this is fresh vegetable farming, which fits almost all the characteristics. Most farmers are dependent on a few suppliers for such items as seed and fertiliser; they sell to a few supermarket chains that have considerable buying power. If prices are too high, end consumers may switch to alternative vegetables or even canned vegetables; almost anyone can start a vegetable farm; and the industry is typically highly diversified and competitive, with many operators.

The point of all this analysis is that if an organisation understands the state of competitive play in its industry, it can attempt to manipulate some of the five forces. In order to increase your organisation's profitability, you might try to:

- reduce the bargaining power of your suppliers (for example, by encouraging more suppliers to start up in the industry)
- reduce the bargaining power of your customers (for example, by locking in long-term contracts)
- prevent new entrants by increasing the cost of entry (for example, by making customers dependent on your proprietary technology)
- prevent customers switching to substitutes (for example, by increasing the costs of switching)
- reduce the level of rivalry (for example, by only chasing a particular market segment or through gaining geographic advantage).

Many organisations have been spectacularly successful at protecting their profitability by manipulating one or more of the five forces. Southwest Airlines reduced operating costs (driven by suppliers) by staying away from expensive airports and using cheaper regional hubs. Wal-Mart used geographic location in areas that could sustain only one operator to prevent other operators from competing with them. Microsoft has the world dependent on its proprietary software and switching to another PC operating system is not an option for most. Intel and AMD own the world of computer chips because it is effectively too expensive for anyone else to set up a competing operation.

However, any action taken by an organisation to enhance its position within its industry can also have an impact on the inherent profitability of that industry; that is, one competitor can effectively take actions that will undermine the whole of the industry. For example, when super-markets first introduced generic no-brand products, it seemed like a good idea. However, it also opened up an avenue for an operator to *exclusively* offer generic products on its shelves. Aldi is one of the world's largest and fastest growing supermarket chains; it only offers its own (and limited) range of generic products. It has consistently undermined margins in the grocery industry in every country that it has entered, while remaining very profitable itself.

Porter provides much more detail on every aspect of the Five Forces model in his book, *Competitive advantage*. Yet even a bare-bones outline of the model can inform a boardroom discussion about strategic directions. Simply by making a rough estimate of the relative strengths of each of the five forces, options for action become apparent. Such actions need to be explored for impact and effectiveness, but even at this 'guestimate' level of analysis, productive discussions will ensue.

Where organisations have the luxury of time and resources, much more detail can be added to the representation of an industry projected on to the Five Forces model. But even an effective first-level analysis will usually deliver significant benefits.

Expanding the Five Forces model

The Five Forces tool can play a support role in various planning activities including:

- *statistical analysis* of an industry or a marketplace (for example, in order to determine the attractiveness of an industry, in assessing the industry's profitability levels, and as an aid to making decisions about whether to enter, remain in or exit an industry)
- *dynamical analysis* (for example, analysing those factors that drive change in an industry—economic, social, demographic and techno-logical changes)
- *scenario analysis* (for example, by developing options and alternatives that may improve the competitive position of the organisation).

Technically speaking, the Five Forces model takes a microeconomic view of the world. To make sense of the world, it relies on factors such as supply and demand; complementary products and substitutes; the rela-tionship between volume of production and cost of production; and market structures like monopoly, oligopoly or perfect competition. Some will argue that this is a very limited view of the world in which business operates.

Of course, all models have limitations and Porter's models are no exception. Some practical additions to the model have been suggested to overcome a number of specific weaknesses. These include:

- *Introducing analysis that relates specifically to industry trends.* For example, in analysing the global airline industry, it can be assumed that there are over 100 competitors. However, it may also be worthwhile to examine how the industry has evolved over time and what is currently happening in the industry (for example, how many airlines are close to collapse or under takeover threat?). This additional data makes the Five Forces model much more dynamic.
- *Considering the role of government.* In many countries, interventions by government have a major impact in some industries. Legislation may well prevent a range of activities from happening, such as takeovers and mergers, that would otherwise be very likely. In any given analysis, it is usually worthwhile to consider the impact of government on the industry under consideration.
- *Considering the roles of buyer's buyers and supplier's suppliers.* Often, these additional players in the value chain impact on the competitive position of an organisation within an industry.
- *Dealing with industry turbulence.* Based on Ansoff's notion of 'levels of turbulence'[6], it seems like good advice to match your strategy to the level of turbulence that prevails in your industry. For example, if the level is high, with discontinuous change happening at unpredictable moments (what Ansoff calls 'a surpriseful environment'), then the organisation must have the capacity to deal with the inevitable surprises. That is, the organisation will need an appropriate strategy as well as organisational capabilities for dealing with the turbulence.

Generic Strategies model

The three generic strategies (cost leadership; product/service differentiation; narrow market focus) are strategic options for any organisation in any industry at a given point of time. Each has its own implications and must be matched to what an organisation is actually capable of achieving. It is not sufficient for a CEO to decide, and then announce, that the organisation will now pursue a strategy of cost leadership—the organisation must be capable of undertaking the strategy. That is why organisations analyse their strengths and weaknesses—it helps to test whether a selected strategy will actually work for it. (When combined with an analysis of the organisation's external operating environment, this is often referred to as a 'SWOT Analysis' of strengths, weaknesses, opportunities and threats). Such analyses are essentially 'reality checks'.

So, each of the three generic strategic options needs to be considered on its merits: is it likely to deliver the results and is it realistic?

The cost leadership strategy

Cost leadership is a traditional route to competitive advantage. The aim is to become the lowest-cost producer within any given industry, because buyers prefer to pay less. A low cost base gives the organisation the option of offering more competitive prices (or if this is not necessary to obtain and retain market share, simply to be more profitable than others). The basis for achieving cost leadership through a low cost base varies from industry to industry. It may relate to proprietary technology, economies of scale, access to low-cost raw materials or geographic location. In most cases, it involves an array of elements which must be juggled to achieve cost leadership.

It is critical with this strategy that 'all other things stay equal'. For example, low cost must not be a trade-off for acceptable quality or minimum levels of customer service. Organisations that try to become cost leaders by sacrificing other core aspects of customer requirements tend to lose business over time and go broke. As Porter puts it, cost leadership must offer 'parity or proximity' to points of differentiation such as quality and service. Porter also warns that the cost leadership strategy is only effective if the organisation becomes the outstanding cost leader in its industry.

The differentiation strategy

Differentiation is about creating uniqueness. In pursuing this strategy, an organisation must offer something to its customers that others don't or can't. The organisation is then able to charge a premium for its unique feature and thus achieve above-average profitability.

Differentiation can arise from many sources and varies significantly from industry to industry. What all the sources have in common is that they are elements of the product or service that is valued by the customer. By definition, this strategy will fail if the basis for differentiation is not valued by the customer. Some common bases for differentiation include:

- product features (for example, exceptional quality—Bang and Olufsen)
- features of the services associated with the product (for example, ease of purchase—Amazon.com)
- brand image (for example, cutting edge design—Alessi).

One critical issue with this strategy is that the cost of delivering the uniqueness must not exceed the premium that can be charged for that uniqueness. Cost can therefore nullify the impact of this strategy on profitability. Differentiators must still control costs relative to the price that can be charged; they must achieve 'parity or proximity' in relation to all other aspects other than the differentiating features.

The key to success with this strategy is to understand your customer base very well and *know* what they will pay extra for. To that extent, there are many possible sources of differentiation, with new ones being dreamt up all the time. Unlike cost leadership, finding sources for differentiation can be a very creative process. For that reason, the task for management is less mechanical and more creative ('creating value for our customers') than it is with cost leadership ('taking costs out of the business'). The process for achieving differentiation is therefore more open-ended and management must move outside the normal parameters for inspiration when thinking about what might differentiate their organisation's products/services from their competitors' offerings.

The focus strategy

The focus strategy is about fine-tuning what an organisation delivers to a segment of a market. The organisation must do this to the point where its offerings are irresistible to that market segment. There are two variants of this strategy, each based on the other two generic strategies. They are *cost focus* and *differentiation focus*. The first variant involves taking a cost leadership position that captures the specific market segment that is being addressed. The second variant involves offering differentiation advantages to a specific market segment. Both these variants have in common the strategy of offering something different to the chosen market segment in comparison with other segments.

An example of the first variant (cost focus) is the Aldi supermarket chain. Aldi's chosen target segment of the grocery industry comprises those customers attracted to the low price of generic products. So, Aldi offers generic products at a price that is much lower than the generic brands available in other supermarket chains. Aldi's product range is limited (hundreds of products as opposed to thousands in normal supermarkets) and is stacked on pallets in wide aisles (as opposed to shelves, thereby reducing stocking costs). Their store locations reflect the segment they are pursuing: low-to-medium income families that shop weekly for large volumes of staple items.

An example of the second variant (differentiation focus) is Lexus. Despite being owned by Toyota, Lexus is pursuing the prestige car market. It offers Japanese quality and reliability, combined with style and performance factors that match European competitors such as BMW and Mercedes Benz. Although it has yet to achieve the prestige associated with the old European 'marques', it is rapidly building market share at their expense with a superior quality product. Note that the Lexus brand is marketed separately from the Toyota brand so that there is no confusion about its position as a prestige product.

To help understand the difference between overall differentiation and focus differentiation, Porter provides the example of IBM as an instance of the former (computers that are widely valued) and Cray Research (super computers for specialist application). Clearly, judgment is required as to whether a market segment is narrow or broad. For example, as IBM computers are linked up, they are starting to acquire super-computer capabilities. This is blurring the line between computers and super-computers, and may have implications for Cray Research in terms of the segment they are pursuing. Thus the line between overall differentiation and focus differentiation becomes blurred.

The focus strategy tries to take advantage of the fact that organisations that are more broadly focused often create opportunities for a competitor who can address the specific and specialist needs of a segment within the overall market. The strategy fails most often if what is offered by the focuser is not *sufficiently* different, either on the basis of cost or differing features. For example, offering a cola drink to a segment such as 20-plus males will probably fail unless there is something truly different about the drink. By contrast, offering caffeine-enhanced drinks to the same segment, who are already used to drinking cola rather than coffee, is likely to succeed (as it has).

Which strategy?

Porter discusses the problems caused by pursuing a mixture of all three generic strategies. Organisations that try to do this tend to get 'stuck in the middle'. That is, by trying to be all things to all customers they end up being nothing special to any of them. This may still lead to profitability if the industry is structurally a highly profitable one. More typically, it leads to pressure on margins and eventual loss of market share to others who successfully pursue one of the strategies in a determined manner.

One solution is to have separate business units that pursue different strategies in the same market. (This is what Toyota does by having a separately branded prestige line such as Lexus. Hotel group Accor does something similar with the Sofitel, Novotel and Formule One brands in the hospitality industry.)

Occasionally, an organisation achieves cost leadership and differentiation at the same time. Three situations seem to offer this possibility:

- *Competitors who are 'stuck in the middle'* and, therefore, easy targets. This situation is likely to be short-term as the competitors eventually realise the threat and start to pursue one specific strategy.
- *Industries where cost is related to market share or to supply chain integration.* If cost advantages are derived from holding large market share, costs incurred in other areas (for example, costs involved in differentiation) can sometimes be absorbed. Where the supply chain is tightly integrated, and the organisation offers products and services up and down the chain, the very nature of that tight relationship may enable both cost leadership and differentiation to be pursued.
- *Industries where major innovations create playing fields that are not level.* For example, when a major technological change reduces the cost of a production process or dramatically reduces other operating costs.

Finally, to provide a *sustainable* advantage, a strategy must lead to advantage in relation to competitors over time. This means that the organisation needs to invest in its capacity to do those things that are required to support the strategy. For example, if the organisation pursues cost leadership it must invest in cost reduction capabilities that will keep it ahead of competitors who also pursue the same strategy.

The risks

There are risks associated with using each of the three strategies—weak points that management must focus on, whether as the basis for attack or defence. These risks can be exploited by competitors, but can also help managers to analyse how to attack a competitor (see Porter's summation of these risks in Table 2.1).

The Generic Strategies model has found ready acceptance in management circles. This does not mean that it is always well understood. For example, some managers still talk about strategies that are in fact not strategies at all, such as 'being the market leader' or 'being first or second in a market segment' or 'being the technical leader in a market'. These are outcomes that may result if the right strategy is effectively deployed. At worst, they may become goals in their own right that can cause an organisation to fail. Being the technical leader is not the same as being the profit leader. If one is connected to the other it is only because technical leadership has led to cost leadership, to differentiation or to focus.

Table 2.1 Risks of the Generic Strategies

Risks of cost leadership	Risks of differentiation	Risks of focus
Cost leadership is not sustained – competitors imitate – technology changes – other bases for cost leadership erode	Differentiation is not sustained – competitors imitate – bases for differentiation become less important to buyers	The focus strategy is imitated The target segment becomes structurally unattractive – structure erodes – demand diappears
Proximity in differentiation is lost	Cost proximity is lost	Broadly-targeted competitors overwhelm the segment – the segment's differences from other segments narrow – the advantages of a broad line increase
Cost focusers achieve even lower cost in segments	Differentiation focusers achieve even greater differentiation in segments	New focusers sub-segment the industry

Observations

Porter's strategy framework is now being challenged. The challenge is coming from industry research (rather than from strategy theory), which suggests that the assumptions on which Porter has based his theories are not wholly in accordance with the real world.

Porter's concept of 'competitive advantage' is based on a detailed analysis of what will work best in a given industry. He argues that organisations must take into account the specifics of their industry in any decision on how to beat its competitors. He claims that some industries are inherently more profitable than others because of fundamental structural reasons. This 'industry approach' provides a licence for some managers to settle for low levels of performance because they argue that they are competing in an industry that is structurally low-profit. The 'industry effect' has been factored into many corporate strategy sessions. However, research over the last 15 years has shown that this industry effect is much over-stated.

Detailed evidence from a range of industries suggests that *internal* organisational factors account for anything up to 10 times the variations in performance than can be explained by industry factors. Given that management has not much control over industry factors, but a great deal of control over internal factors, the implications for management are enormous. Effectively, the licence to hide behind industry factors has been removed. Poor corporate performance can now be laid squarely at the feet of a management team.

As Porter's theories are shown to have feet of clay, an opposing approach is already scrambling to become the next dominant paradigm. The essence of the new approach is for organisations to create sustainable competitive advantage by implementing a value-adding strategy that is relatively unique. This contrasts sharply with Porter's Generic Strategies. Such a strategy will be based on developing and maintaining *unique capabilities* that create a competitive edge.

Gary Hamel and C K Prahalad are most closely associated with the capability view, although they actually focus on only one part of the resources available to organisations: their 'core competences'.[7] Their view tends to exclude other resources, such as physical resources. Interestingly, their approach is neatly aligned with the current fashion for 'knowledge-based' competitive advantage. However, some theorists have argued that tangible capabilities such as intellectual rights and physical resources may well provide a more reliable and secure competitive edge than 'intangible' capabilities. Either way, the capability theorists agree that the edge must be *valuable, rare, unsubstitutable* and *difficult to imitate*.

The catchcry of the capability advocates is to achieve sustainable com-petitive advantage by *competing from the inside out*. In many organisations, the search is on for that unique set of characteristics that will make an organisation succeed regardless of what is happening around it.

User's guide

Porter's models are best used as an aid to a group session where the group is charged with the task of understanding an industry. This may well be part of a larger exercise in determining strategic direction and typically involves answering questions such as: 'Should we enter this industry?' or 'How can we increase our market share in this industry?'

The models can also be used to create a greater level of awareness about industry issues. In other words, the tool is applied simply for an educational purpose. For example, I have conducted sessions with cross-functional groups within an organisation in order to help them understand the strategies that have been decided by senior management teams. The models provided the context that helped the staff to understand what was being done.

Instructions

How to use the Five Forces model

1. Outline the various elements of the Five Forces model.

   This can be made more concrete by using some industry examples to illustrate how each of the five forces impacts on levels of profitability. For instance, pharmaceutical and oil companies are useful examples of high-profitability industries; farming and leisure travel of low-profitability industries (but the choice of industry isn't important).

2. Explore the specific industry that the participants are involved with, teasing out the various factors that impact on profitability.

   - On a flip chart or whiteboard, draw the model for that industry using Porter's Five Forces model.
   - Agree on a rating for the industry for each of the five forces. High, medium and low should suffice in terms of depth. Make sure there is agreement. Talk it out with the group if there is not.
   - Add this information to the model by adding the ratings to each of the forces.

3. Ask the group to consider how to re*duce the impact of each of the forces.*

   - What action could the organisation take?
   - What actions could competitors be taking?
   - What would have greatest impact?
   - What is already happening in terms of medium- and long-term trends?

4. *If the focus of the planning session is specifically on 'industry rivalry', consider the impact of the factors that drive the degree of rivalry:*

- industry growth rate (if high, reduces rivalry)
- high fixed costs (if high, creates competitor opportunities)
- intermittent over-capacity (increases rivalry)
- product differences (low differentiation leads to increased competition)
- brand identity (reduces competitive pressures)
- switching costs (if low, increase rivalry)
- product complexity (reduces rivalry)
- concentration of competitors (few and satisfied means less competition)
- diversity of competitors (if high, increases competitive pressures)
- extent of corporate 'stake' (diversified conglomerates have a lesser commitment to remaining in any given industry)
- exit barriers (if high, increases competition).

5. *Ask the group to consider the implications for action.*

- Select three key actions that would significantly increase the level of rivalry and explore what would be involved to make this happen.
- If appropriate, agree on which actions to take.

How to use the Generic Strategies model

1. *Explain the Generic Strategies model to the group.*

- Resolve issues of disagreement or lack of understanding.
- Provide as many examples as possible for each of the strategies.

2. *Select an industry (usually this will be the one in which the group is currently operating).*

- Discuss what the various competitors are doing.

  - Do any of them have an obvious strategy? If so, what is it?
  - Who is stuck in the middle?
  - What are the opportunities?

3. *Explore, in turn, what would be involved in pursuing each of the three strategies for the organisation.*

- What are the implications?
- What would have to change?
- What would need to happen?

4. *Consider the weaknesses of the competitors.*

- Use Table 2.1 to determine possible lines of attack.

  - How could these be implemented?
  - What are the action steps to make them happen?

Further reading

There really is only one outstanding book on this topic and that is Michael Porter's *Competitive advantage*. The first chapter summarises the Five Forces model and Generic Strategies, and the rest of the book illustrates how to use those concepts.

- M Porter, *Competitive advantage: Creating and sustaining superior performance*, The Free Press, London, 1998.

Notes

1. Henry Mintzberg has rescued the idea of 'making it up as you go along' with his concept of 'emergent strategy'. See H Mintzberg, *The rise and fall of strategic planning*, The Free Press, New York, 1994.
2. A Sloan, *My years with General Motors*, Doubleday, New York, 1964.
3. M Porter, *Competitive strategy: Techniques for analyzing industries and competitors*, The Free Press, New York, 1980.
4. M Porter, *Competitive advantage: Creating and sustaining superior performance*, The Free Press, London, 1998.
5. M Porter, *The competitive advantage of nations*, Macmillan, London, 1990.
6. Ansoff classifies five different levels of turbulence: repetitive, expanding, changing, discontinuous and surpriseful. Each one requires a different response from the organisations competing in that type of turbulence. For example, a 'surpriseful' industry demands flexibility and creativity; a 'repetitive' industry demands stable management based on established precedents. See I Ansoff, 'General management in turbulent environments', *The Practising Manager*, vol. 11, no. 1, 1990, pp 6–27.
7. C Prahalad & G Hamel, 'The core competence of the corporation', *Harvard Business Review*, May–June, 1990, pp. 79–91.

CHAPTER 3

Measuring performance
KPIs and the Balanced Scorecard

Performance management is driven by performance measurement. So it seems surprising that most organisations only discovered the measurement idea recently. People who have more than 10 or 15 years' employment experience may recall the day that management started to speak of 'performance indicators'. Before that time, the talk was of 'financial results' and, more typically, 'end-of-year results'.

These days, organisations operate on much shorter timeframes than they did 50 or even 20 years ago. Management effectively wants continuous reporting on results. In addition, the nature of those results has changed, and continues to change, in response to new management demands. So measurement systems have had to adapt to meet these new demands. Measurement systems based on *performance indicators* have stepped in to fill this need. Once indicators were developed, they were then grouped on the basis of the areas of performance that they measured: the *key results areas*.

Interestingly, once organisations started to measure results based on performance indicators, performance was affected—but so too was management's focus. For example, if management measured sales performance, their focus shifted to that area, often at the expense of other aspects of the organisation. So, to guard against an excessively narrow focus on a handful of indicators, the Balanced Scorecard was developed.

These three tools (performance indicators, key results areas and the Balanced Scorecard) have changed how organisations measure progress towards their performance goals. Although they are not radical departures from what went before, these tools have become so common that it is difficult to find an organisation that does not use them in some shape or form. It is almost reasonable to argue that they are the first of a very small group of management techniques that are part of 'accepted practice'.

Discussion continues on the best way to construct measuring systems based on these three tools. The language used to describe the concepts is not exactly standardised, and there will be further developments and refinements. But most managers agree that the tools are here to stay.

Background

The purpose of performance measurement is to assist performance improvement. These days, unless an organisation improves continuously, it is falling behind. Performance improvement, therefore, is a goal that is mandated by the exigencies of business.

This need for constant improvement accounts for much of the short-term view of many senior managers. Their views are also shaped by the demands of outsiders, such as investment funds and other investors who demand immediate high returns on their investments. All of which explains why CEOs last only a few years in the top job these days. Results are required now, not tomorrow.

It is hardly unexpected, then, that so much change aimed at improving organisational performance often fails to bring benefits or fails altogether. In the words of Cameron and Quinn:

> ... as many as three quarters of re-engineering, total quality management (TQM), strategic planning, and downsizing efforts have failed entirely or have created problems serious enough that the survival of the organisation was threatened.[1]

Such failures are well known to managers and this knowledge only adds to the pressure to perform. It makes managers prey to prescriptions that promise instant results and this provides the perfect breeding ground for fads.

By contrast, key performance indicators (KPIs) seem like a safe initiative on which to focus. This generally involves tightening up a process that already happens in organisations to some extent (measuring performance) and yet it has the ring of modernity about it. When an organisation brings in KPI-based performance measurement, it looks as though it is making progress, but without taking too many risks.

Of course, ordinary performance measures or indicators have been around a long time, although they have been described in many different ways. The breakthrough was to add the word 'key'. This turned the ordinary performance measures from an accounting mechanism into a strategic management tool. The downside of 'key' is that you're only supposed to have a few of them. This meant that organisations had to make decisions about which indicators really mattered. In other words, senior management had to set priorities—making some measures 'key' means downgrading other measures to 'not key'. This choice was very painful for some organisations that were used to running their businesses with a dashboard full of indicators. But to create focus, it had to be done.

In a remarkably short time, businesses all over the developed world happily settled into using the language of KPIs. The most immediate impact was on the staff in those organisations. The age-old principle, 'that which gets measured gets done', ensured that employees started to focus on what was 'key'. The price of this was narrowness of focus. But for many organisations this was an acceptable price for creating an organisation that was very clear about the meaning of performance.

The *Dictionary of Business* defines KPIs as:

> The key measures of the performance of a company, which are monitored and assessed to ensure its long-term success. These indicators help to pinpoint the company's strengths and weaknesses.[2]

The language used in this definition suggests a clear strategic intent. The definition implies that KPIs are linked to an organisation's *capabilities*. A KPI system will identify those capabilities—and the lack of them—fairly quickly, and for all to see. And an organisation's capabilities are what give it an edge.

Interestingly, no one theory, book or guru has driven the KPI phenomenon. It has quickly slipped into day-to-day management language without any overt marketing campaign. The KPI approach has achieved enormous acceptance all on its own. No single writer is associated with the concept and no one consultant or consulting group has become famous through advocating it. The idea of focus seemed so natural in a competitive world that the KPI tool swept all before it. Even a brief glance at the literature on performance management shows its impact on industries as diverse as manufacturing, hospitals and universities.

As the KPI approach drilled down into organisations, KPIs began to drive functional units such as sales, human resources and even research and development. Many organisations developed neatly interlocking and multi-level systems of KPIs.

This approach then travelled well beyond the boundaries of the organisation so that suppliers were judged on the KPIs at the heart of their 'service agreements'. This in turn infected the thinking back inside the organisation to the point that internal service providers (for example, human resources, finance and IT) came to have their performance assessed on the basis of KPIs and their attendant targets.

To make them a little easier to use, KPIs are typically incorporated into a framework that comprises some areas of focus (often called key results areas or KRAs). KRAs lead to KPIs, which then lead to numerical targets. The language varies from organisation to organisation—KRAs may be called key effectiveness areas and KPIs may be called performance measures—but the overall structure is the same, regardless of the actual descriptions used. *KRAs lead to KPIs which lead to targets.*

Many organisations use the KRA/KPI format to structure their corporate plans. The senior managers of the organisation create the top-level version of the KRA/KPI structure, which is then used by the level below to develop their versions. And so on down the organisation, level by level. They call it 'cascading the KPIs down'.

KRAs probably led to the idea of 'balanced scorecard'. Once you group KPIs into areas of activity, the idea of 'balance' becomes evident.[3] All organisations perform on many different levels and in many different ways. So, which KPIs should be used to guide the organisation? Which ones indicate real progress? How does the organisation make sure it is focusing on the correct ones?

Today, KPIs are everywhere. However, what is sometimes overlooked is that not all KPIs are the same. And constructing a balanced collection of KPIs is not always easy.

The tools

Key performance indicators and key results areas

Key performance indicators are measures. Every KPI is a measure of progress in relation to some specific area of organisational activity. A KPI is usually expressed as a *ratio*, though it can be an absolute number. KPIs that use absolute numbers are useful to show long-term results, for example 'total number of days worked without an injury caused'. If a KPI is a ratio, it usually involves comparing one result with another. For example:

- 'Market share' is a ratio of the organisation's share of the market compared with the total size of the market.
- 'Employee turnover' is the number of employees that left the organisation versus the total number of employees employed.
- 'Return on equity' is profit after tax compared with shareholders' funds.
- 'Safety audits completed' is the number of audits conducted versus the number that were planned.

All of these types of ratio measures are usually expressed as a percentage.

After KPIs were introduced into organisations, it became apparent that there was more than one *type* of KPI. For instance, some KPIs provide only historical data. An example from the area of safety is where organisations use an indicator such as 'Lost time injuries'. This KPI is very common in manufacturing organisations and indicates how many times somebody took time off work because of injury. The actual unit of measure may be days lost or hours lost; sometimes the unit used is the number of incidents recorded.

Because KPIs such as 'Lost time injuries' measure what has happened in the past, they came to be called 'lag' indicators. A lag measure tells us what has already happened (in this case in the area of safety) in the recent past. Over time, the data from this KPI can suggest trends (that is, the figures trend up or down) but they are always historical results. Once the results are put on the board outside the factory gate, no one can do anything about the data.

This is quite different from another group of indicators called 'lead' indicators. These KPIs tend to measure what is happening right now in respect of some crucial activity. Once that activity has happened, it is the turn of the lag indicator to measure the ultimate outcome.

In the area of safety, a lead measure might be 'On-time safety audits' (measuring whether safety audits are being carried out when they should be) or 'Personal protective equipment adherence' (whether people are wearing the correct safety gear). These measure the things that ultimately impact on indicators such as 'Lost time injury'. That's what makes them a lead measure—they have a predictive capability.

The difference between lag and lead indicators is that the first can only give you trends about what has already happened in the organisation; the second can indicate what is happening right now that will eventually show up in the results of the first. Most organisations are now trying to design and build more lead measures, mainly because it is a better use of management time to work with such measures. Looking at pages of lag indicators at the end of the month is just contemplating history. Lead measures are simply more useful.

One difficulty is that lead measures are much harder to create. Most organisations are well equipped with systems that generate lag information (such as last month's sales figures or how much was paid out to creditors). But the systems for measurement of lead indicators are often not there. In many organisations, there is little experience in developing and using lead measures. But over time, as experience is being shared, better measures are starting to become available.

KPIs are often grouped on the basis of their common nature. For example, all the safety KPIs can be grouped to show the organisation's progress, in overall terms, in that area of activity. Such a group can then be called a *key results area*, although many other descriptions are used. A KRA such as safety may involve a number of KPIs, for example:

- lost time injuries
- medical expenses incurred
- safety audits completed
- safety training completed.

In any given industry, some common KRAs are typical. For example, in manufacturing, it is common to have KRAs for safety, production performance, quality and training. Service organisations will focus more on areas such as customer satisfaction and sales. Some organisations have many more than four or five KRAs, but more than six or seven tends to create data overload.

Balanced Scorecard

What really pulled all this into some perspective was the publication of Kaplan and Norton's book *Balanced Scorecard: Translating strategy into action* in 1996.[4] This book elegantly puts the case for adding *logic* to your collection of KPIs. Kaplan and Norton argued that KPIs are not independent elements but are *connected*. That is, a KPI in one area (such as maintenance) is connected to KPIs in other areas (such as production performance), which in turn impact on other areas (such as financial performance).

Kaplan and Norton shaped this connectivity into a scorecard based on four major areas of performance measurement:

1. financial performance
2. customer satisfaction
3. internal processes
4. learning and growth.

Each area of the scorecard has a number of key performance indicators, and each area cascades *upwards* to impact on the area *above* it. The notion of cascading is important because it links the areas of the scorecard into a dynamic whole. Instead of having a grab-bag of indicators, the links between them create a structure in which all the parts of the scorecard are connected. For example, measuring your investment in developing the capabilities of your people and the systems they use is a 'lead area' for the effectiveness and efficiency of your internal processes. This in turn can predict what your customers think about your performance, which in turn will predict your overall financial performance. More specifically, training your staff to respond more quickly to customer inquiries (for example, by giving them decision-making powers supported by effective IT systems) will make your internal processes work more effectively. This is almost guaranteed to please your customers, who will return for more. This will generate the most valuable business you can get (return buyers) and that will make you more profitable.

Typically, organisations have few problems in devising indicators for the financial area. Almost all have historical experience on which they can base indicators such as return-on-investment, revenue growth and profitability. Most can also figure out (reasonably easily) indicators for the customer area such as market share, customer retention and customer satisfaction. Even internal processes (with a bit of thought) will generate some useful indicators for activities such as innovation, continuous improvement, productivity and product development. But it is the final area, learning and growth, which creates the most difficulty.

Learning and growth (think of it as 'capability development') is the least tangible area to measure. Likely as not, there will be few historical indicators. Yet it is the powerhouse that drives all the others. The key is to focus on those people and systems-related processes that actually deliver benefits to the organisation. Some of the more obvious ones are areas of activity such as skilling people, systems availability and staff turnover (a shorthand measure of employee satisfaction). One approach to developing indicators for this area is to consider what it is about your systems and your people that truly adds value, and then develop measures for those things. In this area, the indicators will be different for every organisation.

The task of management is to ensure that there is progress in all four areas of the scorecard (creating a balanced organisational effort) rather than focusing on just one or two areas. For example, in the past many organisations focused too much on financial indicators (most of which are 'lag' indicators).

The concept of creating a balanced approach to driving the performance of the organisation has probably been the most powerful management idea of its time. It is estimated that over 40% of Fortune 1000 US companies have installed versions of the scorecard in their organisation in the last 10 years.[5] This is a phenomenal rate of penetration for a management concept.

Observations

KPIs are now so widespread that it is almost heresy to say anything against them. However, they do continue to be misconstrued and misconstructed. They are only a bit better than the types of measures they replaced, although the lag/lead distinction is helpful. Structuring KPIs into key results areas does help management to focus on the things that matter *but they are not a substitute for better performance*—they only report progress towards that goal.

The Balanced Scorecard has been around for about 10 years now and KPIs surfaced a little before that. As I mentioned, the speed of adoption of this management tool has been nothing short of astounding. But as with all management fads and trends, there is always a risk that it will be taken too far.

The Balanced Scorecard has survived most of the situations in which it has been put to work. It has turned out to be an effective and rugged tool for 'translating strategy into action'. And yet ultimately it is only as good as its application. Most organisations spend more time on constructing their scorecard than they do on using it. Many organisations have scorecards that live only in managers' bottom drawers—few make their scorecard 'come alive'.

Part of the problem here is the reason that management turned to the scorecard in the first place. If the motivation is 'to be seen to be doing something', then the initiative probably won't go far. If, on the other hand, there is a real desire to clarify and communicate strategy, track performance in key areas, ensure that action is informed by strategy, and focus the organisation on that which matters, then there is some chance of gaining benefits. The bottom line is to do it for the right reason and then do it very well.

Sometimes organisations are tempted to use KPIs to measure individual performance. This only works for jobs that are very simple to measure. For most jobs, good performance is more than just achieving a handful of performance targets. It may possibly work if you are a sales person with a well-defined territory or a 'cold-caller' doing telephone selling in a call centre. But as soon as your job becomes dependent on other people doing their job (and that is the case for most of us) then KPIs lose their usefulness.

To get the best out of people in terms of performance, you need to turn to employee performance planning (see Chapter 11, Managing performance: Goal-setting). KPIs will fail you in this process because it is quite possible for all the individuals in an organisation to achieve their individual performance standards and yet for that organisation to fail miserably by its own overall measures of performance. There are many organisations in which everyone does the right thing in terms of their personal work standards but the company makes no profit.

Although an organisation's performance can be summed up by a handful of KPIs, try doing the same with your job. In fact, if you do not provide an employee with any formal structure or framework at all, and just ask them how they would like to have their performance judged, the answer is likely to be that they wish to be judged on how they do their work. 'Judge me on whether I have done the things I am supposed to do and how well I have done those things.'

The central issue here is that *how* a job is done is often as vital as the results that are achieved. The behaviour employed to get the job done matters. And KPIs are not very useful at measuring anything but the simplest behaviours. KPIs are for organisations, not for people.

User's guide

Although it is quite possible for a single manager to construct a Balanced Scorecard, this solitary approach loses out on the power of involvement. People support what they help create and so it is with designing and constructing a Balanced Scorecard. In any case, the resulting scorecard is far more likely to be robust and relevant if more than one person is involved in its creation.

Instructions

How to construct a Balanced Scorecard

Any group coming together to build a Balanced Scorecard should follow a few basic steps in the design process:

1. *Establish objectives.*

   Make sure that all those involved in the process of developing the scorecard agree on the reasons for doing it. Such reasons may range from the ordinary ('measure organisational performance') to the more lofty ('communicate strategy throughout the organisation').

2. *Decide who will be involved in the development process.*

   If the scorecard is to be a 'strategic' instrument, then it is critical that the most senior people in the organisation are involved in its development. If the task is delegated to a more junior group or to an outside consultant, it is more likely to fail. In part, the journey is the point.

3. *Decide on the organisational unit to which the scorecard will apply.*

   Depending on the complexity of the organisation, the scorecard may be relevant at either the top or somewhere further down the organisation. For example, diversified businesses often have difficulty in developing a scorecard for the whole of their organisation and instead use business units as the appropriate level.

4. *Decide on the structure.*

   It is usually best to stick with the original four-tier structure proposed by Kaplan and Norton (financial performance; customer satisfaction; internal processes; learning and growth). Variations are possible—but the decision to vary the basic model should be driven by a stakeholder analysis.

   - Review existing measures that may become part of the scorecard by turning them into KPIs.
   - Develop additional KPIs that may form part of the scorecard.
   - Relate all KPIs back to the original objectives for developing the scorecard. You need at least three or four KPIs for each part of the scorecard, and no more than six or seven.

5. *Finalise the scorecard.*

   - Set performance targets for each KPI, and decide how it will be maintained, updated and communicated.

Further reading

With the Balanced Scorecard, there seems no reason to look further than the originators of the concept, Robert Kaplan and David Norton. (I can only assume that in their darker moments these fellows kick themselves for allowing it into the public domain free of proprietary control!)

- R Kaplan & D Norton, *Balanced Scorecard: Translating strategy into action*, Harvard Business School Press, Boston, 1996.

  This was their first book. It tells you everything you need to know for building a Balanced Scorecard for your organisation.

- R Kaplan & D Norton, *The strategy-focused organisation: How Balanced Scorecard companies thrive in the new business environment*, Harvard Business School Press, Boston, 2000.

  Their follow-up book is less successful at creating practical value—it seems an 'extension' work, which is interesting rather than valuable. For briefer descriptions, try:

- R Kaplan & D Norton, 'Putting the Balanced Scorecard to work', *Harvard Business Review*, Sept–Oct, 1993, pp. 134–47.
- R Kaplan & D Norton, 'The Balanced Scorecard: Measures that drive performance', *Harvard Business Review*, Jan–Feb, 1992, pp. 71–9.

Notes

1. K Cameron & R Quinn, *Diagnosing and changing organisational culture*, Addison Wesley, Reading, 1999.
2. *Dictionary of Business*, Oxford University Press, Oxford, 1996.
3. The French have used formal KRA-like scorecards for over 50 years, under the title 'Tableau de Bord'—see http://ideas.repec.org/p/ebg/heccah/0724.html. Kaplan and Norton acknowledge the Tableau de Bord in their book, *Balanced Scorecard: Translating strategy into action* (p. 29).
4. R Kaplan & D Norton, *Balanced Scorecard: Translating strategy into action*, Harvard Business School Press, Boston, 1996.
5. Reported on the web site of the Cranfield School of Management at http://www.som.cranfield.ac.uk/som/cbp/BScorecard.html

CHAPTER 4

Conceiving the future
Scenario planning

Strategy is always based on assumptions, either explicit or implicit. The problem is that sometimes these assumptions turn out to be wrong. When that happens, the entire strategy can collapse. If the strategy was absolutely crucial to the survival of the organisation, then this collapse can have catastrophic consequences.

Assumptions often seem completely reasonable at the time they are made. Typically, they relate to external conditions that impact on the organisation and, even more typically, they are the 'things will stay the same' type of assumption. It is only in retrospect that what seemed generally agreed to be facts turned out to be assumptions.

And unforeseen events do happen. While no-one can stop such events from taking place, organisations can prepare for them. While no-one can predict the events, it is possible to predict that unexpected events will happen. One technique for preparing a defence against such occurrences is *scenario planning*, which differs significantly from traditional planning processes.

Traditional strategic planning tends to follow one of two alternative approaches:

- the rational approach (finding the best strategy through a process of rational analysis)
- the emergent approach (developing the best strategy over time through small incremental changes).

The major disadvantage of the rational approach is that it fails whenever the assumptions that sit behind the analysis turn out to be incorrect. This happens most frequently when unforeseen events occur. The major disadvantage of the emergent approach is that it is reactive, with strategy changing in response to events. This means that the organisation is a captive to events outside its control and it may respond too slowly.

Scenario planning tries to avoid these two extremes by preparing the organisation to deal with *possibilities*. Although it is always the case that there are many different approaches to any particular management tool, in the case of scenario planning the basic steps are generally agreed. However, there is still some disagreement about the purpose of scenario planning.

Background

Preparing for the unexpected and the unknown goes under many names, ranging from contingency planning to prayer. The former seems more appropriate to the business context but the latter also has its exponents in industry. Contingency planning ranges from the short term to the long term.

Short-term plans are most often alternative actions or fall-back positions. In the short term, it is relatively easy to consider the unexpected events that impinge on organisations. This kind of 'what-if' analysis is commonly used in financial forecasting and special tools are available to help with it (such as spreadsheet software like Microsoft Excel). The major virtue of such tools is that their use has spread the message that all projections are based on assumptions. Spreadsheets have forced a generation of managers to think in terms of making explicit their assumptions about the future.

For example, a budget or financial forecast might involve making a judgment about the projected revenue that a company will generate. This may be linked to national economic growth projections. If the economy is expected to grow at 3% in the coming year then, based on past performance, the impact of this will be a given level of revenue. However, if the growth rate is higher or lower, the revenue will rise or fall accordingly. The higher or lower figures can be added to the budget projections in order to analyse the possible range within which the organisation's revenue is likely to fall. Each of these possibilities is a scenario for the future. At best, only one scenario will actually be realised; all the others will not because the assumptions on which they were based turned out to be incorrect. In extreme cases, none of the projected scenarios will unfold because the reality turns out to be different from the range of variations considered.

What makes this kind of short-term scenario analysis worthwhile is that the short timeframe makes most of the assumptions relatively predictable. In the previous example, the economic growth rate is likely to vary within a fairly narrow band—it is highly unlikely to double or halve within any one year. This relative predictability makes the technique dependable. With a short timeframe, we can take past data and use it to make reasonably accurate predictions about the near future.

However, as we stretch the timeframe, the reliability diminishes. Over a period of three years, growth rates may well double or halve. Therefore, our projections need to take into account a far greater range of assumptions, creating ever more possibilities for what may happen. Multiply this by a number of variables (for example, growth rate, inflation rate and debt growth) and the possible outcomes balloon into numbers that are just too great to handle. If an organisation wanted to look even further ahead (say, 5–10 years) then a data-based approach, such as a financial projection, would be worthless. The reliability of projections based on data from previous years declines rapidly as the timeframe is extended.

When the timeframe goes beyond 10 years, most managers and businesses simply give up on using projections. It does not seem worthwhile to project that far into the future with so many variables to consider. Yet many events do take this long to become obvious.

In the last few decades, only a few experts accurately predicted such developments as: the speed of globalisation; the (at times violent) response to this from some parts of our community; the fall of the Soviet Union; the rise in part-time work; the level of female participation in the workforce; or any one of a number of other socio-economic developments. Some events were unpredicted by nearly everyone—the Great Depression in the 1930s, the oil crises of the 1970s and the global Islamic terrorist threat of the first part of this century. Such events can have and have had major impacts on the plans of organisations around the world. Only a few were prepared because they had used planning techniques that gave them the capacity to consider such possibilities and prepare a response.

One such planning technique is *scenario planning*. It became well known because of its role in enabling Royal Dutch Shell to deal with and exploit the 1973 OPEC oil crisis. As the OPEC cartel forced oil prices to levels never seen before, Shell responded by following a plan that it had developed many years earlier for just such a situation. Shell profited from the crisis by taking decisive action while many of its competitors floundered; some of these competitors went broke because they had not thought out a response. As a result, Shell went from being the least profitable to the most profitable global oil company in the world.

Since then, scenario planning has become famous as a tool for protecting organisations against unexpected events and for enabling organisations to exploit opportunities that were unexpected by most. The originators of the technique have become consulting legends in their own right.[1] However, despite the exhortations of these gurus, the tool has become somewhat warped over time as it has been applied by business as a protective device. Some of the gurus even predicted this would happen. They let the genie out of the bottle and as it found its freedom in the world of hard-nosed business and even harder-nosed business consulting, it transformed into a shadow of its former self.

Scenario planning has evolved into two distinct approaches.[2] The first involves considering possible future scenarios because the process helps managers to be more adaptable in their thoughts and actions about how to handle the future. This approach explores the implications of the scenarios simply because it makes managers smarter about the future. It's a bit like going to the gym and getting fit because it will enable you to perform better when you enter a triathlon—the gym sessions are simply a way of developing the necessary capabilities.

The second approach has the same starting point (developing possible future scenarios) but then examines these scenarios in order to develop possible responses. In this approach, scenario planning is not just practising to get better at thinking about the future; managers do it in order to develop plans that will handle the future. It's like working out in the gym because one day you may have to run for your life.

Both approaches involve 'learning by doing', but in the first approach this is the whole purpose of the exercise. In the second approach, it is a means for reaching another outcome, usually in the form of potential responses to potential events. Both approaches recognise that this is a planning activity that involves more play than analysis, more art than science, and more exploration than discovery.

Scenario planning is about the long view (as emphasised by Peter Schwartz in the title of his book, *The art of the long view*[3]). The process is the activity. You have to do it to benefit from it, and no-one can do it for you. It has rules and procedures, but its outcomes are open-ended. Coates compares it to learning how to dance—you have to learn the rules but you do that best by dancing, and you can only get better at it by practising.[4]

The tool

Most organisations want to use scenario planning for strategy testing purposes. This way of using the tool provides illumination with a particular focus (rather than just for the sake of educating the managers in the organisation). It means that the process is more results-focused and action-oriented.

Using scenario planning as a tool for understanding, rather than for action, does not always sit comfortably with the US/UK style of managing organisations. In some cultures that are less focused on immediate outcomes, scenario planning has been used for some time to support the 'long view', with considerable benefit (see, for example, the French version of the process called 'la prospective'[5]).

Scenarios are narrative descriptions of what could happen in the future. These descriptions are internally consistent, and are based on a combination of known and unknown factors. Scenarios are also detailed descriptions of what a situation might look like at some point in the future. Scenario planning provides a route to a world that may become real. It relies on the power of storytelling as a mechanism to integrate complex variables into a coherent, plausible and comprehensive whole. Foretelling the future using stories seems to generate greater realism than simply extrapolating trends based on hard data. Hard data can be part of the scenario, but other contributions come from educated guesses, beliefs, experience, perception and intuition.

There are many different versions of the scenario planning process. The research and popular literature on the process is extensive (see the list of further reading at the end of this chapter) and vigorous debate has taken place on the exact niceties of each of the process steps. The following list is a practical and generic version that will most likely satisfy none of the zealots. It is based on my experience in undertaking this process with various management groups. Feel free to change the steps as seems appropriate to your circumstances.

The actual planning process seems to work best if one of the participants is a facilitator. This does not have to be a professional facilitator; all that is needed is for someone in the group to focus on the process rather than the content of the discussion. This will ensure a more productive discussion. What follows is a summary and brief explanation of the main steps in the scenario planning process and more detail is provided in the User's guide section of this chapter.

1. *Identify a situation or business issue to be explored.*

   Scenario planning is only useful if the timeframe is sufficiently long for the collective imagination to be more useful than data-based projections. Usually, this is 10 years or more. Select a business issue that is relevant over this timeframe.

2. *List the variables that will impact on the situation.*

   Any future situation is the result of a series of variables affecting the current situation. The trick is to identify the most important of these, and consider how they interact to create a possible situation (or scenario). Six to 20 variables seems a practical range to consider for any situation.

3. *Explore the variables.*

   Variables impact on situations in different ways. Not all are equally important and not all impact in the same way. The real impact of all the variables under consideration should be discussed, in order to inform the participants in the scenario process.

4. *Select the 'themes' for the scenarios.*

   A theme provides the basis for a scenario. It offers a trail for developing the scenario. As the theme is developed, it tends to find its own natural direction (as in any creative writing process), following a logic of its own and arriving at a point of detail and specifics that makes sense to the participants. Themes are often derived from a trend such as the ageing of the population. A theme based on that trend might be 'growth in home-based services'.

5. *Create the scenarios.*

   At this point, the scenarios are created and take a particular form. Often a story-like description of a future state (but sometimes more like a narrative or a letter from the future), the scenarios bring together all the ideas generated by the group. Usually, the group knows when a scenario is adequately developed and polished.

6. *Explore the implications of the scenarios for the organisation.*

   Finally, the group needs to consider the implications of each of the scenarios for the current and future activities of the organisation. This is an exploration which may involve people who have not participated in the development of the scenarios. It is where, in response to the scenarios, the organisation considers possible courses of action.

Observations

One of the peculiar things about scenario planning is that, until you have completed at least one such planning session and tasted its impact, it will possibly look a little childish compared to the 'tough' data-based approach to planning (such as the Porter models in Chapter 2). To some people, it looks too much like playing games (and I have found that some managers are almost allergic to game-playing for any purpose). And yet scenario planning comes originally from one of the toughest contexts imaginable: war games.

Some of the very best practitioners of the art of game playing are the military. Even the most cynical five-star general recognises the value of 'if–then' scenarios in a battlefield situation. Long before Royal Dutch Shell used formal scenario analysis to survive several oil crises, the US Department of Defense and the RAND Corporation (under the leadership of Herman Kahn) used scenario planning techniques to develop alternative responses to the terrifying possibilities inherent in nuclear war. If playing scenario games is good enough for military organisations, it may just carry some value for other organisations.

Scenario planning shares some characteristics with other forms of planning. For example, like the 'emergent strategy school', it assumes that the world is largely unpredictable and that we don't know which of the scenarios (if any) will turn out to be real. However, like the 'rational strategy school', it involves applying analytical techniques to work out plans to respond to situations that may emerge.[6]

In reality, most organisations tend to prepare only a handful of critical scenarios, with each scenario describing a different set of future possibilities. Given that hard data and detailed information about the future (the preference of the rationalists) is often difficult to obtain, stories allow a degree of detail that is independent of graphs and tables. Frequently, stories also have a stronger impact on the participants as they provide a richness of descriptive detail not matched by statistics. Many managers will remember a particularly vivid piece of description a long time after they have forgotten a piece of statistical analysis.

Scenario planning is a long-range planning technique.[7] Short-term thinking should be avoided. The actual timeframe varies from industry to industry and from organisation to organisation. Royal Dutch Shell goes out as far as 25 years and, in one instance, as far as 65 years. Most organisations use timeframes of around 10–20 years. Further than that seems to go beyond the life expectancy of most managers!

Given that scenarios are always based on assumptions, part of the planning process involves challenging these assumptions. Challenging assumptions is not always easy. Most managers hang on to their personal assumptions as if they are a life raft in a turbulent storm. But challenged they must be if the organisation is to ponder all the eventualities inherent in the future.

In fact, it is those very assumptions that create the level of surprise in an industry that faces discontinuous change. When the Swiss watch-making industry put a small invention on public display in 1967, without any property rights protection, they had little idea that giving the world free access to quartz movement technology would destroy 80% of their own industry. Their assumptions about the nature of the watch-making industry were so strong that they were incapable of understanding the implications of those assumptions. A little scenario planning back in Neuchâtel in 1967 might have gone a long way towards keeping the Swiss in the watch-making business. (I'm guessing that some time later they did precisely this and reinvented the watch as a fashion accessory—the Swatch. Their industry recovered, but not to the level of dominance it had in 1967.)

To test assumptions, it sometimes helps to make obvious to the participants in a planning session that assumptions do impact on the outcome of the process. Making their assumptions explicit is one way of dealing with that risk. For example, it has been noted that most assumptions about the future fall into one of four categories:

- the future world will be similar to today but better
- the future world will be very much better than today
- the future world will be similar to today but worse
- the future world will be radically different from today.[8]

In practice, most scenario planning exercises are done on the basis of the first assumption. This is mainly because it fits easily within the comfort zone of most managers. Sometimes, it is useful to deliberately adopt one of the other generic assumptions and see how it impacts on the scenarios.

The scenario process does have its pitfalls. It is not very useful without top management involvement (and they may well prefer to have a strategy 'presented' to them rather than be involved in its development). One way to overcome this is to have a less senior group develop the scenarios, but then involve the senior group in the last step of analysing the implications for the organisations. It is a much less preferred approach, but it will still generate benefits.

The process may also fail to generate new options, most typically due to lack of imagination on the part of the participants. It is simply too long term for some. One solution to this is to use a professional facilitator who can ensure that imaginations are stimulated and possible futures more fully appreciated and evaluated. In some situations, I have used professional actors to help stimulate the thinking of a group not used to thinking creatively about what might be.

The process of developing scenarios continues to be refined and redeveloped. One of the more interesting advances comes from the work of Harold Linstone.[9] He argues that the process should take into account the differing perspectives brought to it by the participants. He identifies three major participant groups:

- those connected with the organisation (managers, owners, regulators)
- those who deliver the technologies used by the organisation (internal technical staff, external researchers, academics)
- those who are affected by what the organisation does (customers, the general public, the media).[10]

Each of these groups brings to a scenario planning situation a perspective that typically differs from the other groups on the basis of world view, ethical focus, planning horizon, risk tolerance, technical expertise and many other factors. These multiple perspectives can enhance the scenarios immensely. For example, scenarios created by a particular business can be tested against different perspectives.

It is also useful to keep in mind that scenarios are not forecasts. They are simply too far out from reliable data to be treated as such. This is obvious when you look at the mathematical probabilities involved—in a scenario with 20 variables, if each variable has a 90% level of certainty, the chance of the scenario coming about is 12%. That's why it's not a forecasting tool! The challenge is to accept that this is not a mathematically sound forecasting device but a technique for throwing light on decisions that will never be mathematically based. Scenario planning involves qualitative judgments, not quantitative calculations.

These days, there seems to be less time available for this kind of in-depth consideration of future issues. Some fast-paced versions of the scenario tool are now being developed. For example, David Mercer has published an approach that involves a step-by-step process intended to generate well-developed strategies in a single day.[11] His approach provides an effective design for compressing the following stages into a one-day format (assuming a start date of 2003):

- developing global scenario drivers for 2025
- developing industry scenario drivers for 2010
- developing relevant alternative scenarios
- investigating key turning points and developing strategic responses.

User's guide

Scenario planning is an appropriate tool to use whenever an organisation is concerned about discontinuous change. In other words, as long as change within an industry is reasonably predictable, the traditional rationalistic tools are sufficient. However, if change speeds up and becomes unpredictable, scenario planning comes into its own. Although it won't predict the future, it can help prepare an organisation for how to respond to emerging events.

You don't necessarily need to have access to an expert 'process facilitator' for scenario planning, but it probably helps. Any manager with the interest and the inclination can skill themselves in the facilitation process to the point where they can 'run' a scenario planning session. Using a consultant will shortcut this need but it comes at the cost of not developing in-house expertise (and of course the cost of the consultant!).

Instructions

How to create scenarios

1. *The situation*

   - Select an issue of major significance to the organisation.
   - Decide the timeframe over which the issue is to be explored. Generally, scenarios work best if the timeframe extends beyond the normal planning range. For example, many organisations plan their future successfully over a two to five year timeframe. At 10 years and beyond, their data becomes less reliable so normal (rationalistic) extrapolation techniques break down. That's where scenario planning becomes useful as a technique.

2. *The variables*

   - Develop an exhaustive list of variables that have or could have an impact on the situation identified; use techniques such as informal 'brainstorming'. Discuss their application and relevance to the situation under consideration. Variables can be anything from a slowly emerging trend to a sudden new development; more often, they are the known 'drivers' that make the situation what it is today.

- Check the list for quality. This means that the group considers the relevance, impact and significance of the items on the list. The experience within the group will dictate the calibre and quality of this list, and this makes it critical that the most appropriate people are involved in the process.
- Don't add values to the variables at this stage in the process—that comes later.
- Group the variables on the basis of relatedness or type. There are no rules for doing this other than if it makes sense to the participants then it is right. The aim is to end up with anywhere from six to 20 variables. More than this number creates excessive complexity in constructing the scenarios. Keep talking until there is agreement on this number. If you feel the need to resort to voting, then the discussion is incomplete!

3. *Exploration*

- Analyse the variables for the extent of their impact on the situation under consideration. This should be an open-ended discussion, quite literally an exploration. All participants should feel free to establish exactly what is involved in each of these variables.
- Continue this analysis until the participants are clear about what the variables mean. The purpose of this discussion is to illuminate, not to debate, so it is important to discourage individuals from simply advocating their 'pet ideas'. The order of the day should be questions that clarify and explain, not questions that attack someone else's point of view. The intended outcome of this step is the creation of understanding and meaning.

4. *The themes*

- Make lists of possible themes based on suggestions from the participants. Rearrange the lists, rewrite the words and reformulate the concepts. The ultimate criterion for selecting a set of themes is significance. If the themes satisfy the participants' subjective judgment on significance, then those themes are the right ones. Typically, most themes will cluster around a small number of (related) variables.
- Reduce the list of themes to about five to seven. In a single planning session, most groups can handle about this number. More than this creates too much complexity. By now, the participants should have been deeply immersed in the variables that impact on the situation selected for study.
- Agree on the degree of impact of the variables as they relate to each theme. Some kind of rating system can be useful here but keep it simple. It is only necessary to have broad agreement on relative weightings. For example, a High/Medium/Low type of rating usually

suffices. This step brings out more clearly which of the variables are the most important for a given scenario. Don't be surprised if some variables have almost no bearing on one scenario but are critical to another.

5. *The scenarios*

- Construct the scenarios. This is the hardest part of the process, mainly because it is the most creative part. If the numbers in the group allow, create small groups and have each group write one scenario. The format for scenarios varies but can include: a narrative story; a report of a journey or a site visit; an office memo; a letter; a speech; a news report; a transcript of an interview; or (only once in my experience!) a poem. It is sometimes helpful to agree on a consistent format for all the groups to follow.
- Read the scenarios through with the whole group. The purpose of this is to critique the scenario for internal consistency. This critique should suspend judgment about the likelihood of the scenario becoming real. Instead, the focus of critical analysis at this stage should be on the extent to which the scenario tells a plausible story. The purpose is to remove incompatibilities and inconsistencies, and improve the 'convincingness' of the tale.
- Finalise the scenarios in response to the contributions made. The groups should polish their stories until they are deemed 'satisfactory'. Although this criterion sounds rather vague, by now the participants will know what this means.

6. *The implications*

- Display the scenarios (perhaps on a wall in large format) and consider what each scenario means for the organisation if it were to come about. The scenarios are possible futures. They may or may not be close to what actually happens. What is important is that, if they did turn out to be predictive of the future, then at least one group within the organisation has considered how to respond.
- Ask the group: 'If this was the reality we faced, what are the implications for our organisation?' This discussion typically generates a series of responses by the organisation that can lead to action steps. Some of this may involve actions taken now to prepare in some limited way for the possible reality described in the scenarios. Thus scenario planning becomes a protective planning mechanism that is a bit like insurance— you invest some resources now in case an unplanned but possible event occurs.
- Consider the impact of any proposed action on the scenarios. This means the proposed actions to be taken by the organisation are injected into the scenarios and judgments are made about their impact. Such actions can therefore be tested for effectiveness in bringing about a set of circumstances or preventing them from arising. It is possible

for a different group to undertake this final step; for example, a larger group not involved in the other steps. This spreads the involvement without consuming limited management time.

Further reading

Scenario planning is closely associated with the work done by Royal Dutch Shell; and its ex-employees have written the most interesting books on the subject. Indeed, the four best writers on the subject are all former planning specialists within Royal Dutch Shell.

- P Wack, 'Scenarios: Unchartered waters ahead', *Harvard Business Review*, vol. 5, no. 63, 1985, pp. 73–90.

  Pierre Wack was the founder of the business planning division within Shell that developed the scenario planning technique. His published contribution consists mainly of articles such as this one, which provides the original and classic version of the technique.

- A De Geus, *The living company*, Harvard Business School Press, Boston, 1997.

  Arie de Geus is most publicly associated with the company's research and development of scenario techniques in the 1960s. However, it took him a while to get around to writing this book. It is a bit of a philosophical wander around the modern enterprise, but it is clear that its future orientation is based on the kind of scenario thinking that was developed at Shell.

- K Van Der Heijden, *Scenarios: The art of strategic conversation*, John Wiley, New York, 1996.

  This book by Kees Van Der Heijden is a little more practical. It provides an approach that is based on scenario planning, but takes it one step further by making it part of a continuous process of dialogue within the organisation.

- P Schwartz, *The art of the long view: Planning for the future in an uncertain world*, Doubleday, London, 1996.

  Peter Schwartz's book is also strong on technique and provides possibly the most sophisticated version of the various approaches and subtleties of the process available so far.

Notes

1. See, for example: A De Geus, *The living company*, Harvard Business School Press, Boston, 1997; K Van Der Heijden, *Scenarios: The art of strategic conversation*, John Wiley, New York, 1996; P Schwartz, *The art of the long*

view: Planning for the future in an uncertain world, Doubleday, London, 1996; P Wack, 'Scenarios: Unchartered waters ahead', *Harvard Business Review*, vol. 5, no. 63, 1985, pp. 73–90.

2. J Coates, 'Scenario planning', *Technological Forecasting and Social Change*, vol. 65, 2000, pp. 115–23.
3. P Schwartz, op. cit.
4. J Coates, op. cit.
5. See the work of Michel Godet in *Scenarios and strategic management*, Butterworth, London, 1987.
6. H Mintzberg, *Strategy safari*, The Free Press, New York, 1998.
7. The exception to this is extremely fast-moving industries such as software development or the fashion industry. The application of scenario planning to such turbulent and turbo-charged industries is possibly questionable. By the time the planning process is completed, the scenarios would probably be irrelevant.
8. A Wright, 'Scenario planning: A continuous improvement approach to strategy', *Total Quality Management*, vol. 4, no. 11, 2000, pp. 433–8.
9. H Linstone, *Decision making for technology executives: Using multiple perspectives to improve performance*, Artech House, Boston, 1999.
10. Some of my colleagues also use a 'man from Mars' technique by bringing someone into the discussion who is completely unfamiliar with the organisation and even its industry.
11. D Mercer, 'Robust strategies in a day', *Management Decision*, vol. 35, no. 3, 1997, pp. 219–23.

CHAPTER 5

Changing culture
The Competing Values Framework

Organisational culture is a fashionable topic of conversation in management circles. In a short space of time, it seems to have become the universal explanation of what is wrong with our organisations. Culture is the excuse we turn to when we've run out of other things to blame. All of which naturally leads to the question: What is organisational culture and why are we blaming it for so many problems?

Part of the problem with culture is that it is an attractive but elusive concept. It sounds like something that is powerful enough to explain the complexities of organisational life, but in reality it is rather hard to define. The intangible nature of the concept sets it apart from the very concrete elements that managers usually work with, such as redesigning the organisation's structure or hiring and firing staff. And if it is hard to grasp, it is even harder to change. Some argue that culture can't be changed and others argue that the concept has no useful application for the business of management.

So if culture cannot be seen or touched (although it can be felt!), then maybe the first step towards understanding it better is to create a *picture* of culture. One approach based on this idea seems to be paying dividends. The work of Robert Quinn and his colleagues is founded on the idea that an organisation's culture results from a tug-of-war between a set of *competing values*.[1] Each competing value pulls the organisation towards one of four types of culture:

- a *Clan* culture that values shared beliefs, teamwork and mutual support
- an *Adhocratic* culture that values freedom, initiative and creativity
- a *Hierarchical* culture that values efficiency, predictability and structure
- a *Market* culture that values goal achievement, competitiveness and performance.

The resulting Competing Values Framework allows us to plot the relative strength of each of these four culture types (and every organisation has a degree of all four within its own unique culture), thereby creating a 'culture map' for the organisation. The framework's capacity to graphically demonstrate what an organisation looks like is one of its real strengths.

Background

The notion of culture was brought to organisational studies from anthropology, where it is used to describe societies, both ancient and modern. In particular, the anthropologists' view is that organisations are 'cultural constructs'. The view of an organisation as a *construct* received a major boost in the 1970s, when some adventurous scholars started to look at the modern industrial organisation.

As a consequence, organisational theorists took an interest in what the anthropologists were saying. When discussing the nature of the modern organisation, they began to adopt the language of anthropology, and that language was all about the organisation as a *culture*. Culture was defined in one instance as 'a construct describing the total body of belief, behaviour, knowledge, sanctions, values and goals that make up the way of life of a people'.[2]

Two books put the notion of culture firmly on the management table. *In search of excellence*[3] and *Corporate culture: The rites and rituals of corporate life*[4] (both published in 1982) drove the transformation of culture to an organisational concept: *organisational culture*. The first book linked excellence to a strong and unifying organisational culture, based on a shared vision. The second book added theoretical substance to the growing debate on culture and helped to popularise the concept. This popularisation typically involved looking back to past efforts in the field (as if to provide a pedigree) and so earlier works were rediscovered, such as Ouchi's description of culture as 'the way we do things around here'.[5]

Different approaches proliferated as others tried to unify the debate by creating a holistic approach.[6] Today, the focus is on how to 'operationalise' the concept of organisational culture; that is, make it into something that managers can use. No approach, however, is as successful as the Quinn framework for capturing the choices that organisations make when considering what they are or what they want to be.

The Competing Values Framework (CVF) was developed initially to give managers a tool to understand and change organisational culture within a specific organisation. It derives from the fundamental research conducted by many others and was an amalgamation of the best of that research in a framework that managers could use. It immediately drew criticism from those who believe that culture cannot be changed.[7] Despite all this, Quinn and his colleagues persisted and delivered a framework that is:

- practical (it has been applied in many organisations)
- timely (it has shown that change is possible within a reasonable time period)
- involving (it requires input from many, but especially from those who direct the organisation)
- quantitative and qualitative (it is based on data, both numerical and anecdotal)
- manageable (it can be managed by those within the organisation without outside assistance)
- valid (it has been validated on a number of levels and in many different contexts).

After some 20 years of application, the CVF has proved to be a rigorous and effective tool for understanding organisational culture and driving culture change.

The tool

The CVF is a matrix based on two axes. The horizontal axis indicates where the organisation focuses its attention. It ranges from, at one end, a focus on *internal* issues and the need to create a well-integrated organisation to, at the other end, a focus on the *external* environment. The organisation's position on the horizontal dimension indicates the extent to which it strives to maintain internal cohesion versus local independence. For example, Hewlett-Packard is well known for being the same wherever it operates in the world; at the other end of the spectrum is News Corp, which allows its subsidiaries considerable local independence.

The vertical axis differentiates organisations on the basis of whether they demand stability, order and central control or encourage flexibility, discretion and local initiative. At one extreme, organisations are seen as effective if they are predictable and well-ordered entities; at the other, effectiveness is about being adaptable, encouraging change and being responsive to new ideas. Boeing is an example of the former; Nike is an example of the latter.

The four cultures

The four quadrants of the framework represent four different cultures— four competing but equally valid pictures of organisational effectiveness (see Figure 5.1).

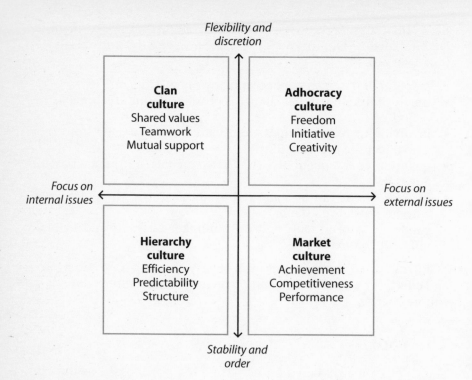

Figure 5.1 The four cultures
Source: Based on the work of Cameron and Quinn[8]

Clan culture

This culture typifies an organisation that focuses on internal issues, especially relating to its people. It deals with such issues flexibly because it is concerned for its people. At the same time, it is sensitive to the needs of its customers.

- It's a friendly place to work where people share a lot of themselves, almost like an extended family.
- The leaders are seen as coaches or even as parent figures.
- The organisation is held together by loyalty or tradition.
- Commitment is high.
- The organisation emphasises the long-term benefit of human resources development and attaches great importance to cohesion and morale.
- Success is defined in terms of sensitivity to customers and concern for people.
- The organisation places a premium on teamwork, participation and consensus.

Adhocracy culture

This type of culture focuses on external positioning, maintaining its competitiveness with a high degree of flexibility and a focus on the individual. It is a dynamic, entrepreneurial and creative place to work, where people stick their necks out and take risks.

- The leaders are considered innovators and risk-takers.
- The glue that holds the place together is commitment to experimentation and innovation.
- Readiness for change and meeting new challenges are important.
- The emphasis is on being at the leading edge.
- The long-term emphasis is on growth and acquiring new resources.

Hierarchy culture

This culture focuses on internal maintenance, with an overriding need for stability and control. It is a very formalised and structured place to work.

- Procedure governs what people do.
- The leaders pride themselves on being good coordinators and organisers who are efficiency-minded.
- Maintaining a smooth-running organisation is most critical.
- Formal rules and policies hold the organisation together.
- Success is defined in terms of dependable delivery, smooth scheduling and low cost.
- The management of employees is concerned with secure employment and predictability.
- The long-term concern is for stability and performance with efficient, smooth operations.

Market culture

This type of culture focuses on external positioning, with a need for stability and control. It drives a results-oriented organisation whose major concern is with 'getting the job done'.

- People are competitive and goal-oriented.
- The leaders are hard-driving, tough and demanding.
- The glue that holds the organisation together is an emphasis on winning.
- Reputation and success are common concerns.
- Success is defined in terms of market share and penetration.
- Competitive pricing and market leadership are important.
- The organisational style is hard-driving competitiveness.
- The long-term focus is on competitive actions and achievement of measurable goals and targets.

Moving to a different culture

There are elements of all four cultures in all organisations but at any one time it is highly likely that only one or two are dominant. In times of change, it sometimes becomes obvious that an organisation needs to move from one dominant way of doing things to another. Some examples of this are:

- In the late 1980s, many manufacturing organisations came to admire the Japanese Clan style of working because it seemed to deliver cost and quality benefits; many organisations tried to adopt Japanese management techniques.
- When many government-owned organisations were privatised in the 1990s, they were forced to adopt a more competitive approach driven by a Market culture.
- When hi-tech start-up companies first open up shop they tend to be extreme Adhocracies, but most soon realise the need to adopt some bits of the Hierarchy culture because otherwise the debts aren't collected and the staff don't get paid.

Sometimes organisations go through cycles of reinventing themselves, often driven by changing market conditions. The global beer and wine group Foster's CUB was, until recently, a sleepy Australian brewer with a somewhat Clan-like management style. It turned to a Market style of management (with a touch of Adhocracy thrown in) to make a relatively unknown (and in Australia not especially popular) beer called Foster's into a world brand. This change was driven by new CEO John Elliott. Having taken the world by storm, it then adopted a Hierarchy style (under the next CEO, Peter Bartels) to consolidate its gains. Finally, the company went back to Market style (under yet another CEO, Ted Kunkel) to reinvent itself as a wine company that also makes beer.

Mapping culture

Each of the four types of culture manifests itself in different but consistent ways of doing things (see Table 5.1).

Organisations can map their current culture by means of an assessment instrument provided by Cameron and Quinn[9]; a slightly abridged version can be found at the end of this chapter. The assessment uses a forced-choice scale where respondents divide 100 points among four alternatives. This forced-choice approach tends to generate fewer extreme responses. By dividing 100 points amongst each of the four options presented, and doing this for each of the six organisational characteristics used in the assessment, it is possible to calculate the relative strength of each of the four culture types. These results can then be plotted onto the four quadrants. For an example, see Figure 5.2, the culture map drawn by a telecommunications company.

Table 5.1 Characteristics of the four types of culture

Characteristics	Adhocracy culture	Hierarchy culture	Clan culture	Market culture
Type of leader	Innovator Entrepreneur Visionary	Coordinator Monitor Organiser	Mentor Facilitator Parent	Driver Competitor Producer
Meaning of success	Innovation Growth Cutting-edge	Efficiency Accuracy Timeliness	Cohesion Morale Teamwork	Market share Achievement Winning
Dominant idea	*Innovation fosters growth*	*Control fosters efficiency*	*Participation fosters commitment*	*Competition fosters productivity*

Source: Based on the work of Cameron and Quinn[10]

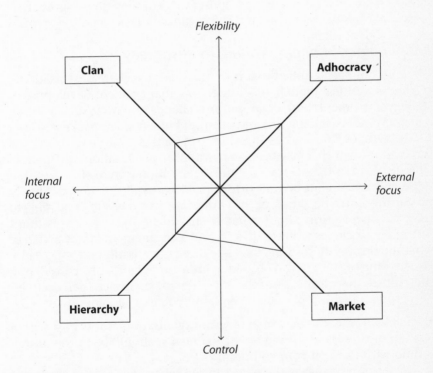

Figure 5.2 Culture map of a telecommunications company

The telecommunication company's culture map shows that the organisation is drawn more strongly towards the Adhocracy and Market cultures, at the expense of the other two types. This suggests an organisation that is out to build market share by focusing on customers' needs, but is possibly ignoring the impact of these actions on staff morale and losing sight of the need to build effective and efficient systems that back up service delivery. Indeed, the organisation is struggling to provide the services it has committed to deliver; the sales function has started to point the finger at the operational functions for failing to follow through on sales commitments. Meanwhile, the operational function is under-resourced and possibly under-valued which, together with the morale issue, is starting to creating serious strains.

The telecommunications company analysed its own needs on the basis of its culture map and realised that it needed to put greater emphasis on retaining customers through improved operations instead of just focusing on getting more customers. The change needed was a bit more Hierarchy in order to deliver a dependable level of operational performance, all of which means there will be a bit less Adhocracy. The sales staff are only reluctantly accepting this but they do recognise that something has to change to stop the organisation from falling apart.

Adapting and changing culture to fit strategy

The CVF has been applied to a host of situations where organisational culture is a critical ingredient—leadership, management development, strategy implementation, organisational change initiatives such as TQM, and many others. But it is first and foremost known as a *culture change* tool.

The most obvious way to apply the tool for this purpose is to examine the culture map that has been drawn for an organisation and ponder whether it is appropriate for what the organisation is trying to do. In that sense, culture mapping becomes a tool for *adapting culture to strategy*. Simply by starting with a depiction of the current culture, it becomes possible to have a conversation about what it should be like (the assessment instrument includes scope to do a second assessment and draw a map of what the organisation *should* look like if the organisation is to succeed.)

This kind of analysis can be made a little more rigorous by considering the culture map from a number of different analytical perspectives. Cameron and Quinn provide several, but you can add your own:

- *Culture type:* compare a map of your organisation as it is now with a map of what it was some time ago, what it should be in the future, and with those of your competitors.
- *Discrepancies:* what is the gap between what your map is and what you think it should be?
- *Strength:* do you have a strong tendency in one direction or is your culture map more balanced and well-rounded; does this matter?
- *Congruence:* re-examine the six aspects of organisational life on which the assessment was made (see the assessment instrument at the end of the chapter) and consider the degree of congruence; is one or more aspect different from the rest?

Making change happen

Assuming that your organisation sees the need for change, describe what the change will mean for everyone in the organisation. You then need to decide how to make the change happen. The map will assist in providing a visual direction for change, a language to describe it, and a tool for measuring progress. But that is not the same as understanding the change and taking action to achieve it. That is a bit more complicated.

Generally, people will only sign up for change if they understand what it involves. This implies that those who drive change need to be capable of *explaining* it to others. Many managers have considerable difficulty with this; they tend to speak in jargon-ridden slogans, probably provided by a consultant or borrowed from a management text. Managers must be able to describe change in a way that will lead to understanding and clarity rather than to suspicion and fear. The best way to do this is to tell stories.

Just as all organisations have stories about the way the place is now, managers need to create stories that are descriptive of what it will be like when the change is in place. For example, let's assume that an organisation wants to move a little up the Adhocracy scale. This may involve a move towards greater customer responsiveness. The organisation wants to give frontline staff greater discretionary power in dealing with customer issues. What the managers need to do is to explain that this means:

- that staff will be making the decisions, not management
- that staff need to use their own best judgment
- that management knows that staff won't always get it right
- that no-one will get into trouble for making a wrong call
- that staff and management need to decide what sort of training they need for their new roles
- that training will be made available
- that managers will still be around to help.

Once again, Cameron and Quinn provide a useful tool to help this process. It involves analysing the broad direction for change that has been selected (for example, more Hierarchy, more Clan, less Adhocracy, same Market) and clarifying *what that change means* and *what it doesn't mean*. Such descriptions are very effective for telling people what the change is about.

As far as making the change actually happen, there are only a limited number of levers that senior managers can pull to achieve cultural change. The two most significant are:

- *Leadership behaviour.* The behaviour of leaders is critical in sustaining a particular culture and it is indispensable in changing it.
- *The systems of the organisation.* Systems constantly reinforce the culture of the organisation. Systems need to be realigned with the desired change so that they reinforce the new way of doing things.

In wanting to change culture, the leadership of an organisation must:

- *Decide which aspects of leadership behaviour require change.* This decision should be made after considering the culture change that is required. For example, the leadership group of an organisation might decide that the organisation needs a bit more Hierarchy, a bit less Adhocracy, while keeping Clan and Market at current levels. These are the leadership behaviours that will generate less 'making it up as we go along' and more 'we plan what we do and we do what we plan'.
- *Decide which systems need to change to drive change towards the desired culture.* This includes rules, policies and procedures. For example, the performance management system has enormous impact on sustaining a given culture. If the organisation needs to be more Market focused but the performance management system rewards Hierarchical behaviour, then the chances are that the system will win out over the strategic decision to become more Market focused.

Observations

Culture is both the most recent and the most complex of management notions on offer. Seen in historical context, it came after the relative simplicity of fiddling with organisational structures, managing by objectives, process re-engineering and a host of other straightforward prescriptions for management success.

Culture seems to offer answers to some really pesky issues such as:

- why employees simply don't wish to be empowered (check the control systems and you'll find that making mistakes is punished)
- why people are always in the meeting rooms for which you've taken the trouble to make a reservation (check the extent to which anyone actually follows any protocol)
- why getting people to put customers first is so difficult (check what happens if an employee fails repeatedly in a task—most likely nothing!)
- why your sales force performs exceptionally well, earning huge bonuses, and yet many leave before their contracts are up (check the extent of teamwork and cooperation on display in the sales depart-ment—you won't find any!).

Culture appears to offer answers where the textbook methods for managing seem not to work. For some, it offers the hope of moulding an organisation to the will of management. The reality is a bit harder, of course. In fact, culture has only ever offered an explanation of what was going on, not a prescription for change. At best, the notion can inform decision making about changes that need to happen within the organisation. It can help those changes happen, but it is not a mechanical tool that will deliver guaranteed results.

Possibly culture's greatest role may be to demolish the idea that managers actually control the organisations in which they work. Some time ago, the image of a boss standing over employees with a constant threat of dismissal was an accurate one. Today, most employees have far greater control than many managers are comfortable with. The discretionary effort required to get most jobs done is ever increasing. To get good performance from people they have to *want* to succeed. So the job of management has changed—from control to influence, from command to lead and from directing to supporting.

This change in role and attendant loss of control is rarely comfortable for those mangers going through it. It means developing a capacity to deal with a host of demands, many of which relate to the competing values that swirl around the innards of our organisations. Managers must learn to manage the resultant complexities and ambiguities.

The sooner we accept that the old mechanical model is insufficient to explain the modern organisation, the sooner we will stop stressing managers. If, instead, we start with a highly dynamic model, full of unpredictabilities and uncertainties, then we at least give our managers a realistic base from which to build their coping strategies. The notion of culture, and specifically the CVF, helps us move towards this kind of model of the organisation. It may be complex, but at least it's real. Having a better model, however, doesn't simplify the task for managers. In fact, many pitfalls remain in managing change (some of which were mentioned earlier):

- the failure to adequately understand what is involved
- the failure to be able to describe the change
- the failure to change leadership behaviour and systems.

Until the organisation is capable of addressing such issues, cultural change will continue to be an interesting idea rather than a real option.

The CVF avoids many of these pitfalls because it provides a map that increases understanding; it outlines what actually drives culture (and, therefore, what needs to change); and it enables a group to draw a picture of what the preferred culture needs to be like. All of this helps to make it one of the few useful tools in the murky business of changing organisational culture.

User's guide

The Competing Values Framework is most effective when supporting a change effort that is focused on organisational culture. Although it has been applied to many other challenges, it stands out as a culture change tool. Because of the effort involved in any large-scale change program, it is likely that a number of people will be involved. The CVF can help to create a common language for the change, and crystallise the meaning of the change.

It is outside the scope of this book to provide a comprehensive overview of how to drive a culture change program (Cameron and Quinn provide such an overview in their book, *Diagnosing and changing organisational culture*). However, working with a group and using the CVF to create a culture map (following the steps in the instructions) can lead to an exploration of the required changes.

As always with group work, it is useful to have a facilitator to guide the process. The group should represent the diversity of views within the organisation; a complete 'vertical slice' is ideal, though not always possible.

Instructions

How to use the Competing Values Framework

1. *Understand the CVF.*

   One of the group should research the model to sufficient depth to be able to explain the Competing Values Framework to the rest of the group. The material outlined in the chapter so far should be sufficient, or supplement it with material drawn from Cameron and Quinn.

2. *Create a map of the current culture.*

   - Use the Organisational Culture Assessment Instrument at the end of this chapter (instructions are provided). Each of those participating in the session should complete it.
   - Plot the averaged results on a whiteboard or flipchart (or use the blank map supplied at the end of this chapter). The resulting four-sided figure represents the current culture of the organisation and shows the extent to which the organisation is 'pulled' towards each of the four culture types.
   - The group should discuss the implications of what they see. Does it feel 'right'? What does it mean?

3. *Map the preferred culture.*

   - Use the assessment instrument a second time, but in response to a clearly identified 'driver for change' (such as 'becoming more responsive to customer needs' or 'becoming more innovative'). The group should indicate what the culture needs to be.
   - Map this on top of the current culture to clearly show any gaps. It is unlikely that the overlay will be perfect.
   - Where there are discrepancies, discuss their meaning. For example, if it shows a need to decrease the Hierarchy aspects of the culture, what does this mean?
   - For each discrepancy, examine the assessment results. Compare the current and preferred scores for each of the six assessment questions. Which of the six areas needs change?

4. *Explore the implications.*

- Clarify what this means and does not mean (see the earlier section, Making change happen). Explore the implications of the cultural shift that is being considered.
- Follow this up with a detailed analysis of the actions that need to be taken to make the change happen.

Further reading

- K Cameron & R Quinn, *Diagnosing and changing organisational culture*, Addison Wesley, Reading, 1999.

I have quoted Cameron and Quinn throughout this chapter. Their book is concise and practical, without being overly academic. It will answer a lot of questions that I have only been able to touch on in this brief summary of their work.

- R Quinn, *Beyond rational management*, Jossey-Bass, San Francisco, 1988.
- R Quinn, *Deep change*, Jossey-Bass, San Francisco, 1996.

Robert Quinn has also written extensively on the role of the manager in organisations. He has undertaken detailed research into the ambiguities, complexities and dilemmas of the job. He relates many of these to managing the contradictions inherent in any organisation that is trying to balance its competing values.

Notes

1. K Cameron & R Quinn, *Diagnosing and changing organisational culture*, Addison Wesley, Reading, 1999.
2. M Herskowitz, *Man and his works*, Knopf, Westminster, 1948.
3. T Peters & R Waterman, *In search of excellence*, Harper & Row, New York, 1984.
4. T Deal & A Kennedy, *Corporate cultures: The rites and rituals of corporate life*, Addison-Wesley, Reading, 1982.
5. W Ouchi & A Johnson, 'Types of organisational control and their relationship to emotional well-being', *Administrative Science Quarterly*, vol. 23, 1978, pp 292–317.
6. D Pheysey, *Organisational cultures: Types and transformations*, Routledge, London, 1993.
7. T Fitzgerald, 'Can change in organisational culture really be managed?', *Organisational Dynamics*, vol.17, issue 2, 1988, pp. 5–15.
8. Cameron & Quinn, op. cit.
9. 'The Organisation Culture Assessment Instrument' in Cameron & Quinn, op. cit., p. 18.
10. Cameron & Quinn, op. cit.

Instructions for the Organisational Culture Assessment Instrument

1. Select the organisational unit to which you want to apply this assessment (it may be the entire organisation). This is a group exercise, but participants must complete the instrument individually.

2. Ask participants to enter the scores for the 'Now' column.

   - For each question, allocate 100 points across the four options, based on how they see the organisation as it is *at the moment*.
   - Using the score sheet at the end of the instrument, each participant must add up all of their A scores and divide the result by six; this will provide the score for the Clan culture. Do the same for B (Adhocracy), C (Market) and D (Hierarchy).

3. Add up all of the participants' A scores.

   - Divide this amount by the number of participants. The result will be the group's *average score* for the Clan culture. Do the same for B, C and D.

4. Plot the group's average scores for each of the four cultures (a blank culture map is supplied at the end of this chapter).

   - Connect the four points to create a four-sided figure. The result is the *current culture profile* of the organisation.

5. To create the *preferred culture profile*, agree on what the organisation needs to achieve (for example, a strategy or an objective).

   - Repeat step 2, entering scores into the 'Needed' column.
   - Repeat steps 3 and 4.
   - Plot the scores onto the same culture map but in a different colour.
   - You can take the analysis to another level of detail by examining the components of the culture. The six questions that form the basis of the assessment instrument will generate data for each of those elements of culture.
   - Draw up a table showing the scores for each question by each of the four cultures. Review the consistency of the scores. For example, the scores for Leadership may differ from the scores for Organisational Glue; what does that mean? Inconsistencies will suggest courses of action for implementing strategies designed to achieve culture shift.

Organisational Culture Assessment Instrument

1. Dominant characteristics: The organisation is...	Now	Needed
A A very personal place. It is like an extended family. People seem to share and give a lot of themselves.		
B A very dynamic and entrepreneurial place. People are willing to stick their necks out and take risks.		
C Very results oriented. Of major concern is getting the job done. People are very competitive and achievement oriented.		
D A very controlled and structured place. Formal procedures generally govern what people do.		
TOTAL	100	100
2. Leadership: The leadership style is characterised by...	Now	Needed
A Mentoring, facilitating or nurturing.		
B Entrepreneurship, innovating, risk-taking.		
C A no-nonsense, aggressive, results-oriented focus.		
D Coordinating, organising, smooth-running efficiency.		
TOTAL	100	100
3. Management of employees: The management style in the organisation is characterised by...	Now	Needed
A Teamwork, consensus, participation.		
B Individual risk-taking, innovation, freedom, uniqueness.		
C Hard-driving competitiveness, high demands and achievement.		
D Security of employment, conformity, predictability and stability in relationships.		
TOTAL	100	100

4. Organisational glue: The glue that holds the place together is...

	Now	Needed
A Loyalty and mutual trust. Commitment to this organisation is high.		
B Commitment to innovation and development. There is an emphasis on being at the cutting edge.		
C The emphasis on achievement and goal accomplishment. Aggressiveness and winning are common themes.		
D Formal rules and policies. Maintaining a smooth-running organisation is important.		
TOTAL	100	100

5. Strategic emphases: The organisation emphasises...

	Now	Needed
A Human development. High trust. Openness and participation persist.		
B Acquiring new resources and creating new challenges. Trying new things and prospecting for opportunities are valued.		
C Competitive actions and achievement. Hitting stretch targets and winning in the marketplace are dominant.		
D Permanence and stability. Efficiency, control and smooth operations are important.		
TOTAL	100	100

6. Criteria for success: The organisation defines success on the basis of...

	Now	Needed
A The development of human resources, teamwork, employee commitment and concern for people.		
B Having the most unique or newest products. It is a product leader and innovator.		
C Winning in the marketplace and outpacing the competition. Competitive market leadership is the key.		
D Efficiency. Dependable delivery, smooth scheduling and low-cost production are critical.		
TOTAL	100	100

Score Sheet

	Scores for A		Scores for B		Scores for C		Scores for D	
	Now	Needed	Now	Needed	Now	Needed	Now	Needed
Question 1								
Question 2								
Question 3								
Question 4								
Question 5								
Question 6								
TOTAL								
Divide by 6								
Culture	Clan		Adhocracy		Market		Hierarchy	

Competing Values Framework culture map
(Use this blank map to plot your results)

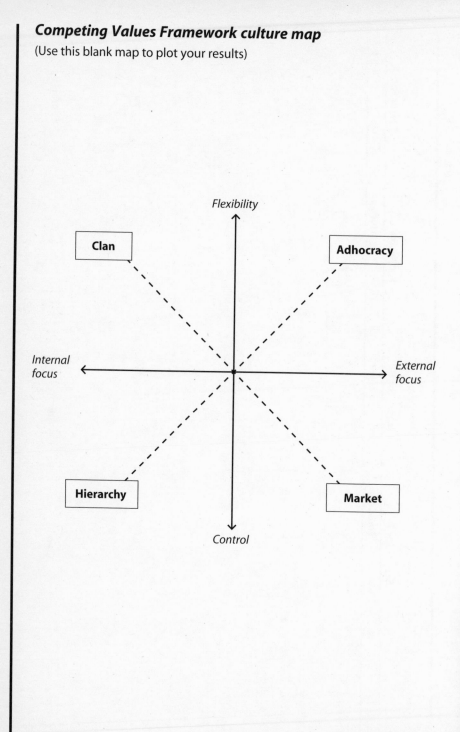

CHAPTER 6

Growing a diversified business
Product portfolio analysis

Many organisations are not single businesses operating in a single market but rather a collection of different businesses with activities in several different markets. In other words, they are diversified businesses. Diversification creates special challenges for organisations because they have to make decisions about how the whole of the business hangs together.

The most important question a diversified business can ask is how to make the organisation as a whole grow and prosper. Inevitably, this means looking at the business units and deciding whether the organisation should support them through investment, or divest them. It may also involve looking outside the organisation for businesses to acquire. Making such decisions is never easy, but it is an ongoing strategic challenge for any diversified businesses.

Those who run diversified businesses ('Head Office') must add value by managing the combination of businesses to maximise the worth of the organisation—they need to make the whole more valuable than the sum of the parts. If the combined shareholder value of the individual businesses is not exceeded by the value of the whole business, then Head Office is not adding value.

A number of tools have been developed (mostly by consulting groups) to help organisations make decisions about their 'portfolio' of businesses. The first of these—and still the one used most extensively in industry—is the *product portfolio analysis matrix*, developed by the Boston Consulting Group.[1] The language of this tool has entered the language of business: Cash Cows, Dogs, Rising Stars and Question Marks.

Product portfolio analysis (PPA, sometimes called Boston matrix analysis or Growth-share matrix) is a relatively simple technique for analysing the contributions made by the various businesses to the future prospects of the organisation. Above all, it is a tool that can drive growth by helping diversified businesses understand where the best growth potential lies. It does this by means of a matrix that contrasts relative market share for a given business with the growth rate for the industry in which that business competes.

The tool allows a diversified organisation to plot all of its businesses onto the matrix. Each quarter of the matrix demands a unique strategic response. For example:

- If a business falls into the quarter that represents high market share and high growth rate, then it is considered a *Star* and should be nurtured.
- Businesses that fall into the low market share and low industry growth quarter are *Dogs* and should be dealt with accordingly.
- Businesses that have low growth rate but high market share generate lots of cash and should be protected; they are the *Cash Cows*.
- Businesses with low market share but in industries that have high growth rates are uncertainties in the portfolio, and they may or may not turn into 'Stars'; they are *Question Marks*.

The PPA does have some limitations and various improvements have been suggested. For example, the consulting group McKinsey (together with GE) developed a more sophisticated version of the matrix that allowed more sensitive ratings to be given along the two axes. However, despite any drawbacks of the original tool, it is still used extensively in industry and continues to provide valuable insights.

Background

Why diversify?

There are various rational reasons why businesses decide to adopt a diversified business model.

- *Economies of scale*. Some businesses can apply a specific set of competencies to a variety of unrelated industries. For example, GE brings general managerial ability to a wide variety of industries.
- *Industry dominance*. Once a business dominates the industry in which it operates, it must look elsewhere for growth opportunities. This is especially so for those businesses in mature, low-growth markets or (in some countries) where government regulation limits market dominance. For example, News Corp dominates the newspaper industry in a number of countries and has diversified into movies, cable television and sports management.
- *Strong cash flow*. Businesses that have strong cash flow (often associated with industry dominance) may want to invest in other industries rather than risk further expansion in their own industry (which could

set off hyper competition that could risk existing profits). For example, following the oil crises of the 1970s and 1980s, many oil companies diversified into other businesses (such as chemicals), although most were unsuccessful and subsequently sold down their investments.

- *Poor cash flow.* Some businesses are unprofitable even though their competitors may be doing well; such businesses may seek to move into other industries in the hope that this will generate better cash flow. For example, many under-performing businesses had a go at becoming 'hi tech' businesses at the height of the dot-com boom in the late 1990s.
- *Industry changes.* Some industries become unprofitable, are changed by government fiat, or even disappear altogether (such as the asbestos industry), forcing businesses to go elsewhere. For example, Australian building products group James Hardie started life as an asbestos producer but, for obvious reasons, branched out.

There are also irrational or non-rational reasons for diversifying.

- *Strategy fads.* The idea that diversified businesses are 'insured' against industry downturns because they have spread their risk across a number of industries is a faddish belief that comes and goes in regular cycles. There is plenty of data to support both the 'diversified insurance' case and the opposite 'focused management' case, and the argument is unlikely ever to be settled. Unfortunately, both cases provide management with the opportunity to promote change for change's sake, the result being regular and largely irrational bouts of diversification followed by divestment back to a core business.
- *Opportunism.* Various businesses (sometimes just the entrepreneurs behind them) thrive on acquiring businesses that are in some way undervalued. An opportunity to make money is perceived and suddenly a new business unit is acquired. In the extreme, these are 'asset stripping' operations, but more often they are simply opportunities to expand. For example, New Zealand spices company Burns Philp acquired Australia's largest grocery manufacturer Goodman Fielder in a hostile takeover because it could see opportunities to make money where Goodman Fielder could not.
- *Ownership/management changes.* Some businesses change course when ownership or management changes. The new owners or managers see better opportunities in other industries and move into those industries. For example, Amcor, the global packaging group, moved into the glass business in Australia mainly because its chief executive came from that industry.

Diversification most often means acquisition. Occasionally a business will diversify through internal development, but this is a very slow process. It seems to happen most often when a business develops (sometimes accidentally) a technology that can lead to a whole new line of business. For example, Australian glass manufacturer ACI developed such a successful information technology capability that it turned it into a separate and profitable line of business. However, even in these circumstances, diversification may be short-lived (ACI later spun off its IT division into a separate company, Ferntree Computing, and went back to focusing on glass).

Acquisition carries many risks and research data suggest that most acquisitions and mergers are unsuccessful. The reasons for the high failure rate are outside the scope of this book. However, the realities are that, successful or not, many organisations prefer the diversified structure over any other business form.

Within the basic strategy of diversification, there are many different options. Researchers have tried to categorise these differences into different conceptual models, although none of these models fully captures what actually happens in the business world. This may well be because of the non-rational reasons for diversification already mentioned, which can be difficult to build into a model. Most diversification models assume rationality on the part of management, which is an assumption that can be hard to justify on the available evidence.

Related diversification

Derek Abell, in *Defining the business: The starting point for strategy*, developed one of the better diversification models.[2] It is a framework for judging the *relatedness* of businesses. Abell's model defines three dimensions for diversification, each representing a type of relationship that can exist between the core and acquired businesses.

1. *Customer use.* The products produced by both the core and acquired businesses are used by the customer in the same way. For example, soft drink customers may also drink mineral water or 'sports water', so soft drink manufacturers often diversify and produce these products as well.
2. *Customer groups.* The products/services produced by both the core and acquired businesses serve the needs of the same customer group. For example, soft drink manufacturers package soft drinks in glass bottles, plastic bottles or aluminum cans; therefore many beverage packaging manufacturers diversify and produce two (sometimes three) types of packaging for the soft drink manufacturing market.
3. *Technology used.* The products/services produced by both the core and acquired businesses involve similar technologies. For example, it is a very logical progression for telephone companies to buy Internet service providers because the businesses involve similar technologies.

If the core and acquired businesses are related in all three dimensions, then clearly there is a high degree of closeness and a good chance of the businesses fitting well together. If they are related in none of the dimensions, then there is a high degree of remoteness and a limited chance of the businesses fitting well together.

Problems arise if the core and acquired businesses are related in only one or two dimensions. For example, in beverage packaging, different packaging products require different manufacturing technologies. Some of these are similar, others completely unrelated. It is unlikely that the one manufacturer will be involved in both glass making and PET plastics and aluminum cans. Glass technology is complex, engineering-heavy and labour-intensive. Plastics and aluminium can technologies are simpler, more hi-tech, and involve few workers. There are few glass-makers in the world, although there are many plastic bottle and aluminum can makers. You may well find a plastic bottle manufacturer that is also in the aluminum can business—but they are very unlikely to be in the glass business as well.

One of the problems with diversification strategy is a psychological one: the innate optimism of managers that they can create value by creating fit. Managers tend to overestimate their capacity to judge what is a good fit and what is not. They tend to see the good bits ('the glass is half full' syndrome) and not the bits that are problematical ('the glass is half empty'). As a result, many acquisitions made to create a diversified business are doomed to failure from day one.

The traditional argument in favour of an acquisition is that it will create synergies that somehow will produce a result that is greater than the sum of the two businesses. The potential source of such synergies is usually areas such as operations (for example, scales of economy in service delivery); marketing (for example, using one sales force to service both businesses); or administration (for example, spreading corporate over-heads more widely). Typically, such synergies turn out to involve cost reductions. That is, the acquiring business is able to shed some of the costs involved in running the acquired business without losing revenue.

Unrelated diversification

There is another diversification strategy that involves a deliberate decision to acquire unrelated businesses. This is relatively common in small economies such as Australia and smaller Asian nations, where the size of the marketplace does not allow a successful operator to expand any further. The typical response to this situation is to enter a new and unrelated market, with no real effort to look for synergies. In larger economies, such as the USA and Europe, this strategy is unnecessary as there is enough room for a single core business to grow.

Unrelated diversification has a number of advantages:

- *Risk spread.* Any business is subject to risk, ranging from predictable cyclical factors to unexpected disasters. By being in more than one business, you spread the risk.

- *Counter-cyclical protection.* By being in businesses that are known to run counter-cyclically (such as having products that will sell in winter balanced by products that will sell in summer), you can smooth out cash flow; a simple example is selling skiwear in winter and beachwear in summer).
- *Financial matching.* Balancing a low cash flow operation with one that is high cash flow, or a business with high debt ratios with one that has low debt ratios.
- *Buying value.* You may see cash flow generating possibilities that are not seen by the current owners of a business.

The tool

Assuming that you have a diversified business, how do you manage the competing demands? Different businesses need different management strategies to ensure a positive outcome for the diversified business overall. Product portfolio analysis (PPA) is a tool for managing this challenge.

PPA was developed by the Boston Consulting Group in 1968 to assist their clients to understand the implications of their 'portfolio' of businesses. It is designed to help create a balanced growth strategy for the diversified business. PPA is based on categorising businesses on the basis of the level of their market share (high or low) and industry growth rate (high or low). There are four categories, each represented on the PPA matrix as a quadrant.

1. High–high quadrant: *Rising Stars*

   Rising Stars (high market share/high growth rate) are the leaders in a given market. But because they are in high growth markets, profits usually must be ploughed back into the business to fund expansion. So they are very desirable businesses to have but they do not actually generate a lot of profit for the diversified business.

2. High–low quadrant: *Cash Cows*

   Cash Cows (high market share/low growth rate) are also market leaders, but because they operate in low growth markets they need little investment to keep them going. As a result, they generate lots of cash that can be used to fund expansion elsewhere. Every diversified business wants and needs a Cash Cow.

3. Low–high quadrant: *Question Marks*

   Question Marks (low market share/high growth) have low market share but in markets that are growing rapidly and, therefore, have enormous potential. However, they need lots of investment to keep them going and to retain their market share. For this reason, they are problematical. Should the diversified business continue to invest in the hope that the Question Mark will become a Rising Star? Every diversified business worries about its Question Marks.

4. Low–low quadrant: *Dogs*

Dogs (low market share/low growth) are the businesses that no-one wants. Increasing market share is usually difficult, expensive or both. Changing the growth rate of the industry is always difficult (although more possible than most organisations think—see below). Dogs are the businesses that the diversified business might consider divesting.

Figure 6.1 is an example of a PPA matrix. Each business in the organisation's portfolio is represented by a circle, with the size of the circle indicating current revenue for that business. The value of the business (for example, in terms of cash flow) can be added to the circles.

This simple four-quadrant approach to analysing the growth potential of the different businesses in the organisation's portfolio provides insight into how to manage the diversified organisation. It opens up the possibility of carefully balancing the cash flows generated by one business

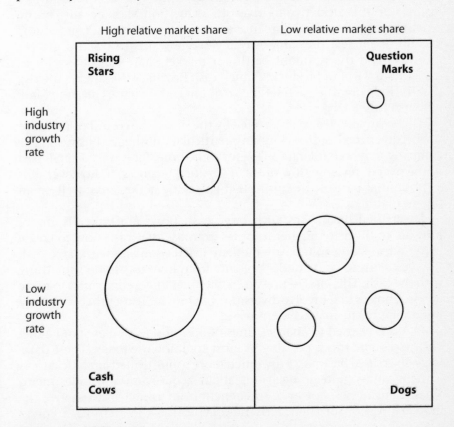

Figure 6.1 A PPA matrix

with the investment needs of another business in order to maximise growth for the organisation as a whole. For example, the cash flow of the Cash Cows can be used to subsidise the investment requirements of the Stars and Question Marks.

More importantly, the matrix can also drive strategic decisions about divestment and investment. For example, clarifying the position of Dogs can help the organisation to make decisions to divest. Typically, divestment decisions are made later than they should be because many organisations make 'emotional' investments in businesses and are then reluctant to admit that their earlier investments were not good decisions. The PPA analysis sometimes makes it easier for an organisation to admit that it is time to cut losses.

The matrix offers the opportunity to consider what needs to happen to make a Question Mark into a Rising Star, or a Rising Star into a Cash Cow. For example, the organisation may decide to invest in a Rising Star in order to protect and increase the Star's market share, knowing that over time this may turn the Star into Cash Cow.

It is much harder to figure out how to turn a Question Mark into a Rising Star. It is attractive to invest in a Question Mark because of the potential to gain market share in a fast growing market. But competitors will no doubt feel the same way (everyone wants to be in a growth industry) and the resultant battle for market share can take a lot of investment without producing much cash flow. There is always the risk that the industry will reach saturation point and then the Question Mark will turn into a Dog.

This analysis will also be affected by the size of the contribution made to the diversified business by any particular subsidiary business. The company may well tolerate a Dog for some time if it is only a small part of the overall revenue flow of the diversified business. If, however, it is a substantial part of the business then taking action may well be an urgent matter.

Diversified businesses with large cash flows are typically under pressure to diversify further in order to utilise that cash flow to create better returns on capital. Any publicly listed company with large cash reserves tends to come under pressure from investors to do something with the cash. This kind of pressure sometimes forces companies to make unwise choices that involve diversification into industries that are largely unfamiliar to the management team.

PPA can be used to analyse 'lines-of-business' as well as stand-alone businesses, and this is possibly its most common use today. These days, large diversified businesses use much more sophisticated analytical tools to help guide strategic decisions about acquisition and divestment. Smaller businesses, however, still benefit from using PPA to analyse the market position of their activities. Typically, the analysis involves examining a range of product or service activities in order to understand where the potential for growth lies. Using PPA in this way is no different from using it to analyse the position of subsidiary businesses within a diversified business.

It is important to remember that PPA is a conceptual tool that helps managers understand their businesses. It is not a substitute for strategy. As a tool, it needs to be supplemented by other forms of analysis before strategic decisions can be made. However, PPA is a useful starting point for a discussion about how to grow the business. It becomes even more useful if supplemented by analysis that focuses on growth options.

Businesses can grow in a limited number of ways. For most businesses, there are only four options, each of which has risks and benefits.

1. *Increased market penetration*

   This contains the lowest level of risk, assuming the business already knows a lot about the market. It can base judgments about what is likely to be successful on its own past experience. However, the gains may be quite limited because the market may be small, the business may already have a large share, and gaining extra market share could be costly.

   The techniques or actions required to gain additional market share may involve marketing campaigns, price reduction, and offering incentives for customers to switch from their current suppliers.

2. *Product expansion*

   This option is more risky than increasing market penetration because it involves making a judgment about which new products will work in a market already well known to the business. It requires a deep understanding of customer needs, supported by tactical actions such as market research and trial marketing. Sometimes, it is as simple as developing new models and versions of old products, or adding features and options to old products.

   A large global business such as Manchester United Football Club uses simple techniques such as creating a new team strip each year, which the loyal fans around the globe purchase in large quantities.

3. *Market expansion*

   This option involves taking an existing product line into a new marketplace. The business will already understand the product line very well but there is a risk in taking it into an unknown market. The product may not work in that new market and the growth thrust may well fail as a result.

   Manchester United FC has been very successful in taking its product lines into Asia, but much less so into the USA, where it competes against a different code of football. Geographic expansion is usually the preferred route for this growth option, but it can also be based on attacking market segments. In the last 10 years,

Manchester United FC has expanded into retail, hospitality (bars and nightclubs) and a wide variety of other niche markets in which its branded products have gained a foothold.

4. *Diversification*

This growth option is the riskiest of all because it involves taking products that are unknown to the business into markets that are unknown to it. It often seems the most attractive option because the new product/ new market combination appears very alluring. However, this may be based on an overly optimistic and ignorant view of that market.

Many organisations learned this lesson the hard way in the hi-tech boom of the late 1990s, when businesses of every conceivable variety decided that they too would succeed in the exciting world of digital technology. Nevertheless, many organisations have diversified very successfully, reinventing themselves in the process. The means for this may be acquisition (lower risk) or development from the ground up (higher risk).

Observations

Although the PPA tool offers a very practical way to analyse the portfolio of the diversified business, it does have limitations. One relates to how to define the industry in which a business operates. It is in fact an arbitrary choice to consider a book publishing business to be in book publishing rather than publishing (the larger industry) or media (an even larger industry). Going in the other direction, many book publishers tend to specialise, so possibly a publisher might be in the non-fiction book publishing business (the smaller industry) or technical non-fiction book publishing (an even smaller industry). Clearly, the numbers associated with estimating an industry growth rate or the market share held by a business can vary dramatically depending on the choice of industry definitions.

Further criticisms relate to the use of only four quadrants. Again, it is an arbitrary choice. Why use only market share and industry growth rate? A subsequent version of the model developed by competitor consulting group McKinsey (together with GE) used 10 factors, providing a rating for 'industry attractiveness' along one side of the matrix and 'business strength' along the other side. This enables much greater accuracy in positioning a business.

Another criticism relates to the assumption that the business must always adapt itself to the market conditions that apply at any given time. This assumption sits behind much strategic thinking, from Michael Porter through to the planning matrices such as PPA. It is almost a tenet of faith that business survival depends on adapting the business to prevailing circumstances. But this is only an assumption, as some researchers and a handful of recalcitrant businesses have shown.

Varadarajan and associates call this assumption 'environmental determinism'[3], which is the tendency to believe that the external environment will determine whether a business will succeed or not. It is the opposite of believing that a business can change its environment and thus succeed. They provide a host of examples of organisations that have adapted the market to their organisation, or at least affected the market to their own benefit, including the following:

- The ready-to-eat cereal market was supposed to mature and decline in the 1980s as the population aged. Kellogg decided to go against perceived wisdom and invested in the market to make it grow. As a result they almost doubled their revenue from 1983 to 1988.
- Based on their experience, Texas Instruments guessed that the cost of manufacturing pocket calculators would drop dramatically. It dropped its prices in anticipation, gaining huge market share and (supposedly impossible) increasing the market growth rate.
- When market forces threatened the US automobile industry, car makers lobbied legislators and obtained protected status for their markets, thereby ensuring market growth for US makers.

By rejecting environmental determinism, some businesses have turned Dogs into Stars and Cash Cows. When baking soda sales declined as the result of women's participation in the workforce (sales of baked products soared as women stopped cooking basic staples at home), the industry had all the appearance of a Dog. Low-price unbranded baking soda used by bakers replaced high-price branded products. The leading supplier of branded baking soda in the US, Arm & Hammer, reinvented itself as a supplier of refrigerator deodoriser, then later as a supplier of carpet and furniture deodoriser, swimming pool disinfectant, bath additives and toothpaste supplements. Each reinvention created a new market and new revenues. Had the company used product portfolio analysis, it would possibly have abandoned the baking soda business.

The PPA tool has had a major impact on organisations trying to understand how to balance a collection of businesses. It has provided reasons for a particular portfolio of businesses to exist and it has helped several generations of managers to make decisions about which businesses to acquire and which to divest. More complex methods have been developed to help with this sort of decision making but none are as elegantly simple as the PPA.

User's guide

The PPA is designed to inform the thinking and decision making of senior managers. As such, it is most typically used as part of a planning session involving a group of managers. It is common for a consultant who has expertise in using the tool to assist, and to provide facilitation guidance to ensure the group achieves a result.

Instructions

How to use product portfolio analysis

1. *Decide who should participate in the planning exercise.*

   The criteria for making decisions on participation usually relate to seniority in the organisation and specialist expertise in planning, strategy and marketing. A typical group might comprise the senior management team, supplemented by various specialists from within or outside the organisation.

2. *Agree the agenda and the proposed outcomes.*

   The meeting facilitator should ensure that there is a common understanding of what is being aimed for in the planning session. For example, one critical issue is whether the group has an advisory role or whether it has a decision-making role. Confusion about such issues can lead to conflict and a failure to achieve the desired outcomes.

3. *The meeting facilitator should explain the PPA tool briefly.*

   It is a very visual tool and drawing on a whiteboard or the like in schematic form will assist understanding.

4. *Draw up a table similar to Table 6.1.*

Table 6.1 PPA data table

Name of business	Market segment	Current revenue	Current market share	Market growth

5. *Enter in the table the names of each business (or line of business) that will be the basis for the discussion. Name and briefly describe each.*

   This sounds easy but, having done this many times, it is obvious to me that many managers do not have a clear understanding of what comprises a business and what does not. The group needs to talk this out until a high degree of clarity and understanding is reached.

6. *Enter data relating to the market segment in which that business operates.*

   Again, this can be a challenge for any group as definitions of what comprises a particular market segment vary wildly. The main aim is to get agreement, even if that is only a working consensus for the purpose of the planning exercise.

7. *Add data about the current revenue generated by the business.*

This is usually readily available. If for any reason it is not, obtain this information as part of the preparation for the planning session.

8. *Add data about the percentage of market share that the business currently holds.*

This is most likely to be an estimate rather than a completely accurate figure. As long as there is broad agreement on the figure to the nearest 10%, then that is sufficient for planning purposes.

9. *Record the group's best assessment of the growth potential of the market segment.*

Frequently, this information is both readily available and very accurate, as independent industry sources often provide such data.

10. *Plot the position of each business onto the PPA matrix.*

Represent the size of the revenue of the business by the size of the circle used to describe the business (a smaller circle means low revenue; a large circle means high revenue). Actual figures can be added to the circles.
    The position of the circle indicates where the business sits in relation to market growth and market share. Its position will place it into one of the four quadrants of the matrix.

11. *Consider the implications of the group's analysis.*

Take care that placing a tag on a business is not confused with making a decision. For example, a business may be a Dog but, as described earlier, sometimes Dogs can be moved into any of the other three categories. The options for growth (see above) can be injected into the discussions to help move the group towards possible decisions on what action to take.

Further reading

- G Hall, 'Reflections on running a diversified company', *Harvard Business Review*, Jan–Feb, 1987, pp. 84–92.

One insider's view of running the diversified corporation comes from George Hall. In this article, he describes the practical issues faced by those who manage complex diversified businesses. He provides a number of guidelines that will assist senior management to handle the issues that arise from diversification.

- R Hoskisson & M Hitt, *Downscoping: How to tame the diversified firm*, Oxford University Press, Oxford, 1994.

Diversification continues to be hailed as a solution or condemned as a route to failure. See this book for a lively discussion on how to extricate yourself from the pitfalls of diversification. It provides both detailed descriptions of how diversification can hold organisations back from success and prescriptions for reducing diversification in an organisation.

- *Harvard Business Review on strategies for growth*, Harvard Business School Press, Boston, 1998.

This book comprises a series of articles on strategies for achieving growth. A combination of academic prescriptions and practical case studies, it covers the field in presenting and reviewing the strategy options for achieving growth.

Notes

1. For more details on the history of the tool see the Boston Consulting Group (BCG) web site at http://www.bcg.com/this_is_bcg/mission/growth_share_matrix.asp
2. D Abell, *Defining the business; the starting point of strategy*, Prentice Hall, Englewood Cliffs, 1980.
3. R Varadarajan, T Clark & W Pride, 'Controlling the uncontrollable: Managing your market environment', *Sloan Management Review*, Winter, 1992, pp. 39–47.

CHAPTER 7

Marketing the business
The marketing Ps

Although the lifeblood of any business is sales, to get sales a business needs to market its products and services. Marketing is a recent function in the pantheon of management specialisations, and it is a relatively new development for organisations to place marketing on an equal footing with operations, finance and administration. It is even more recent for the sales function to be understood as a part of the overall marketing thrust.

Marketing still means different things to different people, but most often it is considered to be the function that covers distribution, advertising and sales promotion, product planning and market research. That is, those functions in a business that directly involve contact with consumers, the assessment of their needs, and the translation of this information into sales. Based on that description, it is obvious that it is a customer-related activity. Yet many organisations still conduct their marketing activities in isolation from their customers. For many, it remains an elusive challenge to put their customers at the centre of their marketing strategy.

One of the most crucial decisions for a marketing function is the mix of elements that will be used to achieve sales within a target market. This concept of a 'marketing mix' is a fundamental part of marketing theory. Given that marketing has a wide selection of techniques available to it, the problem is selecting the right combination of techniques to deliver the best possible results.

In many ways, marketing mix is simply a subset of all the tools and techniques that are at the disposal of the marketing function. For any given product or service in a particular target market, the challenge is to decide which set of tools should be used to achieve the targeted sales outcome. And this is where the problems start. There is typically insufficient data to make such decisions objectively. This is summed up in the old saying that 50% of advertising does not work but no-one knows which 50%.

Marketing mix has become such a familiar term that most practitioners seem oblivious to the fact that there is no generally agreed definition of the term.[1] In particular, there is an ongoing debate among academics as to how to create the right mix. Until recently, the elements that comprise the mix were summed up as 'the four Ps' (product, price, promotion and place), but it has been observed that these four Ps no longer seem adequate to cover the field. Services industries have suggested that the four Ps are too much focused on products, and make no allowance for the special circumstances that apply to the marketing of services. So more Ps have been added to the formula. Almost every writer on marketing has their own favourite additional P. However, there is general acceptance that by adding 'participants', 'physical evidence' and 'process' to the list, the Ps more accurately represent the tool kit of elements that are available to a marketing manager.

As a rule of thumb, most marketing specialists now think in terms of a 7P framework. Some argue that these additions are implicit in the original 4P model, but there seems little doubt that making them an explicit part of the model is a help rather than a hindrance.

The 7P model is a management tool for guiding thinking about how to achieve a targeted sales result. Using the tool will help in the development of a comprehensive marketing strategy that addresses all the required elements (as well as can be judged) that are necessary to achieve sales success.

Background

The idea of marketing mix had been around for some time when, in 1964, Jerome McCarthy formalised it and created the phrase that made it famous: The four Ps of marketing.[2] At that time, product, price, promotion and place were considered the key elements of the marketing mix. Each element consisted of a range of variables to be used in crafting a marketing strategy for a specific product or service.

In a sense, the 4P framework represents a smorgasbord of choice for the marketing manager. It is more a checklist than a calculating device because it acts as a reminder of what could form part of a marketing campaign. It provides little guidance on how to select the elements and the variables that constitute a marketing strategy. At best, it encourages the user to cover all the bases, and make logical or necessary choices (see Table 7.1).

Possibly the most surprising aspect of the 4P framework is that it gained such rapid acceptance in the marketing community. Most

Table 7.1 Traditional formulation of the four Ps

1. Product	2. Price	3. Place	4. Promotion
Quality	Level	Distribution channels	Advertising
Features and options	Discounts and	Distribution coverage	Personal selling
Style	allowances	Outlet locations	Sales promotion
Brand name	Payment terms	Sales territories	Publicity
Packaging		Inventory levels and	
Product line		locations	
Warranty		Transport carriers	
Service level			
Associated services			

students of marketing should be able to rattle off the framework from memory. It is still used by many as a mantra, as if to give the impression that some serious thought is going on!

The framework has found a ready place in the education of marketing professionals and it is almost impossible to find an introductory text on marketing that does not make reference to some version of this model. However, almost as soon as it was promulgated, it was criticised on several fronts. The major criticism came from specialists in the services industry, who considered the framework far too product-focused. As services industries became the dominant sector of most advanced economies, services specialists developed marketing techniques that did not seem to fit into the original framework. The intangible nature of services seemed ill-suited to a framework that emphasises the very tangible characteristics of products.

Some researchers simply wanted to add more elements, such as 'public relations' or 'power' or 'people'.[3] The ease with which some of these suggestions were made indicated that the 4P framework was being treated more as a checklist than a rigorous conceptual tool. It was helpful and handy, but almost anyone could come up with their own version of it. Many did—and proceeded to publish their versions as the best. There really was no way of judging the benefits of one version over another. All of which only encouraged more versions to be published.

Some specifically criticised the framework's focus on the marketing of manufactured goods. Many of these critics argued that marketing services is fundamentally different from marketing products, primarily because services are often intangible, perishable, heterogeneous and inseparable.[4] Possibly the strongest case against the traditional 4P framework came from those who wanted to add extra elements, not just because services marketing demanded this, but because the traditional formulation short-changed product marketing as well.[5] According to these critics, even product marketing covers a lot more than just four Ps.

Another round of criticism came from those who thought the framework did not adequately cover industrial marketing—the marketing of products and services from one business to another business. Their arguments revolved around the complexity of the relationship between within-industry sellers and buyers. Often, the challenge of these relationships is less about marketing and more about account management, with the hallmark being not persuasion (as it is with consumer marketing) but negotiation. For example, the relationship between buyer and seller may well outlast the existence of some branded products, so building the relationship may be more important than building the brand.

In part, these criticisms simply highlight the confusion that surrounded the distinction between products and services. Although in the past it seemed natural and obvious to marketing practitioners to make this distinction, today it seems a rather naïve approach. Almost all products have a service aspect, and almost all services involve tangible goods in some shape or form. As a result, it makes sense to think of products/services as a continuum ranging from one extreme (where the dominant feature is the product) to the other extreme (where the dominant feature is the service). Most products/services sit somewhere in between these two extremes. One view suggests that what is actually being delivered to customers is a bundle of benefits with different mixes of tangible and intangibles elements.[6] The more tangibles in the bundle, the more it looks like products; the more intangibles, the more it looks like services.

More recently, marketing practitioners have turned to formal analytical tools for a better understanding of the needs of their targeted customers. Market research has blossomed into the main driver for the development of the marketing plan. It provides the starting point in that it clarifies what the customer actually wants. This data-driven approach has replaced the older approach of just guessing what the customer wants. Many criticisms are made of market research, but there is little doubt that it has placed the customer at the centre of the marketing plan.

The debate in marketing circles eventually settled down to something resembling a consensus around a 7P framework. This version resolved most of the issues by including additional elements and extending the enhanced version to all marketing, whether product or services, industrial or consumer.

The tool

The 7P framework consists of seven *elements*—these are the broad areas of marketing activity. Within each of these elements, there is a range of specific marketing actions (the *variables*) that can be taken. Marketing practitioners sometimes confuse these two parts of the 7P framework.

A marketing strategy (amongst other things) specifies the elements to be used and the variables that will comprise each of the elements. Most marketing campaigns will address all or most of the elements, but it would be rare for such a campaign to utilise every possible variable. The challenge for marketing managers is to select those variables that will provide the most 'bang for the buck'.

The variables represent the range of choices or options for action that are open to management. There are many to choose from and effective selection requires thought and research. Invariably, this selection is constrained by the amount of money available to implement the strategy. The variables are the actions that will translate the marketing strategy into effect; they present a tactical choice. Taken together, therefore, these action choices represent the tactical marketing plan for a product or service. Table 7.2 shows one well-known version of the variables for each of the elements.

It is immediately obvious from the table that there is room for practitioners to add more variables—no damage is done to the tool if this happens. In that sense, the 7P framework is not prescriptive. It should not be necessary to add more elements, but in the final analysis it would not damage the tool. For any particular business, it may also be worthwhile to tailor the language of the framework to suit the specific context. An organisation involved exclusively in marketing its services over the Internet can modify the content and language of the framework accordingly.

The first four elements are the traditional four Ps: product, price, place and promotion. Adding the three new elements (participants, physical evidence, process) to the framework enables it to be extended to the marketing of services, creates a more comprehensive range of elements for product marketing, and overcomes the limitations suggested by those who focus on business-to-business marketing.

1. *Product*: offering the customers in the target market the right product or service. Each product or service can have a wide range of characteristics. It can be a simple product/service or a complex one with many features. It can have attached to it a range of service-oriented benefits, such as warranties and entitlements. It can be high quality or low quality. Whatever the product/service bundle comprises, it must satisfy the needs of an identified and targeted customer. Generally, it does this by providing features that offer significant benefits to the customer. These benefits always relate to customer needs. Products and services are needs-satisfying offerings that the business makes to its customers.

2. *Price*: always a key issue for customers. In marketing a product or service, it is a key consideration and is linked to the customer's perception of value. That perception is driven by product variables such as brand, quality and value-for-money. Pitching the price

Table 7.2 The 7P marketing framework

1. Product	2. Price	3. Place	4. Promotion	5. Participants	6. Physical evidence	7. Process
Quality	Level	Location	Advertising	Personnel:	(environment)	Policies
Brand name	Discounts and	Accessibility	Direct selling	– Training	Furnishings	Procedures
Service features	allowances	Distribution	Sales promotion	– Discretion	Colour	Mechanisation
(warranty,	Payment terms	channels	Publicity	– Commitment	Layout	Employee
installation,	Customer's	Distribution	Public relations	– Incentives	Noise level	discretion
support)	perception of	coverage		– Appearance	Facilitating goods	Customer
Tangible features	value			– Interpersonal	Tangible clues	involvement
(packaging,	Quality/price			behaviour		Customer
accessories)	interaction			Customers:		direction
	Differentiation			– Behaviour		Flow of
				– Degree of		activities
				involvement		
				– Customer to		
				customer		
				contact		

Source: Based on the work of Rafiq and Ahmed[7]

correctly is a critical marketing decision. As with the other elements, it helps if this is considered in terms of objectives. What are the price objectives for a given product or service? Some of these objectives may focus on achieving a desired level of return (profit objectives) or a desired level of sales (sales objectives). At the next level down, a sales objective may focus on market-share growth, market-share maintenance, or some other market result. The variables (the options for action) should take account of such objectives and the selection of a set of variables that form part of the marketing strategy should be driven by them.

3. *Place:* how the market is physically reached. Products and services reach customers through various distribution channels and by means of a complex web of logistics. Each channel may involve intermediaries who will impact on the perceived quality of the final product/ service that is received by the customer. Each step in the logistics chain can impact on the customer. Some businesses deal directly with their customers (for example, banks); some use one or more intermediaries (for example, wholesalers and retailers). The more intermediaries in the channel system, the less control the provider has over the final perceived quality of the product or service. Further, the width of the channel may determine a range of intangible benefits for the customer, such as convenience and availability.

4. *Promotion*: communicating with the customer. It includes advertising, direct selling, public relations, publicity and sales promotion. Again, the challenge for the marketing manager is to blend these variables into a successful marketing thrust. Within each of these variables, there are many options. For example, sales promotion may include point-of-sale advertising, specials, trials, discount coupons, catalogues, circulars and many other specialised forms of promotional material. Advertising is possibly the best known, most frequently used, and most expensive form of promotion.

5. *Participants*: both the employees of the organisation and its customers are participants in the marketing process. This allows the marketing mix to include the interaction between the two. For example, in service-oriented businesses such as restaurants or airlines, the image of the business is affected by the interaction between service employees and customers. The service delivered is part of the overall product being purchased. Insolent or incompetent service will have a major impact on the customer's perception of the product and probably impact on re-purchase levels.

6. *Physical evidence*: The environment in which the service or product is delivered. It includes any supportive tangibles experienced by the customer. It emphasises that customers use physical clues to assess the quality of the service or product being purchased by them, even when those clues are not necessarily indicative of quality. In particular,

this element is crucial for services businesses that deliver highly intangible services. Credit card companies produce gold-coloured cards because they create an impression of substance. Banks have impressive head office buildings because they create an impression of solidity. Hotels have impressive lobbies because they imply that guests will find luxury elsewhere in the hotel.

7. *Process*: the array of procedures, mechanisms and activities. Any business has choices regarding the processes that will be employed to deliver a product or a service to a customer. Some of those processes will touch the customer and therefore will affect the customer. The customer will make judgments about whether to re-purchase the service or product based in part on this experience. If the checkout times experienced by a customer exceed certain expectations then the customer may avoid that retail shop in the future. If a hotel fails to deliver its services in a reliable manner, then guests may go elsewhere next time. If a bank's procedures for cashing a cheque are too cumbersome, customers may turn to other options for this service. (Of course, the opposite may also enhance an establishment's image; for example, waiting in queues at popular nightclubs for hours only seems to strengthen their attractiveness!)

Observations

Although the 7P framework continues to be a useful tool for guiding marketing strategy, many larger organisations have turned to more sophisticated analytical tools to drive the development of strategy. The 7P framework covers 'the basics' but is not much help in determining which elements and which variables provide maximum impact in terms of sales.

Much of an organisation's general investment in marketing remains an act of faith. Occasionally a campaign can be conducted in such a way as to measure its precise impact, but for most organisations that remains a rare opportunity. All of which may well explain why the 7P framework continues to be used. It seems as good as any tool for making sure that a marketing campaign covers all bases, and it does offer the opportunity to check the alignment between overall corporate strategy and marketing strategies, objectives and tactics.

Organisations can be more rigorous about checking the impact of their marketing activities. For example, in many organisations, marketing tends to be driven by an annual budget allocation. This is about as unstrategic as it is possible to be. Expenditure on marketing should always be treated as an investment, and related back to the gains that are achieved. Some of the links between marketing activity and sales achieved may be tenuous. That does not mean that data cannot be collected that might enable managers to draw conclusions about whether or not their investment is paying off. Marketing practitioners sometimes resist this kind of cost–benefit analysis. The marketing activity still carries consider-able mystique for managers not schooled or skilled in its workings.

At the very least, specific marketing actions should be drawn together into a coherent strategy. General management is perfectly entitled to say: No plan—no investment. The marketing plan needs to make it clear which elements and which variables are being addressed by which marketing actions. Evidence and opinion should be offered as to why actions have been selected. Finally, the marketing plan needs to be integrated into the corporate strategy, with links clearly demonstrated. We may not know what works in marketing but we do know that if the marketing actions are unrelated to corporate strategy, then the marketing investment is unlikely to bear fruit.

User's guide

The 7P framework is a conceptual framework rather than a tactical tool. It generates insight rather than options for action. To make it an action-oriented technique, the 7P framework needs to be supplemented by a mechanism that will translate insight into action. The MIXMAP model created by Claudio Vignali and others at Manchester Metropolitan University does exactly this.[8]

The MIXMAP model takes as its input the strategic direction of the organisation and uses a matrix structure to analyse each of the elements of the 7P framework. The model checks that there is alignment between the variables and elements of the 7P framework (the marketing mix) and the strategies chosen by the organisation. It helps to uncover lack of alignment (when organisations are wasting their investments in marketing) and shows how to achieve a powerful marketing thrust with only modest investment.

Keep in mind that marketing can never be an entirely prescriptive discipline. It provides the interface with the marketplace—an intensely dynamic environment. The marketing strategy must be constantly monitored and fine-tuned using feedback from the marketplace. Marketing plans are never finished.

Instructions

How to use the 7Ps and the MIXMAP model

The MIXMAP model is based on the matrix mapping technique. That is, two axes are drawn, with each representing a high–low range for two identified factors. (Another example of this technique is the product portfolio analysis tool described in Chapter 6, where the two factors are market growth and market share.)

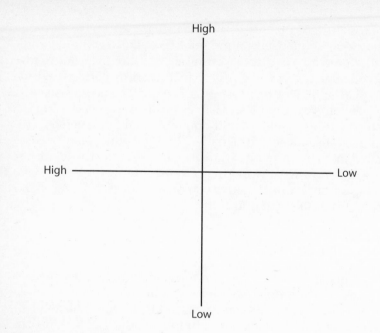

Figure 7.1 The MIXMAP model

The MIXMAP model generates maps with four quadrants: high–high, high–low, low–high and low–low.

The first step in using the model is to have a product/service strategy available. This may have been generated by a separate piece of analysis such as Porter's Generic Strategy option (see Chapter 2) or PPA (see Chapter 6). If such a strategy statement is not available, the matrix can be used to generate one. For example, a very simple analysis can be undertaken using the matrix mapping technique to analyse the various product/service lines of a business on the basis of revenue versus profitability. This will quickly identify lines that are the main contributors to business profitability.

Other possibilities include:

- revenue versus cost (identifies levels of profitability)
- revenue versus market growth (identifies growth products)
- profitability versus market share (identifies market segment profitability).

Once a strategic position is identified, a MIXMAP is drawn for each of the seven elements of the 7P framework. Drawing the map involves these steps:

1. *Agree the products/services to be analysed.*

   This may involve a family of products or a stand-alone product (for example, when a new product has been developed).

2. *Decide which of the elements will be addressed in the analysis.*

Typically, all elements will be addressed, but it is also possible to focus more narrowly (for example, when exploring how to use a new marketing channel such as the Internet).

3. *Agree on the critical variables for each element.*

   • If focusing on the product element, then the critical variables selected from the list shown in the 7P framework in Table 7.2 might be quality and branding. These two variables become the axes for the matrix (see Figure 7.2).
   • If more than two elements are selected, explore the possible combinations for each.

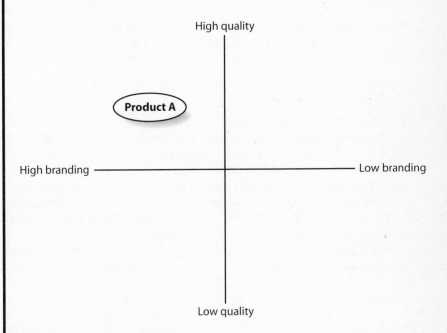

Figure 7.2 Product MIXMAP

4. *Repeat the mapping process for any other variables selected for each element.*

   Unless it causes significant problems for the participants, the process can be simplified by limiting the mapping process for each element to only two variables. This will reduce complexity and, on completion of the mapping process for each element, will generate a total of seven maps.

5. *Once all maps have been completed, analyse the maps for consistency.*

   • Businesses that closely align their marketing variables with their overall strategy will see the product or service under analysis in the same quadrants.

- Businesses where there is little alignment between strategy and marketing tactics will see the product mapped in many different quadrants.
- Where a single map stands out as different, this provides a trigger for analysing why that element is not congruent with all the others.

Further reading

There are plenty of books that can help a practitioner construct a marketing plan. Many of these are useful. However, it still seems to be the case that in this area of management it is OK to make things up as you go along. Many texts invent their own version of the tools and techniques that can be used to construct a plan. If in general management there is a lack of commonly accepted practice, this is even more so in the specialist field of marketing.

- N Paley, *How to develop a strategic marketing plan: A step-by-step guide*, St Lucie Press, Boca Raton, 1999.

This useful and practical text brings together Paley's 25 years of experience in helping organisations develop marketing plans. It includes a computer disk that provides a wide variety of templates that can be used to guide the development process. The book is divided into six parts, each of which tackles a key part of the development process: Strategic section; Tactical section; The strategic marketing plan in action; Checklist for developing competitive strategies; Help topics; Using the templates (computer disk).

The tools and techniques outlined by Paley are carefully integrated into a structured and disciplined procedure for developing the plan. Paley avoids much of the jargon and conceptual effluence usually associated with the development of strategic plans.

Notes

1. For a common (but not necessarily universally accepted) definition see P Kotler & G Armstrong, *Principles of marketing*, 4th edn, Prentice-Hall, Englewood Cliffs, 1989, p. 45: '...the set of controllable marketing variables that the firm blends to produce the response it wants in the target market'.
2. E Jerome McCarthy, *Basic marketing*, Irwin, Homewood, 1964.
3. See W Mindak & S Fine, 'A fifth 'P': Public relations', in J Donnely & W George (eds), *Marketing of services*, AMA, Chicago, 1981, pp. 71–3; P Kotler, 'Megamarketing', *Harvard Business Review*, March–April, 1986. pp. 117–24; V Judd, 'Differentiate with the 5th 'P': People', *Industrial Marketing Management*, vol. 16, 1987, pp. 241–7.
4. See, for example, L Berry, 'Services marketing is different', in C Lovelock (ed.), *Services marketing*, Prentice-Hall, Englewood Cliffs, 1984, pp. 29–37.

5. See M Booms & M Bitner, 'Marketing strategies and organization structures for services firms', in J Donnely & W George (eds), *Marketing of services*, AMA, Chicago, 1981, pp. 47–51; M Rafiq & P Ahmed, 'Using the 7Ps as a generic marketing mix', *Marketing Intelligence and Planning*, vol. 13, no. 9, 1995, pp. 4–15.

6. B Ennis & K Roering, 'Services marketing: Different products, similar strategies', in J Donnely & W George (eds), *Marketing of services*, AMA, Chicago, 1981, pp. 1–3.

7. M Rafiq & P Ahmed, 'Using the 7Ps as a generic marketing mix', *Marketing Intelligence and Planning*, vol. 13, no. 9, 1995, pp. 4–15.

8. C Vignali & B Davies, 'The marketing mix redefined and mapped: Introducing the MIXMAP model', *Management Decision*, vol. 32, no. 8, 1994, pp. 11–16.

CHAPTER 8

Understanding customers
SERVQUAL customer surveys

Providing satisfaction to customers is an intuitively sensible route to running a profitable business. But we have not been very good at measuring whether or not businesses are doing a good job in delivering satisfaction to their customers. Part of the problem is a lack of clarity about the meaning of some of the concepts involved. For example, customer satisfaction is often linked to 'service quality', with some people arguing that they are the same thing. We do not have clear definitions of either concept.

A related concept is 'service excellence', which legendary management propagandist Tom Peters elevated to a status of iconic proportions.[1] There is some justification for this, as the idea of providing excellent service to customers does have the potential to offer a competitive edge. We know that organisations that are very good at offering excellent customer service are very profitable. (Possibly we have not heard from those organisations that were very good at it but went broke!) As usual, putting the idea into effect is a bit harder than just applying a handful of known principles, but research is emerging on how organisations can make the creation and delivery of customer service their core competence.[2]

The fact that researchers are doing this kind of work is the result of a major effort by three researchers in particular to put the issue of customer satisfaction on the management agenda. In 1990, Valarie Zeithaml, A Parasuraman and Leonard Berry published their groundbreaking book, *Delivering service quality: Balancing customer perceptions and expectations*. It encapsulated their previous five years' research on measuring customer satisfaction. For the first time, managers were given a clear framework and a measurement tool they could apply in most situations. The tool, the SERVQUAL instrument, went on to become the pre-eminent instrument for measuring the delivery of quality service to customers.

SERVQUAL has now been applied to a vast range of industries. It is the instrument of choice for researchers, consultants and practitioners trying to understand the perceptions and expectations of customers. Such pre-eminence has, of course, spawned an ongoing debate about the instrument's usefulness. It has been roundly criticised for a wide range of failings, though most of the criticisms relate to the finer points of survey instrument design and construction[3] (in response, Zeithaml and associates changed the structure of the instrument to address some of these points). Overall, the instrument has survived surprisingly well and it continues to help us get useful data about the needs of customers.

Background

SERVQUAL grew out of the profound observation by Zeithaml and associates that customer satisfaction comes about when the gap between what is expected by the customer and what is delivered by the service provider is as small as possible. This 'gap' concept provides the foundation stone on which a whole edifice of service quality can be built. In retrospect, it seems a blindingly obvious idea but—as is often the case— it wasn't really obvious until someone put it into words.

Gaps in customer expectation

Zeithaml and associates expanded their idea by identifying different types of gaps. They explored five key types in some detail:

- the gap between the customers' expectations and management's perception of customer expectations
- the gap between management's perception of customer expectations and what was supposed to be delivered to its customers
- the gap between what was supposed to be delivered and what was actually being delivered
- the gap between what was actually being delivered and what customers were told would be delivered
- the gap between what customers expected and what they perceived they actually received.

It was this last gap that led to the creation of the surveying instrument called SERVQUAL. The gap was summed up in the formula: $Q = P - E$ (*quality is the gap between perception and expectation*). A small gap means that the organisation is providing a high level of service quality.

Dimensions of service

The instrument is based on a framework of five 'perceptual dimensions'. These five dimensions cover the areas in which customers make judgments about the quality of service they receive from a service provider:

- *tangibles*—physical facilities; equipment; staff appearance
- *reliability*—ability to perform the promised services reliably and accurately
- *responsiveness*—willingness to help customers and provide prompt service
- *assurance*—knowledge and courtesy of staff and their ability to inspire trust and confidence
- *empathy*—caring and individualised attention provided to customers.

Survey questions were constructed for each of these dimensions, using a rating scale that enabled respondents to indicate what they *expected* from an industry in general, and also what they *perceived they had received* from a particular service provider. The responses to the survey reflect any gaps, which are expressed as a number. The bigger the number, the bigger the gap and the less satisfied the customer; the smaller the gap, the more satisfied the customer.

In this way—and for the first time—service quality became measurable and quantifiable. Comparisons could be made between different providers within an industry. Organisations could measure improvements (if any) over time in the level of service they provided. Different industries could compare what really matters to customers. Service quality became a numbers game.

The zone of tolerance

Zeithaml and associates continued to develop their model and in the early 1990s invented the 'zone of tolerance'. This concept is based on the idea that there is an area between the level of service that the customer considers *adequate* and the level that is *desired*. For example, if a customer goes to a bank for teller service, the desired waiting time is probably zero, although the adequate level might be up to 10 minutes. If customers repeatedly have to wait longer than 10 minutes, they may well consider moving their business to another bank.

Clearly, the zone of tolerance is situational (that is, it depends on the situation at the particular moment when the service is delivered). Bank customers may well stretch their zones of tolerance to a longer period if they do business in the bank late on a busy Friday afternoon; this is based on their previous experience with the bank situation on Fridays (that is, longer queues). Other factors can also affect the zone, such as promises made by the bank about waiting times.

The zone of tolerance concept can be built into SERVQUAL by asking respondents to make three separate assessments for each of the five dimensions listed:

- minimum (adequate) level of service
- desired level of service
- perception of actual service delivered.[4]

Customer behaviour

Yet another development in the model underpinning the framework occurred in 1996, when Zeithaml and associates published their findings on the connection between levels of service quality and profitability. Their research showed a clear link between the two, and that organisations '... offering superior service achieve higher-than-normal market share growth, that the mechanisms by which service quality influences profits include increased market share and premium prices, and that businesses in the top quintile of relative service quality on average realise an 8% higher price than their competitors'.[5]

This link encouraged the trio to develop a new element of their framework that focused on the customer-behaviour consequences of providing different levels of service. They examined five specific aspects of customer behaviour:

- *loyalty*—the strength of the relationship between customer and provider and the likelihood that the customer will do more business with that provider
- *switch*—the likelihood that the customer might take their business to another provider
- *pay more*—the likelihood that customers continue to buy from the provider even if prices increase
- *external response*—the likelihood that a customer would complain to other (actual and potential) customers about the levels of service received
- *internal response*—the likelihood that the customer would complain to the organisation's staff.

These 'behavioural intentions' have a capacity to impact on the profitability of the organisation supplying services to customers because they are associated with the customer's *intention to remain a customer*. Research shows that, although some of these behavioural factors vary from one industry to another, overall they demonstrate a clear impact on profitability.

This link between behavioural intentions and profitability raises the issue of how much organisations should invest to gain a service edge in order to receive paybacks such as increased customer loyalty or the ability to charge higher prices. Again, research shows that this is a complex calculation that varies significantly from industry to industry. There is a real risk that organisations will over-invest in service delivery without realising worthwhile gains. The gains are there, but the law of diminishing returns applies.

Service Quality Information System

Finally, in 1997, two members of the team provided a fully integrated view of how organisations should listen to their customers.[6] The Service Quality Information System (SQIS) brings together all the different strands of their research over the preceding decade. It suggests that organisations need to listen to their customers on a continuous basis. This demands a dynamic system that is built into the way the organisation does business. Sampling customers for their perceptions should not be an occasional and isolated exercise; it should be built into day-to-day activities.

A SQIS could comprise:

- transactional surveys (satisfaction surveys following a service encounter)
- customer feedback (capturing complaints, comments and inquiries)
- market surveys (involving surveys of the total market, including competitors' customers)
- employee surveys (surveys about how the staff deliver service to customers)
- other methods (for example, mystery shoppers; focus groups; customer advisory panels).

It is hard to over-estimate the impact that Zeithaml, Berry and Parasuraman have had on their field. In some ways, they *are* the field, despite the detractors who criticise some of their research methodologies. Their lasting achievement is the SERVQUAL instrument, which has now been used in many hundreds of industry surveys. More importantly, SERVQUAL has made a transition to operational management in that individual organisations in their thousands use surveys based on the SERVQUAL framework to measure the extent to which they provide service quality. The next time you are asked to complete a customer survey, there is a very good chance that it will be a variation on the SERVQUAL theme. It has become a standard tool of management.

The tool

The SERVQUAL instrument (see the version at the end of this chapter) comprises 22 questions that cover the five dimensions of service quality: tangibles, reliability, responsiveness, assurance and empathy. It is composed of three parts:

- Part 1 asks respondents to indicate what they *expect* from an identified industry.
- Part 2 asks respondents to indicate what they *perceive* to be the level of customer service *actually received* from an identified service provider.
- Part 3 seeks to establish how the respondents weigh the *relative importance* of each of the five dimensions for that industry.

SERVQUAL is a generic instrument that can be applied to any industry and any organisation within an industry (and also to internal service functions within organisations). The data collected in the survey enables an organisation to undertake a number of different analyses and make judgments accordingly. Thus the instrument's fundamental usefulness as a diagnostic tool is its ability to help an organisation understand the strengths and weaknesses of its delivery of high levels of customer service.

Care should be taken in abridging the instrument. It is a complete and validated framework, so reducing the dimensions being assessed or the number of questions used for each dimension risks creating an invalid picture of what matters to the customer. It would be foolish for an organisation to act on such an inaccurate understanding of customer preferences. Of course, some wording can be changed to ensure clarity and to make sure that the respondents understand which industry and/ or which organisation they are being asked to assess.

Organisations sometimes want to add additional questions about areas not covered by SERVQUAL, such as the cost of the service being provided. This can be done, but such questions need to be clearly separated from the basic SERVQUAL framework. In addition, organisations may wish to add questions that elicit qualitative responses (descriptions in words as opposed to ratings by number) in relation to specific areas of customer service that are of current interest to management. Care should be taken not to make the survey too long—customers tend to be willing to respond unless it becomes too onerous to do so.

SERVQUAL is very useful for tracking how an organisation performs over time in delivering customer service. The initial administration provides a useful snapshot of what matters to customers in an industry, how they see a particular organisation performing and the relative weight they attach to the five service dimensions. This can help inform management decisions about where to invest to improve levels of service. However, the survey really comes into its own when it is repeated at a later date to measure the impact of actions taken by management to improve service quality. The repeat administration will uncover whether investment in improvement is working and whether the organisation is staying ahead of the competition (or not).

It should be noted that the importance of the five dimensions will vary from industry to industry; possibly even from customer to customer. However, there is considerable consistency in what is valued most highly by customers (for example, *reliability* is always the most valued dimension). In one wide-ranging assessment, the following relative weightings were found:

- reliability (32%)
- responsiveness (22%)
- assurance (19%)
- empathy (16%)
- tangibles (11%).[7]

If reliability is low, then nothing else matters much to customers. If the organisation keeps making mistakes, then smiles and friendliness from staff are not going to make much difference to the customer's perception of service quality. Yet despite this, reliability is not where management necessarily puts its greatest effort. In many organisations, improving customer service is equivalent to 'smile training' and smart new staff uniforms. If reliability is low, then money spent on such things is simply wasted.

It is also clear that reliability means delivering the basics. Most customers have relatively low expectations about the service they receive. They do not set especially high standards, and they do not look for exceptional service. This is in contrast with many managers, who seem to think that their customers are extremely demanding creatures that are hard to satisfy. The reality is that *most customers simply want a basic service delivered in a competent manner.*

Interestingly, although reliability is the fundamental requirement for *meeting* customer expectations, it is the process dimensions (assurance, responsiveness and empathy) that are the basis for *exceeding* customer expectations. So, the most sensible and broad customer satisfaction strategy is to get the basics (reliability) reasonably right and then build your organisation's reputation on the process dimensions.

Although this outline has focused on external customers, SERVQUAL has also been used extensively to measure and monitor internal levels of service quality. Simply substitute the name of the company with the name of a functional division, such as Accounts Department or IT Help Desk, and the name of the industry with that of the relevant generic function, and the instrument is ready to be used. The analysis process is exactly the same.

Observations

Parasuraman, in particular, has been active in further development of the SERVQUAL instrument. Some of his later work focuses on the trade-off between the costs and the benefits of investing in customer service.[8] He makes the point that some companies are well known for the exceptionally high levels of service quality but rarely do we find out the cost of providing such high levels of service. Is it worth it?

Part of the problem is that service quality and cost of service provision is usually a zero-sum game. That is, an organisation running a customer service division could invest in appointing more customer service staff to provide better service quality (for example, less waiting time for customers), but inevitably this will cost money, thereby reducing the profitability of the business. What is the optimal trade-off between these two variables? Typically, those arguing for cost reduction win the day, and customer service tends to be pitched at the minimum levels that the organisation can get away with without losing customers.

Parasuraman argues that we are looking at this problem the wrong way. Organisations normally calculate their productivity by using a traditional formula that weighs inputs against outputs. In other words, the organisation is entirely preoccupied with what is happening at the producer's end. The customer simply does not feature in conventional productivity calculations. Improving productivity is therefore always about either reducing inputs (costs) or increasing outputs (production levels). This approach to productivity seems inappropriate for a service context where, typically, *the customer also provides input*. A product can be manufactured without the involvement of the customer but you cannot deliver a service without the involvement of the customer.

Parasuraman suggests we should look at productivity as something that also involves inputs and outputs by the *customer*. For example, in a call centre, the customer is contributing to an outcome by providing information, time, effort and (frequently in my experience!) emotional energy. It is possible to calculate the productivity from the customer's point of view by contrasting their input with the output they achieve. An understaffed call centre with long wait times generates a low level of productivity for customers because it requires a great deal of customer input. (Of course, it may very well generate high levels of productivity for the service provider!)

It is possible to combine these two perspectives of productivity into a single framework that accepts that both customer and provider productivity need to be considered. Service quality is the link between the two, suggesting that synergies can be created by looking for mutual benefits rather than accepting trade-offs in service level.

This framework needs further development. For example, no measures have been developed for gauging the contribution of customers to the service delivery process. But the possibility of creating a productivity framework that offers a balanced view of the service process is a significant step forward.

Parasuraman's approach is rather novel and there is little practical application of this concept so far. But it is an innovative example of where the concept of service quality may go in the future.

User's guide

SERVQUAL can be used to measure and monitor various aspects of an organisation's service delivery performance. A number of these are outlined in the following instructions. The instrument itself is a basic skeleton and variations can be made, such as including a major competitor so that the survey measures comparative performance.

Organisations need to decide in advance the purpose of the measuring exercise. The purpose should be made explicit by means of a clear statement by senior managers, and should focus on action (for example, an agreed aim to improve the level of service quality provided by the organisation). Without such a clear focus and commitment, the measuring exercise is pointless.

Instructions

How to use the SERVQUAL instrument

The 22 questions comprising the SERVQUAL instrument cover five dimensions of service quality:

- tangibles (questions 1–4)
- reliability (questions 5–9)
- responsiveness (questions 10–13)
- assurance (questions 14–17)
- empathy (questions 18–22).

Have each respondent complete the SERVQUAL instrument. Transfer scores to the expectation/perception gap calculation table (you will find samples of both at the end of this chapter).

A. The expectation/perception gap for each dimension

1. *Calculate each respondent's gap score for each dimension.*

   - Gap score for each question: for each respondent, for each question, subtract the perception score from the expectation score.
   - Gap score for each dimension: for each respondent, add up the gap score for each of the questions that relate to a particular dimension of service quality (for example, tangibles) and divide by the number of questions (so for tangibles, divide by four).

2. *Calculate the average gap score for each dimension.*

   - For each dimension, add up all the gap scores from all respondents for that particular dimension. Divide by the total number of respondents.

Senior managers should consider this result as the first step in developing a service quality improvement program. It is likely that there will be variations in the five gap scores. Why? What does this tell you?

B. The weighted expectation/perception gap for each dimension

The gap scores for the five dimensions can be weighted on the basis of the relative importance of each dimension. The relative weight for each dimension is derived from the *Relative importance* section in the survey. By allocating 100 points, respondents effectively give a relative weighting to each dimension in percentage terms.

1. *Calculate the overall relative weighting of each dimension.*

    - From the *Relative importance* section, for each dimension add up the total number of points for all respondents. Divide by the number of respondents. (Don't worry too much if the five weightings don't add up to precisely 100. Just use the resultant percentages as a guide—it is often easier if you round them off to the nearest 5%.)

2. *Calculate the weighted average rating for each dimension.*

    - Multiply the gap score for each dimension (see the first step) by the relevant weighting.
    - Compare the scores for each dimension. The highest figure will indicate the area to which management should pay the most attention, as the weighted average rating balances the rating given by customers with the importance placed by the customers on that dimension. It's a bit like balancing the rating you might give to a meal you are served in a restaurant: you might think the fish is of very good quality but that does not mean much if you don't really like fish.

In service delivery, the gap score for the 'reliability' dimension may be comparatively low, but if it is the area that really matters to customers, then the weighted rating may be a comparatively high score.

The results from this third calculation will help management focus on areas of service improvement that truly matter to customers. It helps minimise the possibility of management focusing on less important areas (which, as discussed earlier, is an issue for some managers.)

C. The overall expectation/perception gap for all dimensions

1. *Add up the five averages for each dimension. Divide by five.*

This results in a single figure for how the organisation's service quality is perceived by customers. This type of general score is useful in promoting the issue of service quality within the organisation to employees. It can be made part of a scoreboard that can be updated on a regular basis, using surveys repeated over time to communicate the performance of the organisation.

D. Tracking performance

All of these calculations can be repeated over time. This will enable management to plot various graphs that indicate how the organisation's performance (including the effects of any service improvement programs) is tracking.

Further reading

- V Zeithaml, A Parasuraman & L Berry, *Delivering quality service: Balancing customer perceptions and expectations*, The Free Press, New York, 1990.

All that the practitioner needs to be able to work with the SERVQUAL framework can be found in this book, which is the original text. It is aimed at the general reader as much as at specialist researchers, and provides a host of practical examples backing up the SERVQUAL instrument.

Please note that Zeithaml and associates provided a modified and improved version of the instrument in 1994, and that is the version used in this book (A Parasuraman, L Berry & V Zeithaml, 'Refinement and reassessment of the SERVQUAL scale', *Journal of Retailing*, vol. 67, no. 4, 1994, pp. 420–51).

- T Grapenstine, 'The history and future of service quality assessment', *Marketing Research*, vol. 10, issue 4, 1999, pp. 5–20.

For a lively discussion of the SERVQUAL framework, try this article. It is a report on a special session organised by the Academy of Marketing Sciences to celebrate the 10th anniversary of the publication of SERVQUAL. It is not excessively academic but does bring the originators face to face with some of their critics.

Notes

1. T Peters & N Austin, *A passion for excellence*, Random House, New York, 1985.
2. R Woodruff, 'Customer value: The next source of competitive advantage', *Journal of the Academy of Marketing Sciences*, vol. 25, no. 2, 1997, pp. 139–53.
3. F Buttle, 'SERVQUAL: Review, critique and research agenda', *European Journal of Marketing*, vol. 30, no. 1, 1996, pp. 8–32.
4. V Zeithaml, L Berry & A Parasuraman, 'The nature and determinants of customer expectations of service', *Journal of Academy of Marketing Sciences*, vol. 21, no. 1, 1993, pp. 1–12.
5. V Zeithaml, L Berry & A Parasuraman, 'The behavioral consequences of service quality', *Journal of Marketing*, vol. 60, issue 2, 1996, pp. 31–46.
6. L Berry & A Parasuraman, 'Listening to the customer: The concept of a Service Quality Information System', *MIT Sloan Management Review*, vol. 38, issue 3, 1997, pp. 65–76.
7. L Berry, A Parasuraman & V Zeithaml, 'Improving service quality in America: Lessons learned', *Academy of Management Executive*, vol. 8, no. 2, 1994, pp. 32–53.
8. A Parasuraman, 'Service quality and productivity: A synergistic approach', *Managing Service Quality*, vol. 12, no. 1, 2002, pp. 6–9.
9. Based on A Parasuraman, L Berry & V Zeithaml, 'Refinement and reassessment of the SERVQUAL scale', *Journal of Retailing*, vol. 67, no. 4, 1994, pp. 420–51.

The SERVQUAL instrument[9]

Part 1: Expectations

Based on your experiences as a customer of [industry] services, please think about the kind of [industry] company that would deliver excellent quality of service. Think about the kind of [industry] company that you would be pleased to do business with. Please show the extent to which you think such a [industry] company would possess the feature described by each statement.

If you feel a feature is not at all essential for excellent [industry] companies such as the one you have in mind, circle the number '1'. If you feel a feature is absolutely essential for excellent [industry] companies, circle '7'. If your feelings are less strong, circle one of the numbers in the middle. There are no right or wrong answers—all we are interested in is a number that truly reflects your feelings regarding [industry] companies that would deliver excellent quality of service.

E1: Excellent [industry] companies will have modern-looking equipment.

Strongly disagree   1 — 2 — 3 — 4 — 5 — 6 — 7   *Strongly agree*

E2: The physical facilities at excellent [industry] companies will be visually appealing.

Strongly disagree   1 — 2 — 3 — 4 — 5 — 6 — 7   *Strongly agree*

E3: Employees of excellent [industry] companies will have a neat appearance.

Strongly disagree   1 — 2 — 3 — 4 — 5 — 6 — 7   *Strongly agree*

E4: Materials associated with the service (such as pamphlets or statements) will be visually appealing in an excellent [industry] company.

Strongly disagree   1 — 2 — 3 — 4 — 5 — 6 — 7   *Strongly agree*

E5: When excellent [industry] companies promise to do something by a certain time, they will do so.

Strongly disagree   1 — 2 — 3 — 4 — 5 — 6 — 7   *Strongly agree*

E6: When customers have a problem, excellent [industry] companies will show a sincere interest in solving it.

Strongly disagree   1 — 2 — 3 — 4 — 5 — 6 — 7   *Strongly agree*

E7: Excellent [industry] companies will perform the service right the first time.

Strongly disagree   1 — 2 — 3 — 4 — 5 — 6 — 7   *Strongly agree*

E8: Excellent [industry] companies will provide their services at the time they promise to do so.

Strongly disagree   1 — 2 — 3 — 4 — 5 — 6 — 7   *Strongly agree*

E9: Excellent [industry] companies will insist on error-free records.

Strongly disagree 1 — 2 — 3 — 4 — 5 — 6 — 7 *Strongly agree*

E10: Employees of excellent [industry] companies will tell customers exactly when services will be performed.

Strongly disagree 1 — 2 — 3 — 4 — 5 — 6 — 7 *Strongly agree*

E11: Employees of excellent [industry] companies will give prompt service to customers.

Strongly disagree 1 — 2 — 3 — 4 — 5 — 6 — 7 *Strongly agree*

E12: Employees of excellent [industry] companies will always be willing to help customers.

Strongly disagree 1 — 2 — 3 — 4 — 5 — 6 — 7 *Strongly agree*

E13: Employees of excellent [industry] companies will never be too busy to respond to customer requests.

Strongly disagree 1 — 2 — 3 — 4 — 5 — 6 — 7 *Strongly agree*

E14: The behaviour of employees of excellent [industry] companies will instil confidence in customers.

Strongly disagree 1 — 2 — 3 — 4 — 5 — 6 — 7 *Strongly agree*

E15: Customers of excellent [industry] companies will feel safe in their transactions.

Strongly disagree 1 — 2 — 3 — 4 — 5 — 6 — 7 *Strongly agree*

E16: Employees of excellent [industry] companies will be consistently courteous with customers.

Strongly disagree 1 — 2 — 3 — 4 — 5 — 6 — 7 *Strongly agree*

E17: Employees of excellent [industry] companies will have the knowledge to answer customer questions.

Strongly disagree 1 — 2 — 3 — 4 — 5 — 6 — 7 *Strongly agree*

E18: Excellent [industry] companies will give customers individual attention.

Strongly disagree 1 — 2 — 3 — 4 — 5 — 6 — 7 *Strongly agree*

E19: Excellent [industry] companies will have operating hours convenient to all their customers.

Strongly disagree 1 — 2 — 3 — 4 — 5 — 6 — 7 *Strongly agree*

E20: Excellent [industry] companies will have employees who give customers personal attention.

Strongly disagree 1 — 2 — 3 — 4 — 5 — 6 — 7 *Strongly agree*

E21: Excellent [industry] companies will have the customers' best interests at heart.

Strongly disagree   1 — 2 — 3 — 4 — 5 — 6 — 7   *Strongly agree*

E22: The employees of excellent [industry] companies will understand the specific needs of their customers.

Strongly disagree   1 — 2 — 3 — 4 — 5 — 6 — 7   *Strongly agree*

Part 2: Perceptions

The following set of statements relate to your feelings about [company]'s services. For each statement, please show the extent to which you believe [company] has the feature described by the statement. Once again, circling a '1' means that you strongly disagree that [company] has that feature, and circling '7' means that you strongly agree. You may circle any of the numbers in the middle that show how strong your feelings are. There are no right or wrong answers—all we are interested in is a number that best shows your perception about [company]'s services.

P1: [company] has modern-looking equipment.

Strongly disagree   1 — 2 — 3 — 4 — 5 — 6 — 7   *Strongly agree*

P2: [company]'s physical facilities are visually appealing.

Strongly disagree   1 — 2 — 3 — 4 — 5 — 6 — 7   *Strongly agree*

P3: [company]'s employees have a neat appearance.

Strongly disagree   1 — 2 — 3 — 4 — 5 — 6 — 7   *Strongly agree*

P4: Materials associated with the service (such as pamphlets or statements) are visually appealing at [company].

Strongly disagree   1 — 2 — 3 — 4 — 5 — 6 — 7   *Strongly agree*

P5: When [company] promises to do something by a certain time, it does so.

Strongly disagree   1 — 2 — 3 — 4 — 5 — 6 — 7   *Strongly agree*

P6: When you have a problem, [company] shows a sincere interest in solving it.

Strongly disagree   1 — 2 — 3 — 4 — 5 — 6 — 7   *Strongly agree*

P7: [company] performs the service right the first time.

Strongly disagree   1 — 2 — 3 — 4 — 5 — 6 — 7   *Strongly agree*

P8: [company] provides their services at the time they promise to do so.

Strongly disagree   1 — 2 — 3 — 4 — 5 — 6 — 7   *Strongly agree*

P9: [company] insists on error-free records.

Strongly disagree 1 — 2 — 3 — 4 — 5 — 6 — 7 *Strongly agree*

P10: Employees of [company] tell you exactly when services will be performed.

Strongly disagree 1 — 2 — 3 — 4 — 5 — 6 — 7 *Strongly agree*

P11: Employees of [company] give you prompt service.

Strongly disagree 1 — 2 — 3 — 4 — 5 — 6 — 7 *Strongly agree*

P12: Employees of [company] are always willing to help you.

Strongly disagree 1 — 2 — 3 — 4 — 5 — 6 — 7 *Strongly agree*

P13: Employees of [company] are never too busy to respond to your requests.

Strongly disagree 1 — 2 — 3 — 4 — 5 — 6 — 7 *Strongly agree*

P14: The behaviour of employees of [company] instils confidence in customers.

Strongly disagree 1 — 2 — 3 — 4 — 5 — 6 — 7 *Strongly agree*

P15: You feel safe in your transactions with [company].

Strongly disagree 1 — 2 — 3 — 4 — 5 — 6 — 7 *Strongly agree*

P16: Employees of [company] are consistently courteous with you.

Strongly disagree 1 — 2 — 3 — 4 — 5 — 6 — 7 *Strongly agree*

P17: Employees of [company] have the knowledge to answer your questions.

Strongly disagree 1 — 2 — 3 — 4 — 5 — 6 — 7 *Strongly agree*

P18: [company] gives you individual attention.

Strongly disagree 1 — 2 — 3 — 4 — 5 — 6 — 7 *Strongly agree*

P19: [company] has operating hours convenient to all their customers.

Strongly disagree 1 — 2 — 3 — 4 — 5 — 6 — 7 *Strongly agree*

P20: [company] has employees who give you personal attention.

Strongly disagree 1 — 2 — 3 — 4 — 5 — 6 — 7 *Strongly agree*

P21: [company] has your best interests at heart.

Strongly disagree 1 — 2 — 3 — 4 — 5 — 6 — 7 *Strongly agree*

P22: The employees of [company] understand your specific needs.

Strongly disagree 1 — 2 — 3 — 4 — 5 — 6 — 7 *Strongly agree*

Part 3: Relative importance

Listed below are five features relating to [industry] companies and the services they offer. We would like to know how important each of these features is to you when you evaluate a [industry] company's quality of service.

Please allocate a total of 100 points among the five features according to how important each feature is to you—the more important the feature is to you, the more points you should allocate to it. Please ensure that the points you allocate to the five features add up to 100.

	Points	
1. The appearance of the [industry] company's physical facilities, equipment, personnel and communications materials		Tangibles weighting
2. The ability of the [industry] company to perform the promised service dependably and accurately		Reliability weighting
3. The willingness of the [industry] company to help customers and provide prompt service		Responsiveness weighting
4. The knowledge and courtesy of the [industry] company's employees and their ability to convey trust and confidence		Assurance weighting
5. The caring, individualised attention the [industry] company provides its customers		Empathy weighting
Total points allocated (should be a total of 100)		

Expectation/perception gap calculation table

Dimension	A.1 Respondents E-P gap score					A.2 Dimension average			B Weighted gap	
	1	2	3	4	etc	Dimension total	Number of respondents	Dimension gap	Relative weighting (%)	Weighted average (dimension gap × relative weighting)
Tangibles										
Question 1										
Question 2										
Question 3										
Question 4										
Total questions 1–4										
Average (total ÷ 4)										
Reliability										
Question 5										
Question 6										
Question 7										
Question 8										
Question 9										
Total questions 5–9										
Average (total ÷ 5)										

(continues)

Expectation/perception gap calculation table (continued)

Dimension	A.1 Respondents E–P gap score					A.2 Dimension average				B Weighted gap	
	1	2	3	4	etc	Dimension total	Number of respondents	Dimension gap	Relative weighting (%)	Weighted average (dimension gap × relative weighting)	
Responsiveness											
Question 10											
Question 11											
Question 12											
Question 13											
Total questions 10–13											
Average (total ÷ 4)											
Assurance											
Question 14											
Question 15											
Question 16											
Question 17											
Total questions 14–17											
Average (total ÷ 4)											

(continues)

Expectation/perception gap calculation table (continued)

Dimension	A.1 Respondents E–P gap score					A.2 Dimension average			B Weighted gap	
	1	2	3	4	etc	Dimension total	Number of respondents	Dimension gap	Relative weighting (%)	Weighted average (dimension gap × relative weighting)
Empathy										
Question 18										
Question 19										
Question 20										
Question 21										
Question 22										
Total questions 18–22										
Average (total ÷ 5)										

Dimension average total

C. Overall gap

Divide by 5

Overall gap

CHAPTER 9

Improving processes
Process mapping and management

Process mapping (sometimes called process charting) is at the heart of many continuous improvement techniques, ranging from the very simple, such as 'standard operating procedures' (SOPs) for equipment operators, to the very complex, such as Six Sigma. Process mapping is founded on the premise that if you create a picture or a map of a process, it will be much easier to understand it. Further, once you have a process map in place, you can use it for a wide variety of purposes, from teaching other people to understand the process to streamlining or radically overhauling that process.

One of the many management innovations of the 1990s was the view of the organisation as a complex bundle of processes. This way of looking at an organisation was popularised by writer/consultants such as Hammer and Champy.[1] It was in contrast to the traditional view of the organisation as a collection of separate and distinct functions, such as product development, sales, operations and administration. Because processes tend to straddle functions, the traditional approach can inhibit the efficiency of those processes (as any complaining customer can testify as they are passed from one function to another in pursuit of a resolution to their complaint).

Advances in computing from the 1980s onwards made re-engineering the processes used by organisations much easier, so that even the most complex processes can now be modelled in great detail.

Whatever the process mapping application, it all starts with creating a map of the process. This enables us to reduce the complexity of the process by depicting only the most critical elements. The map is an abstraction (it is *never* the same as the process) but, like any map, it does help get people to a destination. Over time, many different approaches have been developed for creating such maps. There is no 'one best way' to map a process; rather, the approach to mapping should be selected on the basis of whether it will serve the end purpose. For example, if your job is to create a computer program that will accurately replicate the steps in a process currently carried out manually, then it is absolutely critical that every conceivable eventuality and variation is considered and addressed by the program. That is why systems analysts (the people who design computer programs) have developed powerful and sophisticated tools to help them understand processes. The same approach would be overkill if all you're trying to do is to teach a machine operator how to operate a piece of equipment.

In this chapter, we will assume that the purpose of mapping is to *improve processes*. This approach is part of a tradition that goes back a long way and includes the development of assembly lines, process automation, process control and quality improvement. In fact, it was the development of total quality management (TQM) principles that gave process mapping its biggest boost. The rise of TQM is attributed to developments in the Japanese manufacturing industry after World War Two, although US statisticians and quality experts, such as Deming, Juran and Feigenbaum, provided the intellectual horsepower behind most of the TQM tools.[2]

Background

Process mapping has been around for so long that it is hard to know exactly where it came from. It is not closely associated with any particular individual, although General Electric was an early and extensive user of the technique. It is a close relative of other charting techniques, such as flowcharting and Gantt charts, which have also been around for a long time. Charting is generally associated with early developments in computing which, in turn, borrowed the technique from simple forms of logic charting (such as the family tree used in genealogy).

Flowcharting was formalised by researchers at IBM in the 1950s to assist in the creation of computer programs. The flowchart breaks a process into its component steps. It maps each step visually, using special shapes to represent the type of activity involved; for example, a diamond shape stands for a step in the process where a decision needs to be made. IBM developed the standard symbols that denote events in the process flow, such as 'storage' and 'decision point'; these symbols are still used in flowcharting today. Even though the technique has since been developed into more sophisticated versions (such as Unified Modelling Language or UML) and is supported by a wide range of computer packages that make it easier to create the flowcharts, the fundamental ideas of flowcharting have not changed.

Gantt charts are typically associated with project management. The technique allows a project to be broken down into its component parts, which can then be shown as steps in a process that unfolds over time. The main objective is to ensure that the project is completed on time. A Gantt chart enables the user to see the implications of time and budget overruns. In the 1950s, the US navy developed a more sophisticated version, the project evaluation and review technique (PERT), to manage complex projects such as the development of the Polaris submarine. The PERT version shows the 'connectedness' between the project steps, enabling the user to work out the best route through a series of pathways presenting many different choices (this is called 'critical path analysis').

Process mapping is simpler than either flowcharting, Gantt charts or PERT, and this is its strength. A process map has been variously described as:

- a series of connected steps that lead to a result
- a sequence of inputs and actions that lead to an output
- (when used in business) a series of activities that take an input, add value to it and produce an output for a customer.[3]

The common element in these descriptions is that it is a technique that involves *mapping a process of connected steps that lead to an outcome.*

The terms 'process mapping' and 'flowcharting' are used interchangeably by many. The only real differences are that:

- flowcharting is better for *more complex processes* where there are many 'branching' alternatives
- process mapping works better with *more linear processes* that involve fewer choices
- flowcharts are better at showing the *type of steps* involved in the process (process mapping doesn't worry too much about this), enabling the process to be easily analysed (for example, such analysis might show that a given process involves an unusually large number of decision points)
- process maps can show the *input-transformation-output* details, including supplier and customer requirements (for example, for each step they can show who supplies the raw materials needed to achieve a value-adding transformation and exactly what they are).

A process map can be drawn in many ways. Generically, it involves a sequence of steps that lead from one to another until a desired result is achieved. So the simplest map is a series of boxes that each describes a reasonably discrete step. (Flowcharting enables you to indicate what type of step is involved; process mapping usually disregards that.) There is no limit to the length of the sequence of steps but, for ease of understanding, it usually works best if the sequence is a logical and manageable chunk of work. To support descriptions of larger chunks of work, or even a complete operation, you can create a higher level 'overview' process map that maps all the smaller chunks, supported by a separate map for each of those smaller chunks.

Process maps have many different applications:

- process improvement—improving a process so it is safer, faster or requires fewer resources
- process standardisation—ensuring that a process is exactly what you want it to be
- process automation—designing a computer program that will carry out the process
- process management—controlling variations in a process
- process measurement—measuring the performance of each step in the process
- process training—training operators to carry out a process
- process innovation—designing and planning completely new ways of delivering a result
- process redesign—changing a process more radically, and possibly removing it altogether.

These are the major applications, but there are many more. For each one the style of process map used might vary slightly. For example, if the purpose of the map is to improve a process to make it safer, then add to it information that rates the safety of each step in the process. If the map is about cost reduction, add information about whether each step is value-adding or not (this identifies non-value-adding steps which use resources unproductively and can therefore be considered for removal). If it's about speeding up the process, then add information about how long each process step takes.

Types of process maps

There are four different types of process maps: process description maps; process verification maps; process improvement maps; and process redesign maps.

There is some overlap between the type of map used and the reasons for doing process mapping, but these are different concepts. Each type of process map draws a different version of 'reality' (from what we think through to what the ideal version of the process might be); however, the reasons for drawing a particular type of map can vary widely.

Type 1: Process description

This involves creating a map by *describing the process*. Typically, it involves a group of people getting together to draw up a process map of an existing process, based on what they think the process involves. It is a good first step in any mapping exercise, but it tends to be flawed—that is, the process as mapped by the group is not what happens in reality. In addition, groups sometimes are not capable of drawing the map because they cannot agree on what the process is. With any given process, it is quite likely that different people will remember different parts of the process differently. That is why you also need the Type 2 map.

Type 2: Process verification

This involves taking a Type 1 map and *verifying each part of the process by observation*. This is done by direct observation or by other means, such as a videotape recording of the process being carried out. Often, such verification will establish that the Type 1 map has missed out some steps or shows them incorrectly in some way.

One way of limiting the changes that have to be made following the verification process is to involve operators in the development of the Type 1 map. When only managers do the Type 1 map, during verification they often discover that what the operators actually do is quite different from what management thought they did.

This approach can also be used to create processes from scratch (that is, when designing a sequence of operations that has not been undertaken before). The Type 1 map will establish what the designers have in mind, while the Type 2 map will show the practicality (or otherwise) of that design by, for example, building a test model of the process or having experts in similar processes review the new process for practicality.

Type 3: Process improvement

This type of map shows how an *existing process* can be *improved*. The input is a Type 2 map and, after analysis and deliberation, the output is a Type 3 map showing the best way to do the process.

When drawing a Type 3 map, it is important for the group to agree on the objectives of the mapping activity. The criteria for what constitutes improvement should be made explicit. For example, managers will often think of improvement in terms of faster and cheaper, while operators tend to think improvement means safer and easier.

A Type 3 map can be a road map for changing inadequate processes into better ones. However, designing the map and implementing the proposed changes are two quite different things. Make sure that the scope of the group creating a Type 3 map is always clear: 'design only' or 'design and implementation'.

Type 4: Process redesign

The last type of map is the most difficult. Type 4 maps represent the *ideal process*—the best it can possibly be. The aim of the exercise is to draw up the best possible way to carry out a process. It is how you would like the process to be in an ideal world. Type 3 maps may simply be improved versions of a less than ideal way of doing the process.

Redesigning a process using a Type 4 map must be done in the context of overall operations. A Type 4 map is rarely created in isolation, as the process will most likely affect other related processes. If you redesign a process such as how to bill your customers, then it is likely to have an impact on related processes such as debt collection and account management. For this reason, Type 4 maps are usually created as part of a larger project, such as those involving Business Process Re-engineering, Six Sigma or Socio-Technical Systems Work Redesign projects.

More complex models

For some applications, such as process design and innovation, it is critical that almost every conceivable detail is recorded. Maps of this complexity rely on special techniques such as IDEF0 (pronounced 'IDEF-zero'), which is part of a family of sophisticated process mapping techniques developed by the US airforce to map all the requirements of a production system. It is used by experts highly skilled in functional modelling techniques.

Functional modelling represents only one group of modelling techniques. Many other types of modelling are used for specialist applications, including systems modelling (for example, SSADM); information modelling (for example, DFD); dynamic modelling (for example, Petri-nets); and enterprise modelling (for example, CIMOSA).[4]

All of these high-level techniques are recognisable as derivatives of the humble process map. In general management, it is still the simplest of all modelling techniques to help in achieving day-to-day improvements.

The tool

A process is a sequence of steps (usually activities), performed over time and (usually) in a particular space. A process map begins with a picture of these steps. It is traditional to show them as boxes with arrows that demonstrate the flow from one step to the next. You can then add as many layers of additional detail as are needed to satisfy the requirements of the mapping exercise. For example:

- If the purpose is to analyse the physical layout of a process, with a view to reducing unnecessary movement by operators and unnecessary transportation of the product, then data about location and distance needs to be added.
- If the purpose is to speed up the process (for example, to speed up a machine changeover procedure), then in addition to layout data, you might add time data for each step. (To create a really useful machine changeover map, you should add information about whether the step is carried out when the machine is working or not working.[5])

Even a map as simple as the ones described above (a series of steps in boxes showing location and duration of each step) is sufficient to support a number of improvement activities. In addition to reducing unnecessary movements and speeding up the process, you can also:

- decide whether all the steps are needed
- explore whether steps can be combined
- investigate whether steps can be done differently
- check whether those involved in the process are following all the steps accurately
- teach someone how to follow the process accurately.

So even at the simplest level, a process map is a useful management tool. Its usefulness can be increased by adding more layers of data. This will build the complexity of the map but it will also increase its utility. For example:

- On the left-hand side of each box, you can indicate what input is required to carry out each step and who supplies that input.
- On the right-hand side of the box, you can add information about what the output of the box is and who receives that output (for example, the customer).
- You can add further richness of detail by adding information about any standards that the output might have to meet (typically, the customers set those standards).

Often, process maps can also include information about whether the step described in each box adds 'value' to the process or not. 'Value-adding' is an interesting idea that gave rise to its own management fad in the 1980s—'value-adding management'. This involved examining all the steps in an operation, or even a whole job, and removing any that did not add value.[6] In this kind of analysis, value is considered to be added if the step meets the following criteria:

- it adds something that is recognised by the customer as being worthwhile
- it actually changes the product in some way
- it is done right the first time (that is, it doesn't have to be duplicated)
- it is required to be done (that is, for safety, regulatory or ethical reasons).

The reason for adding information about value-adding (it is usually indicated as 'Yes' or 'No') is that it enables you to decide whether you really need that step in the process. If a step is not adding value, then maybe that step can be removed, combined, reduced or replaced. In other words, this is another way of improving the process.

All of this data can be captured in the one process map by completing the *process mapping form* at the end of this chapter. The form provides a handy way of capturing the required information, which then becomes the first cut of the process map. However, to make the most of the mapping process there are some steps that should be followed first.

Preparing to map

At the end of the chapter there is a form, Process mapping: Preparatory steps, to assist you with this exercise.

Step 1: Describe and define the process to be mapped

This step sounds innocent enough, but more process mapping exercises than I care to remember never make it past this step!

Most mapping exercises involve a number of people and most people have a different understanding of exactly what the process is that is to be mapped. Only by writing a description of it can you reach agreement on what the process under review actually is. The words flush out differences in understanding and failure to reach agreement on a set of words usually indicates a serious level of confusion.

This step 'scopes' the mapping exercise. From a practical point of view, it seems to help if you start the description with an action verb such as 'making' (as in 'making a cup of coffee').

Step 2: Establish a start and a finish point

This step involves delimiting the process more exactly. Most processes flow smoothly from the ones that precede them and into the ones that follow them. It is always an arbitrary decision to take a handful of steps and call it a process. But without this, you won't know what you're mapping, so it has to be done. (Following the previous example, are we analysing 'making a cup of coffee' or 'making a cup of coffee and serving it'?)

Look for a logical chunk of work rather than an arbitrary set of process steps. ('Adding sugar to a cup of coffee' seems a bit narrow; 'making coffee' is open to misinterpretation; 'making a drink' seems a bit broad; 'making a cup of coffee for Harry' seems about right.)

Step 3: Determine the output of the process

Most processes have one major output, but there may be secondary outputs to be considered. Sometimes, this step looks obvious ('a cup of coffee'), but some important distinctions sometimes need to be made ('a cup of coffee made in accordance with the preferences of this customer'). These distinctions can make the difference between a satisfied customer and a complaining customer.

Step 4: Identify the customer and understand their needs

This step is closely linked to Step 3. Knowing the customer and their needs provides you with a reference point for various issues relating to standards. These standards usually derive from customers, but they can also come from other sources such as regulatory, safety or other protocols.

The standards are a benchmark for quality; they indicate what is or is not acceptable. (How many, if any, spoons of sugar does the customer want in their coffee?) If there is more than one customer, indicate whether any of them are more important than others. Make sure you truly understand what the needs of your customers are—don't assume you know!

Step 5: Identify the suppliers to the process and define their inputs

This step will tell you what the inputs into the process are and who will provide those inputs. Unlike customers, suppliers don't get to set the standards—you do. To ensure that you get the quality of input that you need, you have to specify the standards that you require (clean cups; freshly ground coffee beans; full-fat and reduced-fat milk; and so on). Each input requires a standard. Standards typically relate to product quality (fresh milk) and service quality (on-time delivery in full).

Step 6: Decide the steps in the process

The most important question at this point in the mapping process is how many steps to include. Once again, a natural chunk of activity comprising 5 to 10 steps seems to work best, but there really is no way of knowing if you need more than that. It all depends on the circumstance. (I make a cup of instant coffee for myself in six steps, assuming all inputs are readily available; I take a lot more if I can be bothered to use my espresso machine.)

It helps if you use action verbs to start each step in the process and keep the description descriptive; if you can't see it, then it's not part of the process!

Step 7: Decide what type of map is required

By following this sequence, you will be ready to create a process map. What remains to be done is determine the *type* of map you want to draw.

The Type 1 map (description) is easiest as it relies entirely on what you think the process is ('here's how I think I make a cup of coffee'). But you need to move to a Type 2 map (verification) if you are going to put the map to use for some purpose ('this is how I actually make a cup of coffee'). It is highly likely that you will discover steps that have been missed or steps that are slightly different from what you thought they were, as you move from Type 1 to Type 2.

Putting the map to work

Now you're ready to put the process map to some real use. Do you want to speed up the process? Do you want to change some steps; remove some steps; combine some steps (how about a heated coffee container with sugar and milk already added)? What about making the process easier (coffee whitener instead of fresh milk)? Do you want to take costs out of the process? (After adding some information about input costs, it is clear that coffee is the major cost so you might buy a cheaper alternative.) The new version of the process can be captured in a Type 3 map (improvement) which shows a better version of the process.

Finally, you may be inclined to attempt a Type 4 map (redesign), which involves looking at the overall context of the process. In a sense, it means starting with a blank piece of paper and designing a better process from scratch. You may need to specify some special criteria (make a coffee in three seconds) and it may need some very creative thinking to make them happen. But the blank piece of paper does present the opportunity to throw away all the traditional notions for completing a process. (By the way, if you think a three-second coffee is impossible, I have seen a vending machine aluminium-can self-heating product which does exactly this!)

Process mapping does not have to be complicated to deliver results. Many (if not most) processes in most businesses have never been mapped and can benefit from a simple mapping process. Many processes were once mapped but the maps have been long forgotten. Process mapping can deliver significant gains without relying on experts or computer software.

Observations

The latest incarnation of TQM is Six Sigma. This gained fame not because it was a new idea (it uses all the traditional TQM tools) but because it was a method of applying TQM to the services industry rather than the manufacturing industry. Companies such as Allied Signal, Motorola and GE gained major benefits from streamlining their non-manufacturing operations and removing non-value-adding steps in their processes. The publicity this received revived interest in the 'heavy' end of process improvement. Six Sigma also seems to have breathed life back into the idea of Business Process Re-engineering (BPR), which uses heavy computer power to automate and streamline high-order information processing activities. BPR was a big hit in the 1990s but faded as the complexities of the re-engineering task became apparent.

No doubt the current interest in the big guns of process mapping and re-engineering will wane over time as organisations discover that Six Sigma is hard work, takes a long time to get right, and involves enormous resources. Although the authors of books on Six Sigma are doing well, and Six Sigma consultants are doing even better, it seems only a matter of time before the fad peaks. Big guns are not for every organisation. Those without a substantial track record in implementing disciplined, well-resourced and long-term plans should not even think about Six Sigma.

On the other hand, every organisation can benefit from the 'light' end of process improvement. This simply involves taking one process at a time, mapping it, and improving it. Granted that it will not deliver the massive savings possible through Six Sigma, but it does have the advantage that it is quick (weeks instead of months or years), immediate (results now, not later), and easy to do (only a couple of people are needed for short periods of time). If this simple approach is undertaken systematically, the overall benefits can be enormous.

Process mapping does not have formal rules but it does help to be disciplined about the mapping process. It can easily be taught to others and, when used in a team setting, gives managers, supervisors and staff an opportunity to reflect on their experience as the 'doers' in an organisation. It can bring quick and practical improvement today, without the need to wait for the input of internal or external 'experts'. We should re-claim this tool for management—it can make a significant contribution to the management function. It is essentially a generalist technique, with the most typical management application being process improvement. Most managers do not invent new processes and they rely on specialists to manage the more complex processes in organisations. However, general process improvement is a managerial responsibility, and I doubt that there is a better tool for managing it than process mapping.

User's guide

A common situation facing managers is where an existing process is not working as well as it should. Usually, this is indicated by a fault report of some kind. The reports might be generated within the organisation, for example, production, quality, customer satisfaction or financial reports. Sometimes they are generated outside the organisation, for example through complaints from suppliers, customers or regulatory authorities. Whatever the source, most managers have no shortage of data about problems. This provides the best starting point for a mapping exercise. Whenever a problem re-occurs, drawing a process map is a good idea.

Instructions

How to create a process map

1. *Having selected a process that appears to generate problems, decide who will be involved in the mapping exercise.*

It is always useful to have the people who carry out the process involved in the challenge of improving the process. They are the 'owners' of the process and generally know most about it. (It may be useful to involve a small team of people. See Chapter 17, Involving employees: Problem-solving teams.)

2. *Decide at the start on the key measurements that are needed to understand the process. The problem will generally indicate what they are.*

For example, if an order fulfilment process is occasionally delivering the wrong product to the wrong customer, it makes sense to focus the mapping exercise on accuracy of information processing within the order fulfilment process. There seems little point in focusing on other measures such as 'on time' delivery or cost of delivery.

3. *Decide the level of detail required for the map.*

Sometimes a broad overview (at a 'macro' level) is sufficient, and in any case, it's a good starting point. Such a map has boxes that contain fairly big chunks of activity.

For the order fulfilment project suggested in step 2, a top-level macro map might look like the one shown in Figure 9.1. This map suggests that if some products are being delivered to the wrong address, some product/delivery information may not be transmitted accurately during the total

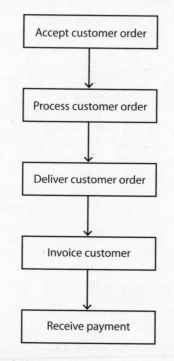

Figure 9.1 The order fulfilment process

process. Complaints are coming in after the delivery stage, so we can rule out the last two steps in the macro process. Errors responsible for mis-delivery may occur at any stage in the first three steps, so each of those steps should be separately mapped.

4. *The process map form that appears at the end of this chapter can now be used to map each of the three steps.*

   This medium level of mapping is sometimes called 'mini-level mapping'. (This is in contrast to 'micro-level mapping', which aims to capture every possible detail about the process.) In the order fulfilment project, this approach would be used if the process was to be automated, for example, by letting customers do their own ordering over the Internet.

   The best way to complete a mini-level process map is to allocate responsibility for collecting and recording information to one person, who then interviews all those who are involved in the process to obtain the relevant data. As the map is built up through these contributions, it needs to be taken back to those who contribute for verification. This iterative process will build the most reliable Type 1 process map.

5. *Turn the Type 1 map into a Type 2 map through verification.*

   Make sure someone walks their way through the full process. (In one exercise, information obtained from a customer was pinned to a person who then followed the physical route normally taken by the information sheet; we abandoned this approach after our carrier spent three days in someone's in-tray!)

6. *The process of verification will generate opportunities for future analysis.*

   For example, it will demonstrate bottlenecks, unnecessary delays, oppor-tunities for errors through data transcription, re-work requirements and so on. The verifier can record all these ideas for future research.

   It is often helpful at this point to go back to the original fault reports and try to identify where the errors have occurred. This tends to indicate weaknesses in the process. Given that the order fulfilment process faults seem to relate to information transmission, look for opportunities where data is recorded or transcribed. These are likely sources of error.

7. *This analysis should indicate weak points in the overall process.*

   In the order fulfilment example, these may well relate to data transcription steps.

8. *Design a Type 3 map, with new steps in the procedure that will reduce or eliminate the opportunity for data transcription errors.*

   For example, reduction can be achieved by adding a data accuracy checking step; elimination can be achieved by redesigning the process so that transcription is removed altogether.

Further reading

- M Hammer, 'Re-engineering work: Don't automate, obliterate!', *Harvard Business Review*, July–Aug, 1990, pp. 104–12.

  Michael Hammer's ideas are encapsulated in his influential HBR article. It is bit iconoclastic but did a great job in putting the focus on process redesign rather than process automation, which was the catch-cry at the time.

- J Huffman, 'The four Re's of total improvement', *Quality Progress*, vol. 30, no. 1, 1997, pp. 83–8.

  In this article Huffman puts the counter case that one single approach is rarely the best.

- R Lee & B Dale, 'Business process management: A review and evaluation', *Business Process Management*, 1998, vol. 4, no. 3, pp. 214–25.

  Try this article for an overview of the current field of business process management. It shows that the field of process management has matured in a relatively short period to become a specialist area for those interested in continuous improvement.

- J Fülscher & S Powell, 'Anatomy of a process mapping workshop', *Business Process Management*, vol. 5, no. 3, 1999, pp. 208–37.

  This article contains an interesting (and rare) description of a complete process mapping exercise. The setting is a Swiss insurance company and the work done in the workshop led to significant changes in the way the insurance company did its work.

Notes

1. M Hammer & J Champy, *Reengineering the corporation: A manifesto for business revolution*, Kogan Paul, London, 1993.
2. For an overview of their impact, see Y Kathawla, 'A comparative analysis of selected approaches to quality', *International Journal of Quality & Reliability Management*, vol. 16, no. 5, 1989, pp. 7–17.
3. R Anjard, 'Process mapping: A valuable tool for construction management and other professionals', *Facilities*, vol. 16, no. 3/4, 1998, pp. 79–81.
4. J Bal, 'Process analysis tools for process improvement', *The TQM Magazine*, vol. 10, no. 5, 1998, pp. 342–54.
5. S Shingo, *A revolution in manufacturing: The SMED system*, Productivity Press, Cambridge, 1987.
6. Recently, this approach has been revitalised as 'value stream mapping' by the advocates of 'lean manufacturing', such as James Womack. See, for example, J Womack, *Lean thinking*, 2nd edn, The Free Press, New York, 2000.

Process mapping: Preparatory steps

Process title:

1. Describe process:

2a. Start point:

2b. Finish point:

3a. Output of process (primary):

3b. Secondary outputs:

4a. Who are the customers?

4b. Standards customers require:

5a. Who are the suppliers?

5b. Supplier inputs:

5c. Standards you require of suppliers:

6. Number of steps required (max. 10):

7. Type of map required:

PROCESS MAP FORM

Title of process: _____

Supplier	Inputs	Standard	Process steps	Value add (Y / N)	Outputs	Standard	Customers
			1.				
			2.				
			3.				
			4.				
			5.				
			6.				
			7.				
			8.				
			9.				
			10.				

Type of value adding: please tick as appropriate (✓)

( ) Customer recognises the value
( ) Done right the first time (not duplicated)

( ) Changes the product
( ) Required by law, contract, or for safety or ethical reasons.

CHAPTER 10

Solving problems
Pareto analysis

There are many problem-solving techniques available to managers, and most of them are powerful tools for reaching a solution. However, one stands out as the powertool to use for deciding *which* problems to solve: *Pareto analysis*. It sorts the vital few from the trivial many. It tells you which problem, if solved, will give you 'the most bang for your buck'. At the same time, it is a simple and easy tool to use and is so flexible that it can be applied in almost any situation. If faced with a problem, Pareto analysis is always a good place to start.

Although the tool is named after Italian economist and sociologist, Vilfredo Pareto (1848–1923), it actually has very little to do with him. It was Joseph Juran, one of the founders of the quality movement, who both created the tool and named it after Pareto.[1] (Juran has since acknowledged that it was probably a misleading attribution[2], modestly suggesting that he should have named the principle after himself[3].) Juran wanted a shorthand description of the phenomenon that, in any given population of effects, only a small number of causes accounts for the majority of effects. This skewed distribution of causes has also been called the *80/20 rule*—it suggests that 80% of the effect comes from 20% of the causes.

Juran applied this *Pareto principle* to a wide range of organisational situations, from quality errors in manufacturing to customer analysis in sales and marketing. For example, in one often-quoted piece of analysis in one company, Pareto analysis found that 10% of the customers accounted for 60% of sales, and the bottom 80% of customers accounted for 25% of sales. This kind of statistic sets the (sales) mind thinking about such issues as where to focus the energies of sales staff; whether to segment the customer base; and how to service the various segments differently.

Since its invention, Pareto analysis has been applied extensively in many fields to sort the most important events from the least important events. At heart, it is a tool for making choices based on priorities. In general management, it is an ideal tool for determining where to place the focus of management attention and action. As a precursor to solving problems, it is both undervalued and unsurpassed. Pareto analysis helps to ensure that managers solve the right problems.

Background

Pareto analysis was developed by Joseph Juran as a quality improvement tool. Juran (along with others such as Deming, Feigenbaum and Crosby) developed an approach to quality improvement that relied on a range of statistical techniques to control production and, especially, quality. Pareto analysis is based on the phenomenon that a high percentage of quality failures have a small percentage of causes. This mal-distribution of events provides an opportunity to sort the vital few from the trivial many. Pareto analysis does not solve problems but identifies which problems have the greatest impact. It thereby generates priorities for management action.

Pareto analysis involves a number of steps, including:

- data gathering
- charting
- analysis and decision making.

Each step in the process is relatively simple but can be applied to almost any problem. Its application to general management is as a focusing tool. By identifying those events that cause the greatest impact, managers can sort the important from the urgent (see also Chapter 20, Managing time: Time-management techniques). In fact, a Pareto analysis of how managers spend their time is likely to show that 80% of their time is spent on the least important things and 20% on the most important things. By applying Pareto analysis to their own time, many managers have been able to refocus themselves on those aspects of their job that have the greatest impact in terms of organisational benefit.

Pareto analysis is frequently used as a rule-of-thumb explanation for any skewed distribution, especially in its popular format as the 80/20 rule. It seems remarkably accurate, even in this informal application. For example:

- 80% of car accidents are caused by 20% of drivers
- 80% of quality failures in manufacturing come from 20% of the process steps
- 80% of household moves are done by 20% of the population
- 80% of all snack foods are eaten by 20% of consumers.[4]

Pareto analysis can be turned into a tool for general management simply by applying the analytical process to a business issue. For example, in any given organisation, it is highly likely that about 20% of the purchase orders account for 80% of the expenditure. That is, a relatively small number of purchase orders involve spending large amounts of money. Put the other way around, the vast majority of purchase orders involve only small amounts of money. Most organisations require at least two people to sign off on purchase orders. If this procedure were to be amended so that only the 20% of orders that involve large amounts of money required two signatures, then tight control would still be exercised over the vast bulk of expenditure. However, requiring only one signature on the 80% of orders that involve small amounts of expenditure would generate a saving of 38% of the time spent on checking and signing purchase orders. In an accounts payable department, this might mean freeing up one person in three.[5]

In particular applications, the numbers may vary slightly but, as an approximation, the 80/20 split is very reliable. For example, the following data comes from a sales and marketing context:

- 73% of sales are generated by 20% of the sales force
- 85% of sales are accounted for by 16% of products
- 77% of sales are accounted for by 22% of customers.[6]

Given this sort of data, management may be inclined to analyse and then consider responses such as:

- examining the activities of the 80% of the sales force that is underperforming (refocus, retrain or reduce)
- reviewing the product range (eliminate products that do not sell)
- reviewing the customer base (eliminate customers that do not buy much).

Interestingly, once such actions have been taken, the 80/20 rule will still apply. For example, even after a massive reduction in the product range, it will still be the case that 20% of the product range will deliver 80% of the income (or thereabouts). The absolute numbers involved will have changed (fewer products) but the relativities within the remaining range will still reflect an 80/20 distribution. This creates the temptation to keep rationalising the product range to the point where we get a diminishing return from the reduction strategy. This quickly turns the reduction strategy into a *reductio ad absurdum* strategy.

Pareto analysis has another drawback. It provides a snapshot that is frozen in time. In other words, it is entirely static. It is only ever true for the instant at which the analysis is applied. This matters, because most organisations exist in a dynamic state. The analysis creates dangers in reducing the product line or customer base to such a skeleton that other opportunities are missed. For example, one of the lesser selling products today may become the biggest selling product in a few years time. At some point in time, Microsoft or IBM was somebody's smallest customer. Only a series of snapshots over time can reveal that a product or a customer has growth potential. Of course managers should focus on the top 20%—but that does not mean ignoring the other 80%, because that is where the future of the organisation may well be found.

Although it is always useful to do a Pareto analysis—unfailingly, it will shed light on a situation—it is at its most powerful when used to investigate problems. Applying the tool to a problem situation is almost the natural first step in solving the problem. The output of Pareto analysis is usually captured in the form of a chart. Pareto charts are histograms that show a frequency distribution from highest to lowest. The Pareto chart will indicate which event relating to the problem occurs most frequently. (If the vertical axis of the graph is changed from 'frequency' to 'costs involved', it will indicate which event is the most expensive.) The chart will usually provide clues as to the root cause of the problem.

Occasionally, a Pareto analysis will generate a chart in which the usual 'Pareto curve' from highest to lowest is not apparent. This does not mean that the analysis has failed but simply that further analysis is required. It suggests that the events used to plot the frequency are not the root cause of the problem. For example, in one case study, examining causes of product defects generated a chart that suggested five out of six defect causes had a significant impact; clearly, the expected Pareto curve wasn't there. A further analysis examined the occurrence of product defects by the work-shift in which the defect was detected. This did show the Pareto effect, with one particular shift (second shift on Mondays) accounting for 45% of all defects for the whole week.

This in turn led to a further Pareto chart on causes of defects generated only by the second Monday shift. The chart showed a clear Pareto effect indicating that over-sized and under-sized product accounted for 90% of the defects. Ultimately, this led to the discovery that insufficient machine warm-up (after the weekend idle period) on the first Monday morning shift was the cause of the defects, which were not identified until the second Monday shift. Changed warm-up procedures eliminated 90% of the defects recorded.[7]

Doing a Pareto analysis invariably leads to insights. For this reason alone, if you face a problem, there is no better first step than Pareto analysis.

The tool

Pareto analysis is best understood by working through an example. The most common applications relate to quality problems, but it can just as easily be applied in other situations. For example, if a manager is faced with an in-tray full of problems, one way of prioritising these problems is to 'Pareto' them on the basis of the benefits achieved if they are resolved. The specific criteria used could be revenue gained, costs reduced or greatest reduction in pressure from senior management if resolved! A Pareto chart drawn on this basis will demonstrate that, at any one time, a small group of problems can generate the bulk of the benefits. Most attention should be applied to these vital few issues.

In keeping with Pareto's origins, the following example draws on quality issues (in this case, quality failure). The process involves collecting data on the frequency of instances of quality failure, categorised by type. For example, an organisation can collect data on the customer complaints it receives and allocate each complaint to a category such as:

- late delivery
- incorrect delivery
- faulty products
- slow service
- miscellaneous.

The data can be collected by means of a data sheet (see Table 10.1).

The next step in the process is to chart these results on a bar chart (technically called a *histogram,* and easily done in a spreadsheet such as Microsoft Excel), showing the causes in descending order of frequency (see Fig. 10.1). (There is no special significance in the descending order, compared with an ascending order, but descending is the traditional approach with a Pareto chart.) The type of event is typically shown along the bottom axis and the frequency is shown along the side or vertical axis.

The chart shows that faulty products are a significant cause of customer complaints. This indicates that this area of failure may be a priority for management. Further analysis could be undertaken to provide more detail. For example, a further Pareto analysis on the category of faulty products may show that one or two types of products account for the bulk of the complaints in this category. Alternatively, a further analysis could be done on the cost of fixing the complaints, which may show that some complaints are very expensive to fix while others are less expensive. This may lead management to focus first on fixing the least expensive problems.

Table 10.1 Data sheet—frequency of complaints

Complaint cause	Frequency
Late delivery	14
Incorrect delivery	21
Faulty products	32
Slow service	11
Miscellaneous	5

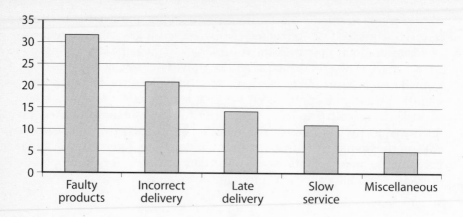

Figure 10.1 Frequency of complaints

There is a tendency sometimes to focus first on the major cause for a quality failure, but this is not always appropriate. For example, easy or cheap to fix are sometimes better criteria than biggest cause. Other criteria that may take precedence over biggest cause include impact on customers, regulatory requirements or greatest cost impact.

Pareto analysis is usually represented with 'categories of events' as the horizontal axis and 'frequency of events' as the vertical axis. However, this is only a tradition. It may well make more sense to use a different measure along the vertical axis, such as 'cost of incidence' or 'extent of impact on customers'. In the previous example, faulty products may be less of an issue with customers than late delivery; running out of stock may cause major problems, whereas sorting a few bad products from the good may be nothing more than an irritation. Only the customer can tell you that.

Frequency is the best option for the vertical axis when both of the following apply:

1. the degree of importance is the same for all categories (for example, all categories create similar levels of difficulty for customers)
2. all other things being equal, the potential for each category to occur is roughly equal.[8]

The first condition would fail, for example, if some customer complaints relate to safety issues. If a delivery involves a product that may harm the customer or the customer's customers, then that takes priority regardless of where it ranks on the Pareto chart. The second condition would fail if the data collected are skewed in some way. For example, if we collect data on customer complaints by day of the week and some days we have twice as many customers than on other days, then the Pareto analysis will also be skewed.

If either of the conditions is not met, then the analysis should take this into account and adjust for it. For example, if the first condition is not met (that is, there is a difference in importance for the categories used), then this can be corrected by adjusting the relative importance of the categories. Let's assume five categories (say: A, B, C, D, E) with each having a different cost impact (say: $80, $20, $50, $100, $25) and each having a different frequency of occurrence (say: 20, 10, 22, 7, 4). This data can be weighted to remove the skewing effect of the different cost impacts (see Table 10.2).

Table 10.2 Weighted cost impact

Category	Cost impact	Frequency	Weighted frequency
A	80	20	1600
B	20	10	200
C	50	22	1100
D	100	7	700
E	25	4	100

A Pareto chart based on the weighted frequency would show that A has the greatest impact (see Fig. 10.2), whereas a Pareto chart based only on the frequency distribution would show C as having the greatest impact.

If the second condition (the potential for each category to occur is roughly equal) is not met, then the data needs to be adjusted to eliminate the skewing effect of the different potentials. For example, if quality

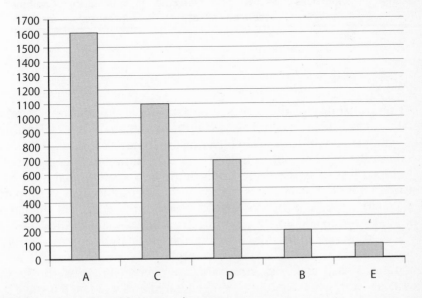

Figure 10.2 Weighted frequency by category

141

errors occur on three different machines (say: A, B, C) generating similar defect levels (say: 6, 5, 4), but each of the machines produces at a different rate (say: 200, 100, 50), then we can adjust the different potentials by calculating a *rate* of occurrence.

Table 10.3 Weighted rate of occurrence

Machine	Defectives	Pieces produced	Defective rate
A	6	200	.03
B	5	100	.05
C	4	50	.08

A Pareto chart based on the defective rate would show that machine C has the greatest frequency (see the data in Table 10.3). (Without the weighting created by calculating the rate, machine A may have appeared to cause the greatest frequency.)

If both conditions are not met, then a combined measure can be calculated. For example, in the machine example in Table 10.3, an importance measure could be added as an extra column. Multiply the defective rate by the importance measure, and you generate a combined measure (see Table 10.4). This calculation shows that machine C creates the greatest impact once the different production rates *and* the different levels of importance are taken into account.

Table 10.4 Combined measure impact

Machine	Defectives	Pieces produced	Defective rate	Importance measure	Combined measure
A	6	200	.03	50	1.5
B	5	100	.05	40	2.0
C	4	50	.08	100	8.0

The availability or the accuracy of data can also undermine Pareto analysis. Lack of data basically stops Pareto analysis in its tracks. Finding the data can be difficult and collecting the data takes time. But data accuracy is a bigger problem in that data collection processes are rarely developed just to satisfy somebody's desire to do Pareto analysis. This means that the data available is not always sufficiently accurate to support the Pareto analysis. If there is any doubt about the quality of the data, you may need to add an extra step in the process—data verification.

With most problems, it is common that the analysis is carried out in several layers, as in the previous example. Where do you stop? It is possible to keep analysing until you are overwhelmed by the sheer quantum of material that has been generated and you reach a stage of 'analysis paralysis'. Although repeated analysis is usually required, three or four layers of analysis should be sufficient for all but the most complex problems. Keep in mind that Pareto does not solve any problems in its own right, it simply creates a focus for problem-solving action.

There are always unique considerations for any problem that is subjected to Pareto analysis. For example, in dissecting a product range to determine which product generates the greatest benefit to the organisation, you need to consider the life cycle of each product. A product in the early stages of its life cycle may generate relatively little cash, but that is to be expected. Eliminating such products from the product range is counter-productive. Instead, consider doing a Pareto analysis on all the products at a similar stage in their life cycle to determine which is realising its potential and which is not.

Pareto charts are always only a snapshot in time and this may create special considerations. Continuing with the product range example, products that are subject to seasonal fluctuations may show up in a good or bad light depending on when the analysis is carried out. This makes it all the more critical to correctly title and date the Pareto chart, if only to make it clear what the chart refers to and when the data was collected.

Observations

Not much goes wrong with Pareto analysis. It is almost never a waste of time to undertake this type of analysis and it almost always generates a degree of insight into the problem being analysed. The tool itself is easy to understand and straightforward to use. It is not based on any complex theory that needs verification and there is little debate about its utility.

It is probably under-utilised in general management, but that is an anecdotal observation; I'm not aware of any studies that have tested it. Given the background of Pareto analysis in quality management, it is probably more prevalent in that area of management than anywhere else. Lately, it has made something of a comeback as part of the renewed interest in process improvement (see Chapter 9, Improving processes: Process mapping and management) and more generally in continuous improvement.

There is considerable scope for it to be used more widely by general management, perhaps under the guise of managing time better (see Chapter 20, Managing time: Time-management techniques), but it can also be used more widely. Various case studies have demonstrated its utility in guiding decisions in areas as diverse as prioritising investment in an information technology project[9], forecasting effectiveness[10], and business process outsourcing[11].

If managers have only one problem analysis tool in their back pocket, I recommend that Pareto analysis should be it.

User's guide

Pareto analysis involves only a small degree of rigour but that should be observed in order to maximise the benefits that the analysis can provide. Using software such as a spreadsheet takes most of the drudgery out of the charting process but increases the risk of data inaccuracy. It often makes sense to get a second (independent) party to verify that the data is correct and has been entered correctly.

One of the less-stated advantages of Pareto analysis is the visual nature of Pareto charts. Rows and columns of data can often hide patterns that become obvious only when they are charted. This also means that information can be shared more easily, such as in a problem-solving group.

Instructions

How to use Pareto analysis

Pareto analysis involves three stages, each with its own discipline:

- Data collection: ensure the data is accurate, up-to-date, and readily available.
- Charting: consider whether the vertical axis should be frequency or some other measure.
- Analysis and decision making: decide whether further analysis through charting is necessary and use criteria to decide which category to focus on.

1. *Data collection*

   - First, make a decision about which problem to focus on.

     Most managers have no shortage of problems that they can tackle. The most fruitful problems for Pareto analysis are those situations that involve unwanted effects from unknown causes. Another way of thinking about this is to focus on situations where there are process failures that cause problems.

   - Select a problem area.
   - Make a list of the events that occur and streamline these by type into a list of categories.
   - Choose a unit of measure that can be applied to these categories (usually this is frequency of occurrence but it could be cost or time).
   - Choose a period of time over which data will be collected and use a data collection sheet to collect the data.

2. *Charting*

   This involves creating the Pareto chart. If done by hand, it means sorting the data into categories of descending order according to the measure selected. The easiest way to do this is to number each category in rank order. (This small step will eliminate the annoying chance of having to re-draw the chart halfway through the process because you've missed out a category!)

If using a spreadsheet, replicate the steps below by adding the data into the spreadsheet and, instead of drawing the chart by hand, select the histogram option from the chart menu.

- Sort the categories in descending order according to the measure used.
- List all the categories in that order along the bottom axis.
- Decide a scale for the vertical axis based on the highest and lowest measure obtained in the data collection.
- Draw a histogram (a series of vertical bars) by adding a bar for each category.

3. *Analysis and decision making*

If the above steps have been followed, you should be looking at a Pareto chart; that is, there is a distinct curve from highest to lowest. Depending on the data (and the scale used) the curve may be more or less pronounced.

- Interpret the result in terms of the 80/20 rule.

    Do a small number of categories account for the bulk of the occur-rences? If so, then you have identified those categories that are most significant. With a relatively simple problem, this may be sufficient to identify where you should take action. With a more complex problem, you may need to undertake further analysis by doing additional Pareto charts. Occasionally this involves collecting more data, in which case the original chart simply indicates where more data should be collected (which is still a useful outcome).

    If there is no curve evident, then the categories selected do not truly indicate the existence of the problem.

- Consider alternatives.

    If you have collected data on the days of the week that your car won't start and no curve emerges, this simply means that there is no causal relationship between days of the week and your car not starting. Re-think the situation and, for example, collect data on the prevailing weather conditions when the car will or will not start. This may lead to a Pareto chart that shows a relationship between weather conditions and the car starting. If that fails, look for other possible categories such as the days that follow lending your car to someone else (include all friends and relatives) or some other series of events that is possibly linked to your car. Eventually, a Pareto curve will be found and that becomes the basis for action.

Further reading

There are many books on Vilfredo Pareto, and none of them are on Pareto analysis. For that you need to turn to the books on quality management.

- B Michael & D Ritter, *The memory jogger*, Goal/QPC, Salem, 1994.

  This is one of the best. It is a collection of problem-solving tools in a pocket-book format. However, almost any book on TQM or problem-solving tools and techniques is guaranteed to contain a section on Pareto analysis.
    Others to try:

- P Capezio & D Morehouse, *Taking the mystery out of TQM: A practical guide to total quality management*, Career Press, Hawthorne, 1995.
- J Evans & M Lindsay, *Management and the control of quality*, Thomson Learning, Mason, 2001.

Notes

1. Juran describes the 'Pareto curve' in J Juran, 'Universals in management planning and controlling', *The Management Review*, Nov, 1954, pp. 748–61.
2. Pareto made several observations about the distribution of wealth in the economy, suggesting that 80% of the wealth appeared to be held by 20% of the population. Juran applied this 80/20 rule to the distribution of quality losses. 'It is a shorthand name for the phenomenon that in any population which contributes to a common effect, a relative few of the contributors account for the bulk of the effect.' See J Juran, 'The non-Pareto principle: Mea culpa', 2001, available from The Juran Institute, Wilton.
3. Reported in K Killen, 'Who was Vilfredo Pareto?', *Purchasing World*, vol. 32, issue 10, 1998, pp. 62–3.
4. R Sanders, 'The Pareto principle: Its use and abuse', *The Journal of Business and Industrial Marketing*, vol. 3, no. 3, 1998, pp. 37–40.
5. This example is drawn from R Stevens, 'Pareto strikes again', *Journal of Systems Management*, vol. 43, issue 1, 1992, p. 21.
6. R Sanders, op. cit.
7. E Fine, 'Pareto diagrams get to the root of process problems', *Quality*, vol. 35, issue 10, 1996, pp. 26–7.
8. J Stevenson, 'Supercharging your Pareto analysis', *Quality Progress*, vol. 33, issue 10, 2000, pp. 51–5.
9. R Craft, & C Leake, 'The Pareto principle in organizational decision making', *Management Decisions*, vol. 40, no. 8, 2002, pp. 729–33.
10. R Garodnock, 'Make better use of your forecasting package using the 80/20 rule', *Apparel Industry Magazine*, vol. 60, issue 10, 1999, pp. 80–1.
11. P Munshi, 'The Pareto principle at work', *Businessline*, 30 December 2002, p. 1.

PART 2

Managing people

CHAPTER 11

Managing performance
Goal-setting

Managing people is almost always about managing performance. Ensuring that employees perform well lies at the heart of the relationship between managers and the people they manage. Although there are many other management responsibilities that involve managing people (such as hiring and training), most of these are carried out in order to ensure performance.

There are many different approaches to managing for performance. Some organisations place their faith in a systems approach; they build complex and sophisticated performance management systems that require managers and staff to complete detailed forms and follow specified procedures. Many people (managers and staff) are intensely dissatisfied with this approach, finding the process cumbersome, intimidating and unproductive.

Other organisations take a more relaxed approach, relying on managers to deal with the matter of ensuring that employees perform well. In such organisations, the expectation is that managers will manage the performance of their staff on a day-to-day basis, rather than as a once-a-year or twice-a-year event. The risk, of course, is that some managers never get around to the more formal aspects of their role, leading to the often-heard complaint that 'my manager never tells me how I'm doing'.

Most organisations are probably somewhere in between. Managers (and maybe staff) are required to complete some formalities (even if only for the purpose of salary reviewing or developing a training plan of some kind) but they are also expected to take day-to-day responsibility for managing staff performance. Whatever the context, a contracting step between manager and staff lies at the heart of the performance management process. A dialogue of some kind takes place, the aim of which is to reach agreement on what the employee will achieve. The quality of that dialogue is dependent on the skills of the manager in managing the conversation, and on the contribution of the staff. The fundamental technique that can bring those two aspects together is the goal-setting process.

As is usually the case in management, many different terms are used to describe the same or similar things. In performance management, goal-setting is sometimes described as 'setting performance objectives' or 'performance contracting'. However, goal-setting is the more common expression and it is the one used in the research literature that is discussed briefly on the following pages. Goal-setting describes *the process of reaching agreement on what will be achieved in doing a task*. It involves measurable achievement—in short, performance.

Goal achievement is part of many spheres of human activity other than business—education, sport, art, war and personal development, to name a few. Even in business, it is as relevant to the whole of the organisation (that is, organisational goals) as it is to individuals. Goal-setting, therefore, has a wider application than just managing people for performance. However, its greatest focus seems to be as a tool for realising performance, including an expectation about how this will be done. For many, goal-setting is about 'forcing' performance. This makes it different to other situations, such as the sporting coach working with athletes who are volunteers.

Part of the problem here is how the parties involved in goal-setting in organisations see themselves and the process in which they are engaged. For the sports coach, the role is a supportive and facilitative one; in business it seems too often to be more of a directive and adversarial one. Often the process itself is something that is to be endured as a yoke rather than exploited as a springboard. The question, then, is whether goal-setting can be transformed into a productive process. The answer is an emphatic 'yes'.

Background

If performance management is the broad process, then goal-setting is the key technique that makes it work. Regardless of whether performance management is carried out informally and irregularly by an individual manager or whether it is part of a systematic approach involving all managers in an organisation working to imposed guidelines, goal-setting will be a key part of the overall process. As long as goal-setting is involved, you're doing performance management. If goal-setting is not involved, then you're doing something other than performance management.

Goal-setting has been extensively studied by researchers. The studies have involved examining the relationship between goal-setting and performance, and have demonstrated very clearly that there is a positive connection. Further, the research has looked at the links between goal-setting and:

- goal difficulty
- goal-setting methods
- goal specificity
- feedback on performance results
- expectation of evaluation.

All this is part of an emerging 'theory of goal-setting'. And although it is too early to make definitive pronouncements on all facets of goal-setting, it seems clear that there are connections and relationships that have now been repeated and confirmed experimentally on many occasions and in many different settings. The broad conclusions from all this research are as follows:

1. *Difficult goals enhance performance.* People seem to respond to the challenge of achieving something that stretches their capacity to perform. This is presumably caused by a motivational factor of some kind but, whatever the causal mechanism, the research shows quite strongly that difficult goals will bring out better performance. This effect is even more pronounced when the goals are set in a participa-tive manner, rather than simply allocated or mandated.[1]
2. *The way in which goals are set has an impact on the level of performance.* Goals can be mandated, self-selected or developed in a participative manner. When goals are easy to achieve, the method used to set the goals does not seem to matter much.[2] But when the goals relate to tasks that are more complex, people perform better if they either select their own goals or if the goals are set in a participative manner.[3] Participation in goal-setting also increases levels of satisfaction about the tasks undertaken and the results achieved.[4] So for simple tasks, it is effective and probably faster to mandate the goals; for more complex tasks, involving people in the goal-setting process will elicit better performance.
3. *Specific goals are more motivating than general or vague goals.* People try harder and perform better if the goals are very specific, and if they include measurable performance indicators.[5]
4. *Feedback has an impact on the effort that people put into doing their tasks.* On its own, it encourages people to perform better. Combined with goal-setting, knowledge about results helps increase performance even more.[6]
5. *If people believe that their performance will be evaluated by someone else, they perform better.* Although self-evaluation is valuable, what really motivates people to do well is the knowledge that someone else will look at their performance.[7]

These broad conclusions can be used by managers in an organisational setting as principles to guide goal-setting. In summary, managers need to:

- involve the other person (at least for all but the simplest of tasks)
- generate goals that stretch the individual
- generate goals that are specific
- build in a feedback mechanism
- include a clear understanding that the level of achievement will be evaluated.

If goal-setting is done in accordance with these guidelines, then there is a likelihood of higher performance than otherwise would be the case. Done consistently by all managers in an organisation, goal-setting can have a significant impact on organisational performance. More specifically, it has been demonstrated to have an effect on profitability. It is not completely clear whether goal-setting *causes* increased profitability or whether more profitable companies just happen also to do a lot of goal-setting.[8] Such a causal link would be hard to prove. However, given the host of evidence that goal-setting improves individual performance, it seems reasonable to assume that there is at least a connection between goal-setting and organisational performance.

Goal-setting can also be done for an organisation, that is, organisational goal-setting as opposed to individual goal-setting. The impact of organisational goal-setting is unclear, because it is usually part of a planning process and we have little data on which planning processes work best. The subject is simply too complex to study in a meaningful way. Although most organisations undertake some kind of formal planning, how this is done in practice and the reasons for doing it vary widely.[9]

At any rate, organisational goal-setting is a fundamentally different process and there is no reason to assume that the principles that apply to individual goal-setting can be translated to organisational goal-setting. The order of complexity is considerably higher, the methods are much more diverse , and the number of variables involved is almost impossible to monitor.

Some organisations—encouraged by various researchers and writers[10]— have tried to systematise the goal-setting process. The idea was to extend the process across the various layers of the organisation so that at each layer there was collective and individual goal-setting. This approach goes under the popular tag of 'management-by-objectives', although in practice many different versions are advocated.[11]

It is claimed that the advantage of the approach is that the whole of the organisation is aligned behind a set of objectives that cascades neatly down throughout the organisation. In reality, most of these systems struggle to achieve consistency and relevance. Most organisational objectives are so interdependent that if one part of the system under-achieves (for example, the sales department fails to achieve its targeted objectives) then all the other parts under-achieve as well (for example, manufacturing falls behind its targets because sales have failed to get the product orders).

Goal-setting in the context of performance management typically involves two participants—the manager and an employee. And it is likely that it will also be used in situations other than performance management. For example, some organisations encourage goal-setting as part of career management or personal development. This may also involve a manager and an employee, but the process is focused on achieving longer-term outcomes.

For the purposes of this chapter, goal-setting is examined as a technique for *performance management of the individual*.

The tool

Goal-setting is an opportunity to focus the efforts of employees on the things that matter. A goal provides employees with a direction and allows them to prioritise their work. This removes confusion and creates clarity, which seems to be appreciated by all those involved in the process. Assuming that the goals are well structured (that is, amongst other things, they are measurable), they also provide employees with the opportunity to evaluate their own performance. Measurable goals make performance evaluation much more effective so that judgments about achievement can be readily made. This feedback about the level of success is highly motivating; generally, people get satisfaction from succeeding.

This goes part of the way to explaining why well-structured goals are effective in driving performance. They appear to create a higher level of motivation than alternatives such as no goals, easy goals or unmeasurable goals.

The goal-setting process unfolds in three stages:

1. preparation
2. agreement on goals
3. follow-up and follow-through.

The preparatory stage can be relatively minor, depending on the level of preparedness of the two participants. The manager needs to have available all the information that is relevant to goal-setting: prior performance, mandated organisational goals, understanding of the employee's capability; and so on. The employee needs to be prepared to contribute to the content of the goal, and to understand how the process will work and why it is encouraged by the organisation. All of this may take some effort if a manager is working with a new or a very inexperienced employee. It can mean very little effort if the manager is working with an experienced employee.

This implies that the manager is clear about the goal-setting process. To ensure a high degree of clarity it can help if the steps in the process are written down in list form to inform new employees and occasionally to remind the more experienced ones. Such a list might answer the following questions:

1. What is the purpose of the goal-setting session?
2. When/where will the goal-setting session take place?
3. What is expected from the employee?
4. What will happen during the session?
5. What will happen after the session?

The list can also include any special expectations that the manager might have. For example, with experienced employees, the manager might require them to bring draft goals to the session. (Some managers prefer to leave the drafting of goals until the goal-setting session to take advantage of any issues that might arise from the review of previous performance. There is no reliable research data indicating which approach is more effective, so it's a personal choice.)

The manager may also want to explain how to construct an effective performance goal. There are two kinds of performance goals:

- those that focus on an *outcome*; for example, a task completed or a result achieved
- those that focus on *how the outcome is achieved*.

Confusing the two types can create problems. For example, a manager might contract with a sales person about a sales result. The sales person then uses inappropriate methods to achieve that result. If the contract between the manager and the sales person only related to outcomes, and not to the behaviour used to achieve them, then the ensuing performance review is likely to generate conflict.

There are various approaches to constructing a performance goal. Most practitioners suggest a format that involves an action or 'doing' verb, followed by a measurable outcome. The outcome could be a result or a task completed. The format, in short, is:

- To (action verb) (measurable outcome).

An example of an initial attempt to construct a performance goal for an employee in a human resources department might be:

- Version 1: *To develop a new staff induction procedure.*

Although this goal follows the format outlined, and the outcome is specific, it is not fully measurable. That is because it fails to meet other criteria for measurability; for example, time limit. To fix this shortcoming, the goal might be changed to the following:

- Version 2: *To develop a new staff induction procedure by 30 June.*

This improves the goal because it is now more measurable and it is also possible to make a judgment about whether the goal is achievable. It can be further improved by checking whether this goal is relevant to what the organisation is trying to do.

Some goals seem far removed from what actually matters to the organisation. The relevance criterion is an opportunity to link the goal to any organisational goals or objectives that need to be achieved. This can be done by adding a link to any known corporate goals to give:

- Version 3: *In accordance with the current corporate plan, to develop a new staff induction procedure by 30 June.*

Whether this goal is likely to challenge and stretch an employee depends entirely on the employee. The goal as it stands might well be an easy goal for some employees (in which case, the manager gets performance but under-utilises her staff) or entirely intimidating for other employees (in which case, she gets stressed employees and under-performance). The aim is to pitch the degree of difficulty at optimal level in terms of the employee's capabilities so that it becomes an *extending* goal.

Finally, it is sometimes necessary to make it clear that the goal is a *required* goal. That is, it is not an optional thing where achievement is at the discretion of the employee.

All these criteria are sometimes summed up in the acronym SMARTER:

- *Specific.* A specific objective either explains a *task* that must be performed ('When dealing with customer inquiries, state your name and the company name, and ask how you can help') or specifies a *result* that must be produced ('To produce this report each month by the last working day of the month').
- *Measurable.* A measurable objective makes explicit the standard used to evaluate performance and either how the task should be done (required behaviour) or the level of achievement (required results). The most common measure is time, but other measures related to quality may also be necessary.
- *Achievable.* An achievable objective is one that is within reach of the employee. Setting excessively high standards of achievement is inviting failure, which can be very de-motivating for employees. Reaching agreement on what is achievable involves two points of view, so it needs to be a shared decision. Employees may sometimes aim for unrealistic targets (both high and low), in which case it is the manager's responsibility to moderate the target to more realistic levels.
- *Relevant.* A relevant objective is one that the employee understands and one that sits within the context of organisational goals. If the employee cannot see the link between the agreed performance target

and their overall job, then they are unlikely to do the task well. The organisational context matters.

- *Time-limited*. A time-limited objective ensures that the employee knows 'by when' the task or the result is to be achieved. The absence of explicit agreement on a timeframe causes more disagreement between managers and employees than almost any other omission.
- *Extending*. An extending objective ensures that the employee is stretched—in other words, the achievement of the task or result will be somewhat of a challenge. This is highly motivating but it requires clear agreement on its achievability.
- *Required*. An objective must be explained as a requirement. It could contain words such as 'I expect you to ...'. At the least, the conversation about the goal must clarify this requirement. It must clearly establish that it is not optional for the employee to meet the objective.

Once the contracting phase has been completed, the final stage is about follow-up and follow-through. It is quite likely that the goals agreed will also involve the manager in some 'deliverables'. For example, employees may need resources to achieve their goals and often it is the manager who has to authorise these. If the manager fails to deliver, the goal-setting has probably been wasted. The manager also needs to follow up on progress. It is rarely a useful managerial tactic to simply wait until an agreed time to check whether the agreed outcomes are being achieved by the employee. By then it is too late to take corrective action. For anything other than the simplest of tasks, this means that the agreed goals should contain some milestone points at which progress is checked by both parties involved in the contracting process.

Observations

Goal-setting is a well-researched topic and the conclusions that can be drawn from the research are sound. Researchers have used many experiments and field studies to demonstrate the power of goal-setting in driving human performance. However, it should be noted that all such research typically involved tasks that were not the usual work tasks for the participating employees. Some of the research tasks were meaningless from the point of view of the subjects. Some of the participants (for example, the researchers) were not those with whom the employees usually work.

What is missing from the research on goal-setting is the real relationship between managers and their staff. This relationship is known to impact on work performance in many different ways. People perform better if they respect their boss and even better if their boss respects them. In the workplace, the person most trusted by employees is their immediate supervisor. The exact impact of this relationship is not completely clear but dissatisfaction with their supervisor is the major reason for people changing jobs. It seems safe to assume that this transfers in some way to impact on the goal-setting process.

In practical terms, what this means is that we also need to factor in the personal relationship between the manager and the employee. If this relationship is not positive, then the goal-setting is likely to be less productive. It will still work, but it may not work as well.

Some performance management systems require that performance goals be divided into separate components such as *performance measures* and *performance targets*. This seems to be a reflection of the measuring systems used to measure organisational performance, where such a distinction makes good sense. In personal performance management, it seems an artificial structure designed more for the sake of appearance rather than any substantive benefit. If the performance goals are structured as outlined (as SMARTER goals), then there is little reason to split them into component parts.

User's guide

Although it is quite possible to do goal-setting in its own right, more typically it forms part of a broader performance management approach. Such processes usually rely on a framework of procedures and guidelines to ensure that performance management issues are dealt with by management on a regular and consistent basis.

There are many such frameworks advocated by and to practitioners. All have advantages and disadvantages and there is really no way to identify which is the best, or even whether one is better than another. Many managers labour under the formalities imposed by frameworks that seriously restrict what they can and cannot do. Others may be concerned that the goal-setting process will not be fully effective without a formal framework to back it up.

What follows is one generic approach to a performance management framework. It is a low-key and modest version, and therefore relatively easy to implement. It is no substitute for quality conversations between managers and employees about the goals that are to be achieved. But for some it may help put some structure in place where they believe it is needed. This approach to performance management relies on three steps:

1. Clarify job understanding.
2. Develop performance goals.
3. Verify required resources.

This simple framework can be expanded to accommodate special organisational or other needs. For example, some organisations want signatures from the parties to record agreement; others want progress steps and milestones included to encourage monitoring of goal achievement; yet others want multiple copies so that others in the organisation will know what has been agreed to. All of these additions can be made. Whether they are truly necessary remains a personal judgment.

Instructions

How to set performance goals

1. *Clarify job understanding.*

   - Verify that the employees' understanding of the job is the same as yours.

     One way of doing this is to ask the employee to explain their understanding. (Some managers take the approach of explaining their understanding to the employee. This is useful, but it does not make certain that the employee understands the job—it is only when employees explain their understanding that managers can be sure what that understanding is.)

   - To assist you with this step, complete the form, Broad Goals, supplied at the end of this chapter.

2. *Develop performance goals.*

   This relies on the two elements that are common to all performance management frameworks, although different descriptions are used for them—*key results areas* and *performance goals*.

   - To assist you with this step, complete the form, Performance Goals, supplied at the end of this chapter.

3. *Verify required resources.*

   It is almost always the case that employees need resources to achieve their goals.

   - Identify what resources are required and how they are to be supplied.
   - To assist you with this step, complete the form, Required Resources, supplied at the end of this chapter.

Further reading

- E Locke & G Latham, *A theory of goal-setting and task performance*, Prentice-Hall, Englewood Cliffs, 1990.

  The research literature tends to be a bit daunting with the struggle for terminological precision taking precedence over readability. For the most accessible approach, try this book. Locke is very much the grand old man in the field of goal-setting research and he has done more than anyone to turn this field of research into something that offers practical guidance.

Most practitioner-focused material is a bit problematical in that the material tends to reflect the personal views of the writers rather than any accepted body of practice. There are many hundreds of books and articles that tell managers how to do performance management in general and goal-setting in particular (Amazon.com lists close to 400 titles on the topic!). Most have little basis in research and are just opinion pieces. The following examples are more useful than most:

- K Smith, *Make success measurable! A mindbook-workbook for setting goals and taking action*, John Wiley & Sons, New York, 1990.
- J Wadsworth, *The agile manager's guide to goal-setting and achievement*, Velocity Publishing, Bristol, 2001.

Notes

1. D Dossett, G Latham & R Mitchell, 'Effects of assigned versus participatively set goals, knowledge of results, and individual differences on employee behavior when goal difficulty is held constant', *Journal of Applied Psychology*, vol. 64, issue 3, 1997, p. 291.
2. C Shalley, G Oldham & J Porac, 'Effects of goal difficulty, goal-setting method, and expected external evaluation on intrinsic motivation', *Academy of Management Journal*, vol. 30, no. 3, 1987, pp. 553–63.
3. P Earley & R Kanfer, 'The influence of component participation and role models on goal acceptance, goal satisfaction, and performance', *Organizational Behavior and Human Decision Processes*, vol. 36, issue 3, 1985, p. 378.
4. Q Roberson, N Moye & E Locke, 'Identifying a missing link between participation and satisfaction: the mediating role of procedural justice perception', *Journal of Applied Psychology*, vol. 84, issue 4, 1999, pp. 585–93.
5. E Locke & G Latham, *A theory of goal-setting and task performance*, Prentice-Hall, Englewood Cliffs, 1990.
6. ibid.
7. S Jackson & S Zedeck, 'Explaining performance variability: contribution of goal-setting, task characteristics, and evaluative context', *Journal of Applied Psychology*, vol. 67, issue 6, 1982, p. 759.
8. D Terpstra & E Rozell, 'The relationship of goal-setting to organizational profitability', *Group & Organization Management*, vol. 19, no. 3, 1994, pp. 285–94.
9. H Mintzberg, *Strategy safari*, The Free Press, New York, 1998.
10. For example, G Odiorne, *MBOII: A system of managerial leadership for the 80s*, Pitman, Belmont, 1989.
11. For a recent version, see the Japanese planning system called 'hoshin kanri': M Betchtell, *The management compass: Steering the corporation using hoshin planning*, Blackhall, Dublin, 2002.

Broad Goals

Describe how your job adds value to the organisation. How does it help to achieve organisational plans?

List the broad goals that you need to achieve over the current planning period.

What is the relative importance of each of these broad goals (indicate by a percentage)?

Performance Goals

What are the key results areas in which you need to deliver results?

What are the performance goals you have agreed with your manager for the current planning period?

Required Resources

What special resources do you need to achieve your goals?

What support do you need from others to achieve your goals?

CHAPTER 12

Enabling others
Empowerment

Empowerment is a simple concept that is difficult to put into practice. The idea is to get other people to do the things they are able and willing to do and that you believe need doing. But in practice this implies a degree of autonomy and self-direction that sits uncomfortably with notions of management control. It suggests that, as a manager, you place your faith (and maybe your own career prospects) in the hands of other people who are less experienced than you. And it requires you to sit back and, occasionally, let people make mistakes that you could have avoided.

All this creates risk. And as a professional group, managers are notoriously risk-averse. So, in practice, empowering other people involves risk management and developing risk tolerance. Managers who learn to tolerate a little more risk and trust their people, and who also manage that risk in a considered way by using appropriate techniques, gain the benefits of an empowered workforce. And those benefits are substantial. One large-scale award-winning industry study in the USA concluded that businesses that practise workplace empowerment are more profitable, generate more sales per employee, and have less staff turnover.[1] Studies in other countries have found similar results.[2]

So why haven't more managers and organisations taken up the empowerment challenge? The answer to that question is not clear, but a number of factors seem to have contributed. For a while, in 1990s, empowerment became a management fad and almost everyone in management was talking about it. It got to the point where most people were heartily sick of the expression, especially when little changed in the organisations that claimed to be encouraging workplace empowerment. Consultants jumped on this bandwagon (maybe they were driving it!) and managers were harangued from all quarters (books, speeches, articles, videos—even novels!) to start empowering people. Inside organisations, support staff, such as human resource professionals, advocated the idea while line managers were the ones supposed to make it work. It was made to look easy and those who tried it were disappointed that it took more than a minute to create an empowered workforce.

Worst of all, everyone under-estimated the resilience of organisations in maintaining the old order. Empowerment is a fragile thing. It does not take much to undermine it, whether it is being practised individually by a manager or collectively by an organisation.

Many approached the idea as a mechanism that could be bolted on to organisations, a bit like an electronic control device is bolted on to a piece of equipment. It doesn't work like that and it is the wrong analogy. Empowerment is more like a living and growing thing. Think of it like a plant that has to be nurtured, cared for and supported. To empower other people, managers have to think of themselves as gardeners rather than as mechanics. And that mind-shift is not easy. Empowerment starts with managers.

Background

Part of the problem with empowerment is the word itself—especially the 'power' bit. Power is a subject with emotional overtones and undertones in most organisations. All organisations maintain power structures, although the source of the power wielded by individuals can range from coercion ('Do this or you will be sacked') to expert power ('Do this because this is the best thing to do').

Most managers exercise positional (sometimes called 'legitimate') power, which means that their power and authority derive from their position in the organisation's hierarchy. Some managers are able to exercise other sources of power as well, such as reward power ('Do this and I will reward you') and referent (or charismatic) power ('Do this because I ask it').[3] The source of power matters, because it will make the concept of empowerment either very easy or very difficult for managers to accept.

Managers who see their power as something that needs to be hoarded and protected will have a difficult time with the empowerment process. It comes down to attitude. If you think that the only thing that stands between you and the hordes of savages on the shopfloor or in the front office is your power to control them, then empowering them is clearly a threatening idea, possibly bordering on the insane. If you think you stay in control only because you can use the power you have to manipulate and wrangle your staff, then empowerment is probably not going to be your thing.

The irony, of course, is that most of the changes that have affected workplaces in the last 20 or 30 years have consistently diminished the capacity of managers to control employees. Several factors have contributed to this trend. Most organisations now have far wider 'spans of control' (the number of people reporting to a supervisor or manager) than they used to have. And most organisations now rely on the majority of their employees being 'knowledge workers'; that is, workers who use their brains rather than their brawn—and brains are hard to control!

Possibly the most significant reason for the lessening of managers' control is that jobs are getting more and more specialised. In many organisations, managers may not even be able to do the jobs of their staff; they have become completely reliant on the expertise of their staff. Finally, information technology has given employees a degree of power within organisations unmatched in the past. If a machine operator could bring a production line temporarily to a halt in the past by throwing a spanner in the works, that is nothing compared to what workers can do to today's IT-dependent organisations.

So those managers placing their faith in getting results from their staff by wielding their authority in order to control are probably fooling only themselves. At best, managers can influence the outcomes achieved in their organisations. One of the best ways to do this is by getting people to do the things that need to be done because they want to do those things. This may not involve the overt exercise of power but it works a lot better. Many managers realise this and the 'control freak' in most organisations is a thing of the past (with plenty of exceptions, of course!).

Most managers already use empowering techniques to get things done. What the advocates of empowerment are arguing is that they could do it a lot more, and get better results as a consequence. It needs a little bit more of a mind shift to achieve this higher order of empowerment, but such an empowering culture has made some organisations a preferred employment destination.

One way of achieving this mind shift is to change the language that we use to describe empowerment. We need to stop thinking that empowerment is about 'sharing power'—it is not, or if it does involve sharing, it is the kind of sharing that does not diminish what is being shared. Researchers call this type of sharing a 'non-zero sum' outcome, where one party shares with another but does so without losing anything. This contrasts with the outcome in other arrangements, where if one party gains then the other party loses; these are 'zero sum' games involving trade-offs or, in the extreme, winners and losers.

One example of a non-zero sum outcome is what happens when we share knowledge. As I share all the tools and techniques in this book with you, you have gained that knowledge, yet I have not lost it. I still have the same knowledge that I had before I shared it with you by writing it down. The only difference is that you now also have that knowledge. Knowledge shared is *not* knowledge halved.

'Non-zero sumness' is a very inelegant expression for one of the most elegant concepts that has ever been developed (for its relevance to everything from evolution to the development of human civilisation, see Robert Wright's *Non-zero: History, evolution and human co-operation*[4]). It has direct application to the conundrum of how to empower other people because it provides a solution to managers' fears that power shared is power halved.

Based on the idea of playing a non-zero sum game, here's how to think about empowerment:

Empowerment is a way of giving others the capacity to do things for themselves.

It does not mean giving up your power as a manager, but it does mean giving power (the capacity to act in a self-directed manner) to others. You build up the capability of others without losing anything yourself. And in the process, you will probably enhance your standing as a manager because people want to work with managers who know how to strengthen others.

If all this still sounds a bit fluffy, then think about what happened when we were in school. Teachers turn children into adults, which is the best of conversion processes! They do this by helping them to grow from within. Most knowledge can only be learned by people who want to learn. Teachers help people to learn, and the best teachers make people want to learn more and more. By doing this, teachers are not diminished in any way. They do not give up anything in the process of helping others learn. Teachers enable others and (in most cases) gain enormous satisfaction from that. The teaching metaphor is a good one for managers who want to empower others.

This may all sound very modern, trendy and progressive, but it's actually been around since the early part of the twentieth century. It was advocated by the earliest founders of modern management theory. The outstanding writer and theorist in this field was Mary Parker Follett (1868–1933) who wrote some of the most powerful arguments for the empowered workplace. The language she used might not be exactly the same as that used by writers on empowerment, but the conception was certainly hers. Follett wrote about 'power-with' (as opposed to the notion of 'power-over') as 'a jointly developed power, a co-active, not coercive power'.[5]

By framing it in this way, the notion of 'power' in empowerment becomes a self-developing capacity that is encouraged by the manager. It is more closely related to personal development than it is to authority. With the concept of 'power-with', Follett both predates and encapsulates the fundamental issue in so-called 'empowerment programs'—that the process is not about power, but about enabling others to develop their abilities.

Peter Drucker—the management guru's management guru—called Follett a 'prophet of management'.[6] For inspiration about the benefits of empowerment, it seems that we only have go back 100 years or so.

The tool

Empowerment is less a tool than an approach to working with people. It involves a number of techniques and methods that combine to create an effect *over time*. It is important to note that it is not an instant technique. It takes time to make empowerment work, because it takes time to build up the required levels of *communication* and *trust*. Empowerment only works if the level of trust between those involved in the process is high and the channels of communication are open. You need very little of either to issue a command; you need lots of both to drive empowerment.

Several different approaches to implementing empowerment have been proposed. One of the most influential is that offered by Ken Blanchard and colleagues.[7] It is a practical and effective approach, providing you can cope with the way it is presented, which is the 'short industrial novel'. Blanchard made this format famous with *The one minute manager*[8], which sold in the millions, so maybe we shouldn't disparage the format. However, some people are simply allergic to the simple tales of almost magical results that are achieved by his one-dimensional characters. What really matters is that Blanchard's three-step framework works.

Blanchard summarises the route to empowerment as:

- Share information.
- Create autonomy through boundaries.
- Replace hierarchy with teams.

Each of these steps is expanded into a number of steps that can all be completed in the typical organisation, although the degree of difficulty will vary from situation to situation. This means that empowerment will take longer for some managers than it will for others.

Share information

This step is based on the sensible idea that empowering ignorant people is dangerous! If people are to make decisions and act on their own initiative, then they need to be competent to do so. This requires knowledge about the business. It starts with what Blanchard calls 'the big picture stuff', but also includes 'the little picture stuff'. Essentially, it means sharing all that can be shared, working on the principle that most information can be shared if we abandon the idea that information is power.

For many organisations, to do this is a big ask. Tradition has it that information should only be shared on a 'need-to-know' basis.

Empowerment demands that we turn this upside down and work on the principle that everything should be shared unless there is a very good reason not to do so (such as privacy issues or commercial confidentiality). More and more organisations are now doing this. People within the organisation are typically briefed about how the business is going. Sharing strategy plans, budgets and performance data is no longer the daring idea that it was 20 or 30 years ago. Most organisations can and should do more, but many have already started on the path to creating an informed workforce.

Sharing information has a number of impacts other than creating an informed workforce:

- It creates trust, because employees appreciate that they are being told stuff that is important.
- It makes information into a common coin within the organisation, rather than a secret handshake that only a privileged few understand.
- People are far less likely to share sensitive information if they have been told what it is and understand that it is sensitive. Some managers fear that critical information will be revealed to competitors by staff. However, if you begin the empowerment process with that fear as your starting point, it may be best not to proceed any further until your level of paranoia has reduced!

Sharing information was the basis for the *open book management* philosophy that came from the remarkable story of the Springfield Re-manufacturing Company. This company practically made sharing information with its employees an art form.[9] The company's turnaround to profitability was directly attributed to its investment in business literacy for all its employees and to sharing virtually all information within the business. This theme was picked up by many other organisations and by now the link between organisational performance (including profitability) and information-sharing has been firmly established.[10]

Create autonomy through boundaries

This principle is based on the idea that you create freedom by creating a framework within which people are authorised to make decisions. Define the boundaries and you remove uncertainty and create clarity. People are unlikely to use their initiative if they don't know the limits of what is allowed, and managers only invite conflict if they do not clarify boundaries.

The boundaries start with the big picture. Employees need to know what the game plan is for their organisation if they are to make a sensible contribution to realising that plan. So make sure everyone understands what the organisation is trying to do and how it is going about doing that. If you as a manager can't get sensible answers from your staff to the question: 'What are we trying to do here?', then don't start empowering people. Do start educating them!

How the game will be played also matters. One of the boundaries is about acceptable behaviours. Some organisations have started to define what is and what is not acceptable behaviour within the organisation (see Chapter 1, Strategic intent: Vision, mission and values statements). Defining behaviours (and the values that drive those behaviours) is not easy, but managers need to provide guidance even if this is difficult. Start with the rules of behaviour that matter to you. For example, if you have a high need to be kept informed of progress on the tasks carried out by employees, try the line 'use your best judgment but keep me informed'. This discourages the employee from asking the manager for permission but it requires close communication on what has transpired. Managers need to invent their own versions of these sorts of communication rules.

If necessary, in complex situations or where the manager aspires to a high level of autonomy, it will be necessary to develop formal structures that define precisely what an employee is empowered to do (two examples are provided in the User's guide section of this chapter).

Another technique for creating boundaries is to provide training. This has the advantage of creating consistency amongst a group of people who perform common tasks. If, for example, a group of employees are to be asked to authorise customer refunds (a task that might previously have been done by management), then it makes sense to train those staff in the principles and procedures to be followed in making refund decisions. It will create consistency, confidence and a willingness to use personal judgment.

Once authorities and accountabilities have been transferred, it is important for managers to follow through and check that the accountabilities are being exercised effectively. Handing over accountabilities is not an invitation to stand back and watch people fail. The managers should be held accountable for how well they have transferred accountabilities to staff.

Replace hierarchy with teams

One way of making the transition to an empowered workforce easier is to use teams. The virtues (indeed, the wisdom!) of teams has been well expounded in recent years.[11]

It is not entirely necessary to use teams to empower employees, but in practice it seems to have become the preferred route. There are several reasons for this. Teams create a comfort zone for employees when they are first asked to start exercising authorities that they did not have before. The uncertainties associated with this transfer seem to be eased by having colleagues around who are going through the same difficult process.

Effective teams share their knowledge and expertise so that less experienced or skilled members are supported. Teams also bring a diversity of individual traits and capacities that enable tasks to be shared according to the interests and capabilities of the team members.

Setting up teams is a larger topic than this chapter will allow but, briefly, for any team to function effectively, a number of fundamentals must be agreed to by the whole team. The most important ones are:

- team goals
- team performance scoreboard
- team ground rules
- meeting rules and procedures
- team records system.

Most of the reasons why teams do not function effectively can be traced back to these five elements. Whether you are working with an existing team that has some problems, or with a team that is just being established, the first place to start is with these fundamentals. You need to check that each of these five elements is properly in place and being used by the team. If you can help the team to sort out its shortcomings in these areas then you will have helped them to remove their biggest barrier to high performance.

Most critical of all is the role of the manager in the process of handing accountabilities over to the team. Some managers have approached this task with all the enthusiasm of a dump truck—a kind of dump-and-run approach to empowerment—and it simply doesn't work. Accountabilities need to be handed over in a disciplined and planned manner. At each hand-over, the manager needs to check that the team is ready (that is, it is willing and able to take on the accountability). Thereafter, the manager needs to check that the team is handling the new accountabilities capably, and provide support if it is not. Only in the extreme does support mean taking the accountability back. More typically, support means access to training, to expertise and to advice. Don't do the job for them; help them do the job.

The business case for teams is by now well established but if anyone needs reminding, try Jeffrey Pfeffer's marvellously angry overview of the business benefits of teams, *The human equation*.[12] Pfeffer is angry because of the disparity between what the research shows are the pay-offs of putting people first and the conventional management practices in most organisations. There is not a single piece of research that backs up the business benefits of autocratic management, and an overwhelming mountain of research that shows that an empowering management style builds business profits. Yet many organisations and many managers still opt for autocracy (sometimes without being aware of it!).

Specifically on teams, Pfeffer recites from studies that show the business benefits of teams. A few examples of these benefits are:

- on-time delivery improved from 40% to 99% (Honeywell)
- 15.4% increase in sales revenues for a customer service team (Bell Telephone)
- US$52 000 per team savings in indirect costs for network technicians (Bell Telephone).

Additional support for the process

Pfeffer argues that in addition to empowering people by sharing information, creating autonomy through boundaries, and replacing hierarchy with teams, managers and organisations should also:

- provide employment security
- recruit the right people
- base payment on organisational performance
- invest in training
- reduce status distinctions within the organisation.

These actions certainly help support the empowerment process, but they are not so critical that it can't be done without these additional steps. Empowerment is a tool that individual managers can turn to even when their organisation does not explicitly back the idea.

Observations

Although not every organisation is ready for, or capable of implementing, self-management for employees in its fullest sense, every manager can implement the empowerment concept at some level. It does not need to be announced as an initiative (it probably works better if it isn't!) but it does need to be a considered effort. That is, you can't just start on a whim. As with most management tools, empowerment needs to be planned and the plan executed.

Some managers claim to have tried the empowerment approach and found that it did not work for them. In every instance where such a claim was made to me, I have asked those managers to show me their plan for implementing empowerment. Without exception, these managers did not have a plan. At best, they had read or heard about the idea, and had made a half-hearted attempt to involve their staff in a discussion about the issues involved. Failure seemed almost inevitable.

If these managers had taken the same laissez-faire approach to designing a new information system or introducing a new piece of technology into an organisation, they would have been reprimanded (if not sacked!) for tackling a major project without a plan. Yet, somehow, when it comes to people-based initiatives such as empowerment, it seems acceptable to all involved to make it up as they go along.

There is nothing difficult or complex about empowerment. It is as obvious as it looks. Indeed, it is a simple idea. But it is a difficult idea for managers unused to the demand that they change themselves before they try to change others. It has been observed by many before me that the introduction of empowerment into a workplace is actually not about the employees, but about the managers.

User's guide

Two specific tools are useful in supporting managers to take a disciplined approach to empowerment. Both tools involve managing the handover process and clarifying understanding of who is accountable for what.

The first tool, the *Accountability Matrix*, is mainly a planning tool that details who will be responsible for what accountabilities in the future; it enables managers and employees to work together to decide a handover plan that essentially works back from that future state.

The second tool, the *Responsibility Grid*, examines each accountability that is presently held by employees and clarifies what is involved in its execution. This tool enables managers to know who, among all those involved in carrying out a specific accountability, is actually responsible for what.[13]

It is possible to complete versions of the two tools for an individual rather than a team. The range of accountabilities will be far narrower but, for sufficiently complex jobs, it will help clarify the respective roles of management and employee.

Instructions

How to use the Accountability Matrix

An example of an Accountability Matrix for a production team appears at the end of the chapter.

1. Decide who will work on the design of the matrix. It can be developed in a number of ways, but the best way seems to be for a representative group from the teams or front-line staff and from management to simply talk it out until agreement is reached.

   - Agree on which accountabilities are already in the desired quadrants. Decide which accountabilities should be moved to the desired quadrants in the next 6–12 months.

2. *Draw up an appropriate list of accountabilities.*

   - Make a list of all the accountabilities that impact on a team, regardless of who actually has carriage of those accountabilities.

3. *Create the Accountability Matrix.*

   - Select a timeframe to which the matrix will apply; for example, three years. This provides the timeline over which the empowerment process will unfold. It turns the matrix into a description of the future state of empowerment to which the planning group aspires.

- Allocate each accountability to the appropriate quadrant of the matrix on the basis of where that accountability should sit at the end of the timeframe:
  - *Givens* (the externally mandated accountabilities; for example, legislative or corporate accountabilities)
  - *100% management* (the accountabilities that are solely owned by management)
  - *100% teams* (the accountabilities that are solely owned teams)
  - *50/50 shared* (the accountabilities shared by management and teams).

How to use the Responsibility Grid

This grid lists all the major accountabilities that impact on a team and indicates who is responsible or involved with those accountabilities. It indicates a timeframe and clarifies the level of self-management that is in place at any given time. The grid is useful whenever there is confusion about who does what in or around the team because it identifies the person actually responsible.

An example of a Responsibility Grid for a production team is provided at the end of this chapter.

1. *Draw up a list of relevant accountabilities.*

   These may derive from the Accountability Matrix or from some other source. The list has to be specific and relevant to a particular team.

2. *Have the team and the manager (along with anyone else who should be involved) review the list to make sure it is comprehensive and accurate.*

3. *Draw up a list of all those who fulfil a role that has an impact on the team (for example, team members, team leader, team manager, plant manager, technical specialists of various kinds, committees and so on).*

4. *Make sure the team understand the* levels *of accountability:*
   - R = is *responsible* for doing
   - S = *supports* others in doing
   - I = is kept *informed*
   - V = has power of *veto*.

5. *Ensure that the team and others involved reach agreement as to who has responsibility now for each of the accountabilities.*

6. *Record this information on the Responsibility Grid.*

7. *Identify accountability areas that will change in the given timeframe (for example, over the next six months).*
   - Add this information to the grid (for example, by using different colours such as black for current, red for prospective).
   - Try to reach a consensus decision.

Further reading

- K Blanchard, J Carlos & A Randolph, *Empowerment takes more than a minute*, Berrett-Koehler, San Francisco, 1996.

  Given my previous comments, it will come as no surprise that I recommend this book by Ken Blanchard and colleagues.

- K Blanchard, J Carlos & A Randolph, *The 3 keys to empowerment: Release the power within people for astonishing results*, Berrett-Koehler, San Francisco, 1999.

  If the idea of the 'industrial novel' format is too much to bear, then try this alternative from the same team.

- J Pfeffer, *The human equation*, Harvard Business School Press, Boston, 1998.

  Jeffrey Pfeffer still offers the best business case for investing in people, and unleashing their capabilities within the organisation. But a warning: Pfeffer will make you feel rather silly for not having done all this stuff long ago!

Notes

1. M Huselid, 'The impact of human resource management practice on turnover, productivity, and corporate financial performance', *Academy of Management Journal*, vol. 38, no.3, 1995, pp. 635–72. The HR practices considered in this study align closely with the notion of empowering employees.
2. L Bilmes, K Wetzker & P Zhonneux, 'Value in human resources', *The Financial Times*, 10 February 1997, p. 10.
3. J French & B Raven, 'Bases of social power', in D Cartwright (ed.), *Studies in social power*, University of Michigan, Ann Arbor, 1959.
4. R Wright, *Non-zero: History, evolution and human co-operation*, Abacus, London, 2001.
5. H Metcalf & L Urwick (eds), *Dynamic administration: The collected papers of Mary Parker Follett*, Pitman, London, 1941, p. 101.
6. P Graham, *Mary Parker Follett—prophet of management: A celebration of writings from the 1920s*, Harvard Business School Press, Boston, 1996.
7. K Blanchard, J Carlos & A Randolph, *Empowerment takes more than a minute*, Berrett-Koehler, San Francisco, 1996.
8. K Blanchard & S Johnson, *The one minute manager*, William Morrow & Co, New York, 1982.
9. J Stack, 'Springfield Remanufacturing bought the company and learned to play the game of open-book management', *National Productivity Review*, vol. 13, issue 1, 1994, pp. 39–52.
10. T Davis, 'Open-book management: Its promise and its pitfalls', *Organizational Dynamics*, vol. 25, issue 3, 1997, pp. 6–20.
11. J Katzenbach & D Smith, *The wisdom of teams*, Harvard Business School Press, Boston, 1993.
12. J Pfeffer, *The human equation*, Harvard Business School Press, Boston, 1998.
13. As far as I can determine, this idea was first proposed in R Beckhard & R Harris, *Organizational transitions: Managing complex change*, Addison-Wesley, Reading, 1977.

Example of a list of accountabilities

Work accountabilities for a production team

- Acquire major equipment
- Allocate work to teams
- Allocate work within teams
- Appoint team leaders
- Communicate between teams
- Communicate within teams
- Continuously improve work processes
- Control waste
- Decide major changes
- Decide plant layout
- Determine corporate policies/ budgets
- Develop new designs, products and technology
- Ensure adherence to environmental practices
- Ensure common work practices across the site
- Implement legislative requirements (environmental)
- Implement legislative requirements (health and safety)
- Implement legislative requirements (industrial relations)
- Liaise with external customers
- Maintain plant
- Make discipline decisions
- Make firing decisions

- Make hiring decisions
- Make leave decisions
- Make training decisions
- Manage amenities (lunchrooms, etc.)
- Measure team performance
- Meet quality standards
- Negotiate supplier agreements
- Order materials
- Order and control stock
- Organise team area housekeeping
- Plan site production
- Plan plant budgets
- Set discipline policies
- Set hiring policies
- Set internal environmental policies
- Set internal health and safety policies
- Set internal quality standards
- Set leave policies
- Set team goals/objectives
- Set team performance targets
- Set training budgets
- Set working hours
- Undertake rework

Example of an Accountability Matrix

Accountability Matrix for the production team (year 2005)

Givens

- Corporate policies/budgets
- Legislation (environmental)
- Legislation (health and safety)
- Legislation (industrial relations)

100% management

- Plant budgets
- Supplier agreements

50/50 shared

- Allocation of work to teams
- Appointment of team leaders
- Arranging major equipment acquisition
- Decisions on major changes
- Decisions on plant layout
- Development of new designs, products and technology
- Discipline decisions
- Ensuring common work practices across the site
- Firing decisions
- Hiring decisions
- Liaising with external customers
- Managing amenities (lunchrooms, etc.)
- Planning site production
- Setting discipline policies
- Setting hiring policies
- Setting internal environmental policies
- Setting internal health and safety policies
- Setting internal quality standards
- Setting leave policies
- Setting team goals/objectives
- Setting team performance targets
- Setting training budgets
- Training decisions

100% teams

- Adherence to environmental practices
- Allocation of work within teams
- Communication (between teams)
- Communication (within teams)
- Continuous improvement of work processes
- Control of waste
- Maintenance of plant
- Making leave decisions
- Materials ordering
- Measuring team performance
- Meeting quality standards
- Setting working hours
- Stock control and ordering
- Team area housekeeping
- Undertaking rework

Example of a (partial) Responsibility Grid for a production team

Responsibility Grid

Actors / Decisions	Team members	Team leader	Team manager	Plant manager	Production planning	Maintenance	Logistics	HR
Allocation of work to teams	I	I	R	V	S			
Appoint team leaders			R	V				S
Decide plant layout	I	I	I	R				
Develop new designs, products and technology			I	R	S	S	S	
Major equipment acquisition			I	R				
Make discipline decisions	R	R	I					S
Make training decisions	I	R	S					S
Make firing decisions	I	I	R	V				
Make hiring decisions	R	S	V					S
Manage amenities (lunchrooms, etc.)	R	S						
Plan site production	I	I	S	S	R			
Liaise with external customers	I	R	S					

Key:

R = Responsible (initiates)   V = Right of veto   S = Support (required from)   I = Kept informed

CHAPTER 13

Developing self-awareness
Multi-rater (360-degree) feedback

In the 1980s and 1990s, organisations started to change from highly structured pyramid-like hierarchies towards flatter and leaner shapes. The autocratic management styles that suited a pyramid structure won't work in the modern organisation with its wide spans of control, high levels of self-management, and a workforce that relies on motivation rather than control. Management styles needed to change.

Change is difficult at the best of times, but behavioural change is more difficult than anything else. Many things get in the way of the best intentions to do things differently. Behaviour is largely driven by habits—and habits are hard to change. Some managers didn't want to change. Some managers didn't know how to change. Some managers didn't think they needed to change. Something was needed to bring objectivity to the process of deciding whether, and how, managers should change their style. Into this vacuum came a tool that is now almost universally known as *360-degree feedback*. Researchers prefer to call it multi-rater or multi-source feedback.

The feedback idea is based on the notion that, if managers receive feedback on their behaviours from a number of different sources (usually, their boss, their peers and their staff), then it is more likely to be accurate, accepted and specific. This approach is different to the feedback that managers might receive in a performance appraisal with their boss.

By involving more people and structuring the rating process, the feedback is immensely strengthened. The feedback is also anonymous, as the raters' perceptions are typically aggregated into an overall score (or at least an overall score for each group of raters). This makes it much easier for people to be honest in their assessments. Finally, such feedback is normally done for developmental purposes (helping someone get better at what they do) rather than for administrative purposes, such as salary review or performance appraisal.

Multi-rater feedback is not without its problems though, because:

- It has to be introduced carefully so that people know what is involved.
- It can give rise to false expectations about how quickly managers will change their behaviours.
- The data collection process can be cumbersome and, at its worst, completely unreliable.
- The quality of the feedback can be dubious and even damaging, especially if the survey questions are open-ended rather than structured.
- Research on the effectiveness of the technique is not universally supportive. (For example, there are no significant studies that compare multi-rater feedback with other development techniques such as assessment/development centres or personality profiling.)

But there is no doubt that multi-rater feedback has become the standard management tool for helping managers understand the impact of their personal ways of doing things. In most organisations in English-speaking countries, it has become part of how management development is achieved.

Background

There is no general agreement on a definition of multi-rater feedback. Most researchers describe it in very general terms; for example, as an approach for gathering behavioural observations from various layers within an organisation that are then fed back to the person being rated. Within this very broad description, there are many variations. Some insist that the ratings must be obtained in a structured way and that all raters must complete the same questions. Some insist that the observations made by raters should only include observable behaviours, while others include assessment of personality factors and traits. Although most agree that raters should include boss, peers and staff, many also include other raters such as the boss-once-removed, external customers and suppliers, internal customers and suppliers, and skip-level employees. Some argue that self-assessment should always be included, while others argue that this is not always necessary.

The purpose of multi-rating feedback is also debated. Some researchers claim that it is simply another form of performance appraisal. Others claim that it is strictly about development and growth. This debate is linked to the terms used to describe the process. Descriptions include: stakeholder appraisal; full-circle appraisal; multi-source assessment; group performance appraisal; and multi-perspective ratings. For the purpose of this book, I will use the description *multi-rater feedback* because it is most descriptive of the process (despite the likelihood that '360-degree feedback' will remain the popular tag).

Multi-rater feedback became popular when researchers in the 1980s started to focus on how senior managers learn. They discovered that managers learn by doing.[1] Some of the most worthwhile research on this topic came from the Centre for Creative Leadership, in North Carolina, and led to some general principles that seem obvious today, but at the time provided a radical new basis for leadership education and development.[2] They found that:

* Feedback on behaviour is an important stimulus for personal growth.
* The most effective leaders are those who think of themselves as learners and who welcome opportunities to improve.
* It requires special effort to get honest and open feedback from others because most organisations are 'feedback shy'.

At the same time as these findings were published, two other management tools became very popular—employee attitude surveys and customer satisfaction surveys. Driven by the interest in organisational culture (see Chapter 5, Changing culture: The Competing Values Framework), employee attitude surveys were intended to let management know what the workforce thought about the organisation. This often included a section on what they thought about the managers in the organisation. A logical next step was to introduce a survey tool that focused exclusively on management behaviour, and specifically on managers identified individually by name. Similarly, customers were discovered by management in the latter part of last century, and were promptly invited to give their views on how well the organisation was meeting their needs. Customer feedback mechanisms, especially the satisfaction survey (see Chapter 8, Understanding customers: SERVQUAL customer surveys), were soon part of everyday management. Put the survey technique together with management development and the management feedback survey was born.

What made the idea really take off was the combination of problems that it seemed to solve. First, senior managers do not like to do performance appraisals of the managers that report to them, especially about those elements of the appraisal that involve non-quantifiable aspects of management performance, such as personal style, behaviour and professional development. The survey takes senior management a step away from those aspects by involving many others in the assessment process and making it a structured process, as opposed to a one-on-one conversation.

Second, middle managers don't trust the opinions of their senior managers when it comes to observations on how they manage their own staff. The main objection is that senior management rarely sees middle management in action with their staff and, therefore, are not in a position to make accurate observations.

Third, human resource management professionals are well aware that both senior managers and middle managers make very flawed judgments about their own and others' performance. They overrate; they underrate; and they forget to rate. All of which makes it a very attractive proposition for the HR professional to implement a standardised system that works to a timetable and spreads the subjectivity over a lot of different raters.

Clearly, the multi-rater feedback survey was a tool whose time had come. It has penetrated business with great speed and thoroughness. The 1998 report from the American Society for Training and Development found in its annual benchmarking survey that 73% of companies use multi-rater feedback surveys.[3] Another report suggests that 90% of Fortune 1000 companies use them[4], as do almost 100% of Fortune 500 companies[5]. In Europe, these percentages are lower but rapidly catching up.

The reasons for introducing multi-rater feedback systems vary widely, which is why managers need to be clear about what the purpose of the process will be for their organisations. They include:

- *personal development.* The most common purpose is as a personal development tool.[6] This is where the focus is on creating managers' awareness of their strengths and weaknesses so that they can commit to making changes in behaviour that will lead to improved managerial performance. This may be part of a formal system that the organisation has devised and which applies to all managers in that organisation, but it may also apply to a single manager participating in a management development program.
- *cultural change.* Another relatively common application is as part of a change program that targets organisational culture. Many models that guide cultural change accept that managerial behaviour is one of the few levers that organisations can pull to change culture (for one example, see the Competing Values Framework in Chapter 5). In this application, the purpose is to align management behaviour with the preferred organisational culture. The feedback is a control mechanism designed to make sure that managers are adhering to the new ways of working, including the new ways of managing. If, for example, an organisation wants to move towards a culture that is more focused on teamwork, then the multi-rater surveys provide an opportunity to enforce the managerial behaviours that are supportive of teamwork.
- *performance evaluation and remuneration.* This is contentious, mainly because managers are generally uncomfortable with the involvement of their staff in the evaluation of their overall performance. This concern only increases when the manager's pay and/or bonuses are at stake.
- *promotion and succession planning.* The use of multi-rater feedback to assist with formal promotion or succession planning decisions is still relatively rare. Informally, however, the results from feedback reports are often taken into account in determining such decisions, sometimes without the full knowledge of the managers involved. Some of this

has the potential to undermine the developmental benefits that accrue from the process.

- *team development.* This is one of the fastest growing applications for multi-rater feedback processes. Teams can include management, project and even functional teams. The purpose is to enhance the level of teamwork that is exercised within the team. The multi-rater feedback is sometimes combined with other forms of self-awareness raising, such as personality profiling or work-style assessments. In this application, it is typical to involve only those who are within the team. When everyone in the team gets feedback from everyone else in the team then issues about people's roles, work style and approach are rapidly resolved. It can quickly help a team move towards a high degree of teamwork.

It is important to clearly articulate the purpose behind introducing and using the feedback process, as it will affect the perceptions of those involved in the process. For example, several pieces of research found that raters would have rated their managers differently if the rating were to be used for performance evaluation instead of the stated purpose of performance development.[7]

The tool

At its simplest, multi-rater feedback systems involve only four major components:

- *the survey instrument.* It can be a standardised commercial survey or a customised version designed specifically by the organisation.
- *raters representative of those with whom the recipient interacts.* Typically the feedback recipient's manager, two to four peers, four to eight staff, and any others that seem useful to include, such as customers or suppliers.
- *the recipient of the feedback.* Typically a senior or middle manager in the organisation who may be part of a group participating in the process or an individual involved in a professional development program.
- *the feedback session.* It may involve a coach or adviser (internal or external), although in some situations there is no other party involved, and the feedback is simply provided in report form to the recipient.

An approach to designing and developing a multi-rater feedback system is described in the User's guide section of this chapter. The steps shown are designed to avoid pitfalls and problems that have become apparent over the last 10 years, as organisations have implemented their particular approaches. Here are some of those problems and some suggestions on how to avoid them.

Managers resist participating

Some managers feel threatened when the concept of multi-rater feedback is first presented to them. This is less likely these days as more and more managers become aware of, and familiar with, the technique. The problem tends to be worst in organisations that are strongly hierarchical, and for those without a clear understanding of why the process is being undertaken, or both.

Most instruments are linked to a model that represents desirable managerial behaviour, such as a participative and consultative approach to management. If a survey based on such a model was carried out in an organisation that instead valued or practised controlling and directive behaviour, it would inevitably create tension, stress and even fear. Organisations need to be very clear as to the reasons for adopting multi-rater feedback. If such reasons cannot be clearly articulated, do not proceed with the technique.

Negative feedback

It is inevitable that some managers (if not all) will receive negative feedback. Some managers have difficulty in coping with criticism and such feedback may well de-motivate them rather than motivate them to improve.[8]

Multi-rater feedback raises the stakes in terms of managerial behaviour. It is very personal and directly touches the manager's concept of self. Multi-rater feedback sits on the fine line that divides the organisational and the professional from the personal and the private. Some see it as sitting on the organisational side of the line, but many see it as an intrusion into their personal space. Therefore, multi-rater feedback needs to be handled in a sensitive manner. Top executives should be prepared to demonstrate their willingness to participate (on several occasions I have witnessed an organisation halt the feedback process after the CEO received his feedback!). Confidentiality needs to be emphasised and respected, and the purpose should always be developmental rather than administrative.

Flawed survey instruments

Designing and developing survey instruments is not as simple as it may appear to the lay person. Many survey forms developed informally by consultants and HR practitioners are seriously flawed. These flaws include the use of inappropriate scales, unvalidated behavioural descriptions, non-behavioural descriptions and poor user instructions.

Further, the multi-rater approach possibly has some structural issues that better survey design will not resolve. These include the participation of inappropriate raters (for example, those who do not regularly observe the recipient); raters relying on memory to make a judgment (hence the recency phenomenon, where recent events are more easily recalled); and raters' inability to conceptualise the behaviour described.

Many of these chronic structural problems can be difficult to overcome. To avoid them:

- use only validated instruments
- select raters carefully and inform (and preferably train) them as much as possible
- in the feedback sessions, focus on the broad patterns rather than the minutiae of the raters' feedback.

Unrealistic expectations

Many involved in the feedback process expect instant results. This is not realistic as it takes a long time for managers to change ingrained behavioural patterns. Merely using the multi-rater surveys in an organisation sometimes leads to an expectation that managerial behaviour will change. Staff, in particular, sometimes expect overnight transformations in their managers.

As part of the communication strategy that goes with the introduction of multi-rater feedback, everyone needs to be informed that this is part of a longer-term process. And this point should be emphasised at every opportunity during the process.

Poor quality feedback

The perceived value of the process is directly linked to the quality of the feedback process. If the communication of feedback is seen as a positive experience, then generally the participants express satisfaction with the process. This makes it important for organisations to ensure that the feedback session is as effective as possible, even if this means paying for trained staff to be involved in the process.

Simply providing recipients with a copy of the report detracts from the overall experience and will typically lead to participants dismissing the whole process as another management stunt. On the other hand, the greatest satisfaction seems to come from recipients who have had an opportunity to discuss their understanding of the feedback data, and its implications for behavioural change.

Organisations should invest in this stage of the process by making sure that skilled coaches are available to facilitate the feedback discussion.

Rater inconsistency

Many managers have trouble understanding why raters would rate them differently. This apparent inconsistency sometimes leads managers to dismiss the feedback as not useful. As part of the introduction of multi-rater feedback, managers need to be informed that inconsistency can be expected because:

- raters have different degrees of exposure to the recipient
- the recipient may behave differently with different raters
- raters perceive behaviours differently and bring different expectations to the rating process.

Part of the value of the feedback process lies in exploring these differences and working out how to deal with them.

Failure to develop action plans

Although most managers see the feedback they receive as valuable, many do not take the next step and commit to actions to address areas of weakness. This means that the process is largely a waste of time—the multi-rater feedback becomes interesting rather than useful.

This can be overcome by requiring the manager to develop a learning strategy or action plan based on the feedback received. Because managers learn by doing, such plans should focus on on-the-job learning activities. Managers have various options for learning, including:

- *experiential learning.* This involves seeking out opportunities to practice new ways of doing things that are based on the feedback received, and/or consciously approaching aspects of the managerial routine as opportunities for applying something that has been learned from the feedback process.
- *ongoing feedback.* Once the idea of feedback is in the workplace, it is much easier to approach co-workers and ask for feedback on an informal and ongoing basis. This may consist of the manager, when a task is completed, asking how they performed.
- *coaching.* Finding another person with whom the manager can have regular conversations about their self-development activities. Occasional conversations with someone who understands what the manager is attempting to do appears to have a major impact on long-term behavioural change.
- *personal development.* Seeking out training opportunities that align closely with the development plan. This can be as simple as reading books, but can also include training programs, conferences and special projects.

Observations

Multi-rater feedback is still a relatively new tool. Many questions remain about its effectiveness and usefulness as a management tool, although its current popularity cannot be denied.

It has been well established that many managers change their behaviour when they participate in multi-rater feedback processes. The unresolved issue is whether the change is caused by the feedback or the exposure (through the process) to a preferred set of behaviours. Several studies claim evidence that simple exposure was enough to induce change and that the feedback reports had no actual impact.[9] Others claim evidence that, without the reports, there is little change in behaviours.[10] At this stage, it is simply unclear how change is induced as a result of the feedback process, or even whether it is actually induced at all.

This is only one of many issues that remain unresolved. There are others that are not yet explored, such as the long-term impact on the development of leadership behaviours or the impact of managers taking responsibility for their own self-development. Despite this, as can be judged from its rapid acceptance by organisations and managers alike, there are real benefits to be gained from multi-rater feedback:

- The process draws attention to the preferred behaviours that the organisation wants to see applied in the workplace. It helps to clarify what those behaviours are and improves communication about those behaviours. This has been observed to improve a number of organisational processes such as teamwork, work relationships and mutual respect.[11]
- The process supports organisational efforts aimed at increasing the extent of employee involvement in the organisation. This in turn appears to have an impact on employee relationships.[12]
- Employees genuinely believe that the feedback is of assistance in developing their capabilities as managers.[13]
- There is evidence that the process improves productivity in organisations.[14]

On the face of the evidence, multi-rater feedback is here to stay.

User's guide

Although there are many different versions of multi-rater feedback, most have many elements in common, particularly where the broad purpose of the feedback system is to provide development support.[15]

Instructions

How to design a multi-rater feedback system

1. *Decide the purpose of multi-rater feedback in your organisation.*

   Organisations or managers considering the introduction of the tool should be clear about whether it is to be used for employee development purposes or for performance assessment purposes. This decision has an impact on the design of the survey, and on the attitude of the people involved in the process. Communicate the purpose to all those involved so that everyone is clear as to what is at stake.

2. *Select the survey instrument.*

The choice is between designing a survey instrument in-house and purchasing one from a commercial provider. There is some evidence to suggest that the in-house survey is more effective because it can include company-specific elements, but it is also expensive to develop. It requires expert knowledge in survey instrument development, although there is no guarantee that such expertise has been applied to the commercially developed tools either. Many consultants peddle their own instruments with dubious validity and reliability characteristics.

The benefit of the better-known commercial instruments is that they are validated. More importantly, they are standardised, which means that results can be compared between managers and, for each manager, over time. This opens up the opportunity to compare the results for a particular manager with a 'normed' sample of managers with similar managerial jobs.[16]

3. *Decide the behaviours that are to be included.*

The behaviours to be included can come either from a generic model or from the organisation's own strategic intent statements, such as value statements (see Chapter 1, Strategic intent: Vision, mission and values statements).

The first approach involves making a commitment to a model and usually the survey instrument follows logically. For example, I like to use the Leadership Practices Instrument which is based on the model developed by James Kouzes and Barry Posner, authors of the best-selling book, *The leadership challenge.*[17]

The second approach involves the more complicated step of deciding which behaviours the survey should focus on, translating these behaviours into statements, and creating a rating scale. This type of work is best left to specialists with experience in survey design.

4. *Decide who will be rated.*

Top-down implementation of multi-rater feedback surveys sends a signal to everyone in the organisation that the organisation is serious about this improvement technique. Most organisations target their top management layers. However, there are different opinions about how far down the organisation the technique should be pushed. The issue is mainly about front-line supervisors, where the 360-degree nature of the technique requires that front-line employees be involved in the process.

In practice, in some organisations it can be a risky thing to expose front-line supervisors to the anonymous feedback of a group of their staff. It can be misused as an opportunity to score points rather than to provide honest feedback. Each organisation needs to make a considered decision on this issue.

5. *Inform the participants.*

When multi-rater surveys are first introduced in an organisation, the concept needs to be communicated and explained to all those involved. Managers being rated need to understand the purpose and the boundaries of the exercise. Similarly, the raters need to understand the why and the how of the process.

6. *Decide who will rate.*

Typically, raters are chosen by the manager who is the recipient of the feedback. The raters can be chosen from anyone within the 360-degree 'circle' around the manager: boss, peers, staff and others.

Selection by the recipient has been criticised as offering the potential for managers to select those who will give 'good' reports. Providing the developmental nature of the exercise is emphasised, this is rarely a problem in practice.

The total number of raters is usually in the range of 6–12 so there is quite limited opportunity to 'stack the deck'. In any case, if the application is developmental, what does the manager gain from doing this?

7. *Organise the distribution process and report generation.*

Survey forms can be distributed physically or electronically to all those who are participating in the exercise. Lately, various Internet-based surveying services have become available that have considerably speeded up the surveying process.

The key issue with the distribution process is to maintain confidentiality at all times and to maintain the perception of confidentiality.

The survey responses then need to be processed (usually by means of processing software) to generate a report. Commercially available surveys typically include such software as part of a package which will also include information about how to handle the subsequent feedback stages.

Reports typically show the recipient's self-assessment for each behavioural area or behaviour, and compare this with averages (sometimes broken down into subgroups) of the ratings made by the other raters. It is this gap that will inform subsequent development discussions.

8. *Feed back the feedback.*

The feedback session should be carried out by someone experienced in handling development discussions. This could be done by suitably qualified in-house staff or by external consultants; in either case, the role is one of performance coach.

The session should use the data contained in the report to identify areas where the recipient of the feedback could strengthen their performance as a manager. Areas of strength should be agreed to balance the discussion.

The outcome should focus on behaviours that could be adopted or modified. This may also lead to the identification of training opportunities that can assist with behaviour change.

Follow-up sessions should be planned and built into the action plan.

9. *Follow through.*

The action plan should be formally followed up to ensure that managers follow through with their commitments to improve their leadership performance. The performance coach could schedule further discussions and ensure that training commitments are carried out.

Another element that could be considered at this stage is whether to repeat the surveying process in order to determine if any improvements have occurred. Typically, this would be done at least a year later, and the frequency of repetition may form part of the overall procedures governing the process.

Further reading

There are many books and articles available on multi-rater feedback. As usual in management, most of these are by self-appointed experts or by authors pushing a particular version as the best, for no reason other than they happened to have designed that version.

- P Ward, *360-degree feedback*, Institute of Personnel and Development, London, 1997.

  This is a reasonably independent and objective look at how to build a 360-degree feedback system. It covers most of the issues and is well written.

- R Lepsinger & A Lucia, *The art and science of 360 degree feedback*, Jossey-Bass, San Francisco, 1997.

  Another thorough and reliable guide that includes several case studies and shows how the tool has been applied to achieve various organisational benefits.

Notes

1. M McCall, M Lombardo & A Morrison, *The lessons of experience: How successful executives develop in the job*, Lexington Books, Lexington, 1998.
2. E Lindsey, V Holmes & M McCall, *Key events in executives lives*, Technical report no. 32, The Centre for Creative Leadership, Greensboro, 1997.
3. L Bassi & M Van Buren, 'The ASTD state of the industry report', *Training and Development*, vol. 53, no. 1 (supplement), 1999.
4. L Atwater & D Waldman, 'Accountability in 360 degree feedback', *HR Magazine*, vol. 43, no. 6, 1998, pp. 96–102.

5. J Ghorpade, 'Managing five paradoxes of 360-degree feedback', *Academy of Management Executive*, vol. 14, no. 1, 2000, pp. 140–50.
6. Towers Perrin, *360-degree feedback: The global perspective*, Towers Perrin, London, 1998.
7. M London, A Wohlers & P Gallagher, 'A feedback approach to management development', *The Journal of Management Development*, vol. 9, no. 6, 1990, pp. 17–31; D Waldman & D Bowen, 'The acceptability of 360-degree appraisals: a customer–supplier relationship perspective', *Human Resource Management*, vol. 37, no. 2, 1998, pp. 117–29.
8. R Kaplan, '360-degree feedback PLUS: boosting the power of co-workers ratings for executives', *Human Resource Management*, vol. 32, nos 2 & 3, 1993, pp. 299–314.
9. L Smither, M London, N Vasilopoulos, R Reilly, R Millsap & N Salvemini, 'An examination of the effects of an upward feedback program over time', *Personnel Psychology*, vol. 48, no. 1, 1995, pp. 1–34; R Reilly, J Smither & N Vasilopoulos, 'A longitudinal study of upward feedback', *Personnel Psychology*, vol. 49, no. 3, 1996, pp. 599–612; P Dominick, R Reilly & J McGourty, 'The effects of peer feedback on team member behaviour', *Group and Organization Management*, vol. 22, no. 4, 1997, pp. 508–20.
10. L Atwater, P Roush & A Fischta, 'The influence of upward feedback on self and follower ratings of leadership', *Personnel Psychology*, vol. 48, no. 1, 1995, pp. 35–9; L Atwater, D Waldman, D Atwater & P Cartier, 'An upward feedback field experiment: supervisor's cynicism, follow-up and commitment to subordinates', *Personnel Psychology*, vol. 53, no. 2, 2000, pp. 275–97.
11. ibid.
12. T Garavan, M Morley & M Flynn, '360-degree feedback: its role in employee development', *The Journal of Management Development*, vol. 13, nos 2 & 3, 1997, pp. 134–48.
13. J Hazucha, S Hezlett & R Schneider, 'The impact of 360-degree feedback on management skills development', *Human Resource Management*, vol. 32, nos 2 & 3, 1993, pp. 325–51.
14. M Edwards & A Ewen, *360 degree feedback: The powerful new model for employee assessment and performance improvement*, AMACOM, New York, 1996.
15. The generic model presented draws heavily on A McCarthy & T Garavan, '360-degree feedback processes: performance improvement and employee career development', *Journal of European Industrial Training*, vol. 25, no. 1, 2001, pp. 5–32.
16. Norms are a way of validly comparing one result with other results. For example, a manager might receive a relatively high score (say, 6 out of 10) from her employees for, say, a behaviour like coaching and supporting. But if a 'normed' population of similar managers on average receives a higher score (say, 8 out of 10) then she really has not performed very well. The 'raw score' looks impressive but once it is compared to a norm, it looks much less impressive.
17. B Posner & J Kouzes, *The leadership challenge*, John Wiley & Sons, New York, 1995.

CHAPTER 14

Selecting people
Behavioural interviewing

People are the lifeblood of all organisations. Adding new people to an organisation is not unlike having a blood transfusion. If the new blood is not a good match, the body will suffer, and ultimately reject the transfusion. That is the risk all organisations take when they recruit new people. It follows, then, that it is important to make the right choice about whom to employ. The cost of getting it wrong can be substantial. And yet many organisations do not invest adequately in ensuring that they make the right selection decisions.

This is all the more surprising when you consider that we do know how to make better selection decisions. The real surprise is that our knowledge about how to get it right is often ignored. In simple terms, when offered the choice between what works (structured interviewing) and what does not work (informal and unstructured interviewing), many managers and many organisations choose the latter.

The reasons for this are unclear. Many organisations are slowly turning to structured interviewing and reaping the benefits of a selection process that is significantly more likely to provide the right candidate. But this change in attitude and approach is happening only slowly. As a candidate for a job, you are still far more likely to face an unstructured interview than a structured one.

Part of the problem is what researchers call 'the illusion of validity'.[1] Put simply, this means that many managers believe that others might not know how to use an informal interview to select the right candidate but they do! Even when made aware of the research evidence that shows that the informal interview has very low reliability in selecting the candidate most likely to succeed in the job, managers put this evidence aside and continue on their merry way with the unstructured interview. Even worse, the recruitment industry (which, over the last 20 years, has largely taken over the early stages of the selection process for organisations) takes much the same point of view: 'Others may get it wrong but we get it right'.

So this chapter is for those who are more interested in getting it right than maintaining their false illusion of being interviewers with a sixth sense for making correct selection decisions.

Structuring interviews can be done in a number of ways, but the single most powerful technique is *behavioural interviewing*. In essence, this involves asking candidates to describe their own previous behaviours when faced with situations similar to those related to the job under consideration.

A related technique is *situational interviewing*, which is not quite as effective, but is useful when interviewing people who have little previous work experience. It involves asking questions that require candidates to indicate how they *would* handle situations that are similar to those related to the job.

Both these techniques substantially improve the process of making the best possible selection decision.

Background

The limitations of the job selection interview have been well demonstrated over the last 10 years or so.[2] Common weaknesses include:

- stereotyping of candidates (using very limited information to decide that a candidate is of a certain type)
- primacy effects (remembering the beginning of the interview better than the rest of the interview)
- personality similarity effect (believing that people like ourselves are the most competent)
- negative information weighting bias (exaggerating the importance of information that reflects poorly on the candidate).

Despite these known shortcomings, interviews remain popular for various reasons including:

- They perform functions other than selection, such as selling the organisation to the candidate, and persuading and negotiating arrangements with the candidate.
- They are accepted by managers and candidates as valid because interviewing is a known technique and easier to understand than other more technical techniques (such as competency profiling or personality testing).
- They are low in cost compared with other techniques such as tests.

As a result, most organisations continue to use the interview technique, and so researchers have focused on how to make it more effective.

It is generally agreed that the best approach is to make the interview more structured, which can happen in two ways—via content or via the evaluation process.

Elements that impact on the *content* of the interview include:

- basing questions on job analysis
- asking each candidate the same questions
- limiting prompting of candidates by the interviewer
- using better types of questions, such as behavioural or situational questions
- using more questions
- disallowing questions by candidates.

Elements that impact on the *evaluation process* include:

- rating each answer on a scale
- using behaviourally-based rating scales
- taking detailed notes
- using multiple interviews
- using multiple interviewers
- using the same interviewer(s) for all candidates
- not discussing candidates between interviews
- providing interviewer training
- limiting unsolicited information by candidates
- using a rating system for each question/answer rather than making a broad overall judgment.[3]

Interestingly, several of these structuring elements are very much disliked by managers and candidates. For example, both candidates and interviewers have problems with limiting prompting, longer interviews and preventing questions from candidates.

The elements that most improve interview content are the use of job analysis, using the same questions and using better types of questions. The elements that most improve evaluation are rating each answer, using behaviourally-based scales and interviewer training.

Question type has a major impact on an interview's reliability in predicting likely job performance by a candidate. The two question types that seem to have the greatest impact are *behavioural questions* and *situational questions*.

Situational questions are essentially hypothetical questions about how the candidate would deal with a given situation. Those situations are usually related to the requirements of the job. This type of question is based on the idea that a candidate's *intentions* are a good guide to how they would be likely to behave in a given situation.

By contrast, behavioural questions are based on the *past experience* of the candidate. This type of question asks candidates to describe how they behaved in given situations in the past. Once again, those situations should be relevant to the job. The idea is that past behaviour is a good guide to future behaviour. For example, if a job requires persuasiveness, then a behavioural question might ask the candidate to describe what they did when they were required to persuade somebody to change their opinion or agree to do something. The aim is to uncover what candidates did previously in this kind of situation and the level of skill they applied.[4]

Research suggests that behavioural questions can improve the effectiveness of the selection interview by a significant factor.[5] Some of this research was set in real organisations, using measures such as supervisor satisfaction with the appointed candidates, and candidates' subsequent performance. Other studies have compared behavioural questions with situational questions and this suggests that behavioural questions are more effective.[6]

Overall, the effectiveness of behavioural interviewing is very similar to proven techniques such as assessment centres (the most intensive and comprehensive of all the selection techniques used by selection specialists) and work sampling techniques.[7] However, these latter two selection techniques are expensive, whereas behavioural or situational interviews are inexpensive.

Behavioural questions are more effective than situational questions as an interview technique and have a number of advantages, including:

- *flexibility*. Behavioural questions are more flexible than situational questions because candidates can be encouraged to expand on their answers. Such questions allow candidates to explain their real-life experiences and behaviours. Probing questions can be used to explore additional detail behind the answers provided.
- *fairness*. Behavioural questions are fairer to candidates, in that any relevant real-life experiences (not just work-based experiences) can be nominated by the candidate in explaining how they have dealt with situations.
- *veracity*. Answers to behavioural questions are difficult to fake; follow-up questions can be used to probe for detail which is typically difficult to supply if the candidate is making things up. (Answers can also be verified independently and candidates are usually aware of this, which assists truthfulness.)

The extent to which behavioural interviewing is used by organisations is not completely clear. One UK study suggests that, in 1994, only 3% of the 400 organisations selected at random from the Times 1000 list of companies used the technique.[8] However, the technique has spread rapidly since that time, especially through the use of 'proprietary' versions of the approach. For example, author and consultant Paul Green has been very influential in advocating behavioural interviewing; a video based on his approach is reputedly the world's best-selling training video on selection interviewing techniques.[9]

Even more influential has been the branded version of the technique developed by consulting and training group, Development Dimensions International. Their 'Targeted Selection™' program has been used by thousands of organisations around the world to train managers in a structured interview process that is built around behavioural interviewing.[10] Because of the branded name, some managers and organisations using the system are unaware that they are actually using a form of behavioural interviewing.

Whatever the label used, there is little doubt that behavioural interviewing is the most cost-effective technique available to managers involved in the selection of employees for recruitment or promotion. The technique is 'in the public domain' and does not really require commitment to a proprietary version in order to make use of it in an organisation. It can be taught in a few hours (or simply by reading this chapter!) and, if applied consistently, will significantly improve the chance of selecting the candidate most likely to perform well in the job.

The tool

Behavioural interviewing is more than just asking behavioural questions. The structure of the interview process should include several of the other elements already mentioned. The simplest reliable behavioural interview structure should include the following elements:

- competency-based behavioural questions
- common interviewer(s) and questions for all interviews
- use of agreed rating scales for all questions.

These three core elements can be amplified by other elements that enhance the effectiveness of the interview process (such as interviewer training or using multiple interviewers) but these are optional rather than essential.

Elements may also be added for reasons other than selection, such as negotiating conditions with the candidate or promoting the organisation to the candidate. But such elements should not be confused with the three core elements that will ensure that the interview is structured and behavioural.

Taken together, these three steps will structure a selection interview to maximise the chance of selecting the candidate most likely to succeed in the job.

Competency-based behavioural questions

Interview questions need to be related to the job. Although this may seem obvious, in practice candidates are regularly asked questions that are wholly unrelated to the job. Even recruitment specialists are known to have their 'favourite question' for eliciting that insightful response from candidates. When challenged to justify such questions, these practitioners usually fall back on a mumbled response about their 'experience over many years'. This is usually an excellent signal that they are under the spell of the 'illusion of validity'. They believe it but cannot explain why it works or how it works, or demonstrate that it works.

The alternative is to design all questions so that they relate to the specific requirements of the job. (There is still plenty of room in the interview to do things other than select the best candidate for the job, such as impressing candidates or negotiating conditions of employment; just don't confuse this part of the interview with the selection part!)

The requirements of a job are best defined through a structured process, such as job analysis, but if this is not possible the interviewer can fall back on job descriptions or even the advertised requirements for the job.

Some questions can elicit information that is relevant to more than one skill area. It can, therefore, be useful to use a matrix to both capture the questions, indicate which skill areas they relate to, and also record the rating given by the interviewer (see the sample Behavioural Interview Matrix at the end of this chapter).

Common interviewer(s) and questions for all interviews

Using common interviewer(s) for all candidates automatically brings a degree of consistency to the judgments that are being made. If the interviewer is not highly skilled, at least the same judgments are being brought to bear. Of course, it would be far more effective to use skilled interviewers, so it is always worth investing in training for interviewers. If, however, the same interviewers cannot be used with all candidates (and exigencies do sometimes make this impossible) then training interviewers becomes a critical piece of insurance. The training will bring a degree of consistency that will otherwise be missing.

Using common questions has much the same impact as using common interviewers. It brings consistency through standardisation. This does not mean that the interview becomes inflexible. In fact, one of the advantages of behavioural interviewing over situational interviewing is that the interviewer has the opportunity to explore answers provided by candidates and seek amplification of the responses provided. Such probing will frequently uncover the detail that demonstrates a candidate's real experience and behaviour. Skilled interviewers will steer a highly interactive conversation but always come back to the same core questions with all candidates. This commonality creates the basis for fair comparison.

The questions should be written out in advance and made available to all interviewers. All questions should be asked of all candidates. Interviewers should be made aware that candidates may have previous and relevant experience that is not job-related. Organising a mothers' group to do fundraising for a local childcare facility requires many similar skills to business-oriented activities such as project management. It's the skills that matter, not the context in which they were applied.

Agreed rating scales used for all questions

Rating scales substantially improve the consistency and reliability of candidate evaluation. They also assist in maintaining consistency between different interviewers who may be involved in the selection process. The consistency comes from using a common scale that is understood by the interviewers. In other words, it's not just about devising the scale but also about making sure that the interviewers know what the scale stands for.

The rating scales do not have to be very sophisticated. A scale from 1 to 5 is sufficient to distinguish between the level of experience presented by candidates. The most critical aspect is for interviewers to agree about what each of the steps in the scale stands for. That is, if a rating of 3 stands for 'competent', what does this mean in the minds of the interviewers? The simplest way of clarifying this is for the interviewers to consider descriptions of the skill being used and allocate a rating to that description. Some organisations have developed their own definitions and descriptions of what the various rating options stand for. These explanations are very helpful in maintaining consistency.

Observations

It is important to remember that behavioural interviewing has limitations. It is not a perfect tool that is guaranteed to deliver a good result. Selecting people for a job will always be fraught with many uncertainties. Behavioural interviewing simply swings the odds more in your favour. It increases the chances of getting it right, but any selection decision is always a gamble.

The limitations of behavioural interviewing become apparent when you consider the two assumptions on which it is based. The first one is that behaviour patterns are consistent over time. This is based on the assumption that the best guide to future behaviour is past behaviour. This assumption is probably true, but the evidence is not completely conclusive. Past behaviour is never a completely accurate guide to future behaviour because people do change over time. This, after all, is the basis for a wholly separate industry—the self-improvement industry, which advocates that people can change themselves and can escape past behavioural patterns. So, although it is generally a reasonable assumption, it still remains an assumption that has a question mark over it.

The second assumption behind behavioural interviewing is that candidates can be compared fairly on the basis of their past behaviour. Even assuming that past behaviour is a guide to future behaviour, the reality is that candidates have different past experiences. Some will have experiences that are directly relevant to the behavioural requirements of the job under consideration and others will have far less or more limited experience. This limitation is sometimes amplified by how well candidates can recall and describe their past experience. Those who cannot 'tell their story' may be compared unfavourably with those who can.

All this is not to say that the other selection techniques are without blemish:

- *Situational interviews* assume that a hypothetical response is a good indicator of future behaviour, even though we know that intentions are not always a reliable guide to actual behaviour.
- *Ability tests* assume that a test can fully and adequately capture all the relevant aspects of a job.
- *Personality profiles* assume that what we call personality is a stable construct that can be measured accurately by any one test at any one time. Further, they assume that personality traits can be accurately linked back to job performance, when in many cases they cannot.
- *Assessment centres*, the most reliable of the techniques (and the most expensive), are based on the assumption that the array of tests and exercises a candidate has to complete will adequately capture what is entailed by the actual job.

So, all selection techniques have limitations. However, taking all those limitations into account (and accepting that we will get it wrong on plenty of occasions), there seems little doubt that behavioural interviewing is the most reliable, cost-effective and acceptable technique for selecting people for jobs.

User's guide

Interviewing is only one part of the selection process. Other aspects (such as referee checking and ability testing) are also important. But traditionally the interview has been the crucial step in the process, at least for many managers. It is the step that is most under the control of the manager, and least likely to be manipulated by candidates.

As with all other steps, the interview must be planned in advance. If the behavioural approach is to be followed this may involve a little more time for preparation, most of which is spent on crafting the questions to be used in the interview. If more than one interviewer is to be involved, then some time will also be needed to ensure that the interview procedure is coordinated.

The following steps indicate what is involved in preparing and executing a structured interview.

Instructions

How to prepare a selection interview

1. *Derive competencies or skill areas for the job (job analysis).*

   Job analysis is the preferred technique for generating the skill areas in which a job-holder should be proficient. It identifies and determines (in detail) the particular job duties and requirements as well as the relative importance of these duties for a given job. An important aspect of job analysis is that the analysis is of the job, not the person. While job analysis data may be collected from incumbents through interviews or question-naires, the product of the analysis is a description or specifications of the job, not a description of the person.

   Job analysis will generate the behavioural requirements that are critical for job success. However, sometimes it is not possible to undertake job analysis, in which case it may be necessary to rely on a job description.

   - Verify what the critical behaviours are, using the position description as a prompt (for example, by interviewing the person who will be managing the job-holder or who managed their predecessor in the job). The simplest approach is to ask what the job-holder is required to do.
   - Follow up any answers that describe what the job-holder should be like (that is, answers that are about personality traits) by asking what this means in terms of what people are expected to do. For example, if a manager seeks a person who is 'highly motivated' and a 'self-starter', use probing questions to uncover what this means in behavioural terms. Ask questions such as: 'So what would they be doing that requires this high degree of motivation?'

   Whatever the method used, the outcome should be a list of skill areas that are critical to the job and that will form the basis for a selection decision.

2. *Develop behavioural questions for each skill area.*

   Once a set of skill areas has been identified, the next step is to develop a set of questions that will encourage the candidate to describe experiences they have had that involved using these skills. For example, if a job involved project management skills, a behavioural question related to that might be: 'Tell me about a situation in which you had to use project management skills'.

   The degree of specificity of the question can be varied with the requirements of the job. For example, if the job was a specialist project management position in the field of IT, the question could be varied to: 'Tell me about a situation in which you had to use project control techniques to manage an IT project'.

The key to behavioural interviewing is the way in which the questions are structured.

• Derive each question from a specific skill area. On average, most jobs involve four to seven major skill areas.
• If the job is complex, divide each skill area into sub-areas. For each sub-area, devise one or more questions that require the candidate to describe their actual previous experience. The question should direct the candidate to relate specific events in which they were required to deal with some aspect of a job. Use phases such as:
  – Tell me about a situation where you …
  – Have you been involved in a situation where …
  – How did you handle instances of …
  – Have you had to …
  Include follow-up probes such as:
  – What did you do?
  – Can you give me an example?
  – What happened?
  – How did you respond?

3. *Develop rating scales.*

The critical issue in developing rating scales is to achieve consistency over time, both for each interviewer and between different interviewers. This means that the meaning of each rating needs to be clarified.

The best way to achieve common understanding is for the interviewers to rate sample descriptions of the skill being applied and then compare their judgments.

The words don't actually matter too much and are largely a matter of personal preference. What does matter is that the interviewers agree on what those words mean.

• Describe each rating in some detail. What does it mean when an inter- viewer rates a person as 'competent' in project management techniques? The answer to that question needs to be commonly shared by all the interviewers. To reach this level of common understanding, the inter- viewers could discuss their understanding until consensus is reached.
• Alternatively, develop standard descriptions for each of the ratings that clarify what is meant by that rating. This is more time consuming but it is also more effective. Standard descriptions make it much easier to train interviewers in applying the appropriate standard. Writing the descriptions is made simpler if industry skill standards (now common in many industries) are available.

4. *Ensure that the same questions and interviewers are used for all candidates.*

• Train the interviewers in the questions that are to be used. Experienced interviewers will not require much training, although their previous experience may incline them to add their own questions. The purpose of the training is to discourage such ad hoc questions unless they are follow-up questions to those agreed for the interview.

- Alternatively, supply the list of questions to the interviewers and instruct them to use only those questions with all candidates.

In many organisations, matters such as how the interviews will be conducted are mandated as part of a policy on recruitment and selection processes.

Further reading

There are few good resources available on behavioural interviewing. Many of the popular books on selection interviewing are based on limited research data, often written by self-appointed 'experts' who simply push their personal preference for how such interviews should be conducted.

- N Anderson & V Shackleton, *Successful selection interviewing*, Blackwell, Oxford, 1993.

This is one of the best books that is based on research (and therefore recommends the behavioural interviewing approach). Anderson and Shackleton are two of the best researchers in the field of selection interviewing techniques. The book is comprehensive and readable, but solidly based on research data. Subsequent research has confirmed the basic soundness of their approach.

- D Rosenberg, *A manager's guide to hiring the best person for every job*, John Wiley & Sons, New York, 2000.

Deanne Rosenberg covers the gamut of the selection process, including behavioural interviewing. This book offers a wide range of techniques and approaches, without the fanfare style that too many other books adopt, and it offers a simple system for preparing and executing selection interviews.

Notes

1. H Einhorn & R Hogarth, 'Confidence in judgment: resistance of the illusion of validity', *Psychological Review*, vol. 85, 1978, pp. 395–416.
2. N Anderson, 'Eight decades of employment interview research: a retrospective meta-review and prospective commentary', *European Work and Organisational Psychologist*, vol. 2, no. 1, 1992, pp. 1–32.
3. M Campion, D Palmer & J Campion, 'A review of structure in the selection interview, *Personnel Psychology*, vol. 50, no. 3, 1997, pp. 655–702.
4. For more detail on behavioural questions, see J Barclay, 'Improving selection interviews with structure: organisations' use of 'behavioural' interviews', *Personnel Review*, vol. 30, no. 1, 2001, pp. 81–101.

5. For those who are technically minded, the research suggests that behavioural interviews have a validity ranging from 0.32 to 0.61 compared with 0.10 for traditional unstructured interviews. See T Janz, 'Initial comparisons of patterned behaviour description interviews versus unstructured interviews', *Journal of Applied Psychology*, vol. 67, no. 5, 2001, pp. 577–80; C Orpen, 'Patterned behaviour description interviews versus unstructured interviews: a comparative validity study', *Journal of Applied Psychology*, vol. 70, no. 4, 1985, pp. 774–6.

6. M Campion, J Campion & J Hudson, 'Structured interviewing: a note on incremental validity and alternative question type', *Journal of Applied Psychology*, vol. 79, no 6, 1994, pp. 998–1002; E Pulakos & N Schmidt, 'Experience based and situational interview questions; studies of validity', *Personnel Psychology*, vol. 48, 1995, pp. 289–308.

7. N Anderson & V Shackleton, *Successful selection interviewing*, Blackwell, Oxford, 1993.

8. See J Barclay, 'Employee selection: a question of structure', *Personnel Review*, vol. 28, no. 1/2, 1999, p. 139.

9. P Green, 'Behavioral interviewing', *Executive Excellence*, Nov 1991, pp. 10–11.

10. See DDI's web site at www.ddiworld.com

Behavioural Interview Matrix: Sample for an IT Project Manager

Rating scale: 1–5 (from low to high)

Questions	Project management skills	– project management techniques	– team management	– client relations	Business acumen	Communication skills	IT systems knowledge/skills
Tell me about specific project control techniques that you have used to manage a difficult project.							
Have you ever had to deal with a difficult team member? How did you handle that situation?							
Tell me about how you dealt with demanding customers on previous projects that you were involved in?							

CHAPTER 15

Controlling tasks and projects
Project management techniques

Project management involves the application of various tools and techniques that have evolved over more than 100 years of development. As it became an ever more technical discipline, with ever more technical tools, project management became something of a management specialisation. This 'technicalisation' of project management hides the fact that at its core are some very simple but powerful techniques for getting things done. These core techniques are powerful tools that can be applied in general management on a day-to-day basis as easily as in large-scale projects.

Computer software turned project management into a technical art form, making it more and more difficult for generalists to apply the tools of project management without knowing the ins and outs of the software. Whenever management tools get locked into a PC application, they seem to become unapproachable for many managers. In reality, you do not need to know how to use Microsoft Project to use project management tools and techniques. In fact, there are advantages in *not* using software, such as being able to involve a group more easily (computers exclude people; wall charts and whiteboards include people.)

Lately, project management has made something of a comeback as a general management tool, due partly to the changing nature of organisations in the twenty-first century. Many critical organisational issues, including strategic alliances, mergers, acquisitions and restructures, now demand a project management approach. So, many managers are now involved in a managerial role that is project-based and project skills are becoming more and more valuable to organisations.[1]

Project management tools are simply too useful to be left to project management specialists. Many managers use such tools as a matter of routine to manage their daily round of tasks, meetings and small projects. Most managers work on projects most of the time, and to use techniques to manage small and medium projects makes just as much sense as to use them for large projects. It does not require a computer or an understanding of software. To make the most of these tools, it simply requires a little knowledge and some discipline.

Background

Project management is a set of techniques that are used to control a complex undertaking. Such undertakings (projects) usually involve making sure that a wide variety of activities happen in the right order and on time to ensure that an end result is achieved. The more complex the undertaking and the more activities that have to be coordinated, the more useful project management becomes.

A typical project may involve many different people, cost lots of money and use a variety of resources in order to build or create something. Examples are:

- completing a large construction project, such as an office building
- building a complicated piece of machinery, such as a factory production line
- writing a complex piece of computer software, such as a payroll system.

However, projects of any size can benefit from the discipline that project management techniques provide. Each of the techniques is capable of being applied quickly and simply, without all the bells and whistles that might accompany them in a larger project. Project management will help you find the best sequence in which to carry out all the individual activities to ensure that the project is completed on time, within budget and to a specified standard. However, project management is also useful whenever you need to complete something that has a beginning, middle and end.

Each project tends to go through a series of separate phases which, when taken together, form the project cycle. The phases are sometimes known as the *SPEC* cycle, where:

- S = *specifying* the project
- P = *planning* the project
- E = *executing* the project
- C = *concluding* the project.

This SPEC cycle is important—skipping over one of the steps is likely to lead to difficulties. For example, many projects fail because people skip the specifying stage. Other projects seem to go on forever because no-one knows how to wrap them up and reach the concluding phase. There is no better way to guarantee failure than by failing to SPEC your project. This step is actually a project management technique in its own right.

Every project has its built-in limits. You are unlikely ever to be involved in a project that gives you unlimited resources and unlimited time, and where no-one cares about the quality of the work you do! These limits, or *project parameters*, usually relate to three areas: quality, resources and time. Each parameter is measured and controlled differently:

- *quality* by specifications
- *resources* by budget
- *time* by schedule.

If you are the project manager for a project, your main preoccupation will be with these three parameters and their associated control mechanisms. Normally, the details of each are stipulated by the person who has appointed you as project manager, whether that is a client or a senior manager. For example, clients or senior managers usually want something of a given quality, costing a certain amount of money, and delivered by a certain date.

All this is contained in the 'project contract', however informal that might be. If you are your own client (that is, you set up the project and you are carrying it out), then it still pays to go through the discipline of specifying the project and stipulating the parameters to ensure a quality outcome.

Occasionally you may find yourself in the fortunate position of carrying out a project where 'money is no object' or 'you can take as much time as you need' (although rarely both). However, I have never heard of a project where the quality was totally unimportant!

There are six steps involved in the process of specifying a project:

1. Analyse the task or problem.
2. Write the project definition.
3. Write the project objectives.
4. Write the project outcomes.
5. Consider all options and alternatives.
6. Decide a course of action or approach.

In many ways, this planning stage is the heart of project management. After all, project management is a planning tool. That is why it was invented and that is what it does.

The tool

Project management involves using a number of different techniques, some being alternative ways of achieving a similar result. The key techniques are:

- activity charting
- Gantt charting
- PERT charting
- critical path analysis
- resource control.

Gantt charting and PERT charting are alternative ways of creating a road map for your project (also see Chapter 9, Improving processes: Process mapping and management).

Activity charting

In order to plan the quality conformance, cost and duration of your project, you need to subdivide it into smaller chunks of work. Each chunk or activity, because it is relatively small, can have estimates attached to it for quality, resources and time. Reducing the project to activities is called *activity charting*. Usually, any complex project will have a number of layers where activities are subdivided into a further layer of activities (this is called a *work breakdown structure*). Simpler projects will have only one layer.

There are no fixed rules about how many layers you have or about the size or number of the activities to which you need to reduce a project; the rule of thumb is to reduce it to activities that you can accurately assess for quality, resources and time. If you cannot estimate with confidence, then that is a good sign that the activity should be broken down into smaller units.

For example, if you were planning a small project such as building a garage, then the activities might be as outlined in Table 15.1.

Table 15.1 Example of an activity chart for building a garage

Garage: Activity chart		
Foundations	Excavate footings	1
	Prepare footings	2
	Pour concrete	3
Structural	Erect walls	4
	Fix roof	5
	Install external windows/doors	6
Interior	Erect internal walls	7
	Carry out electrical work	8
	Plaster walls/ceiling	9
	Paint walls/ceiling	10
	Fit fixtures	11

Our project has several layers and is broken down into logical activities. For example, each of these activities could be carried out by a separate contractor.

Planning for quality is the foundation of any project. Managing a project is like building a house—it is vital to make sure that the foundations are solid before building up the walls and roof. To carry the building analogy a bit further, the purpose of quality planning is to make sure that you get what you need. When you pour a concrete slab that is supposed to be able to withstand a certain pressure, quality planning will ensure that you don't end up with a slab that can only withstand a lower pressure.

Quality planning ensures that the final product of the project will conform to the specifications that were established in the first phase (specifying the project). If the quality is less than that nominated in the specifications then, at worst, your building may fall down or, just as bad, your client or senior manager may not accept the building. In many ways, quality is the most critical of the three parameters. Your client may not be happy about cost overruns or about time overruns. But they will be very unforgiving if your project simply doesn't achieve what it is supposed to.

The NASA project to put a man on the moon—one of the mega-projects which actually led to the development of formal project management methodology—cost more than was planned and took longer than planned. But it was still considered a success because it achieved what it was supposed to achieve; it put Neil Armstrong on the moon. However, can you imagine the reaction to the project if they had failed to get him back off the moon?

You can plan for the control of quality by writing a complete set of quality specifications for each activity on your activity chart. This means that you must:

1. specify the nature and quality of the materials to be used
2. specify the tests to be carried out to verify step 1.

Table 15.2 outlines the quality specifications for the garage discussed earlier.

Table 15.2 Example of quality specifications for building a garage

Garage: Quality specifications	
Footings	
1	Pour concrete footings around the perimeter of the garage to a depth of 600 mm and width of 450 mm, reinforced with 15 mm diameter steel rods.
2	Pour two intersecting centre beams to a depth of 450 mm and width of 450 mm, reinforced with 15 mm diameter steel rods.
3	Concrete to withstand 25 MPa* after 28 days.

*The internal strength of concrete is usually measured in megapascals.

Gantt charting

The old adage says that time is money. It is certainly true when you consider that many projects contain penalty clauses that stipulate how much the project manager has to pay to the client if the project is not completed on time. But even if your projects do not contain penalty clauses, there are many other obvious reasons why they should be completed on time—gaining further work, keeping the client happy and gaining a good reputation as a project manager.

To plan the *time* for a project, you once again start with the activity chart. For each activity, calculate:

- how long the activity will take to complete
- the earliest time it *can* be started
- the latest time it *must* be started.

Since the accuracy of the time schedule will depend on the accuracy of the time assessment for each activity, make sure that you get accurate estimates. That means you may have to ask others who know this better than you do.

Time estimates for projects are notoriously difficult to get right. The problem is that a minor variation in one activity can have a significant impact on the overall project. Even worse, a lot of small variations can add up to an enormous delay in time for the total project.

There are various techniques for dealing with time estimates. Practical and accurate experience is the best source of advice. Using a time range rather than a fixed duration is another approach. In complex projects it may be necessary to use mathematical models to calculate likely time estimates. There are two major techniques for charting the time estimates for a project: Gantt charts and PERT charts.

Named after the industrial engineer who invented the technique, a *Gantt chart* is like a bar chart with the bars running horizontally across the page. Each activity in a project has a bar drawn across the page indicating when it starts and when it finishes. All this is drawn on a simple calendar showing dates. Taken together, all the bars indicate which activities can overlap (that is, those that can be done at the same time) and which cannot be started until another has been completed. From the beginning of the first bar to the end of the last bar, they give you an overall estimate for the duration of the project.

Figure 15.1 shows what such a chart might look like for the garage project. You will see that one of the useful things it tells us is that two of the activities can be carried out at the same time. (To test your ability to read the chart, which two activities can be carried out concurrently?)

The Gantt chart can also contain information about the progress of the project by adding a second (and different-looking) bar for each activity that shows the *actual* time taken for that activity. This feature allows you to track how the project is going, and gives a progressive idea of whether the project is on schedule or not.

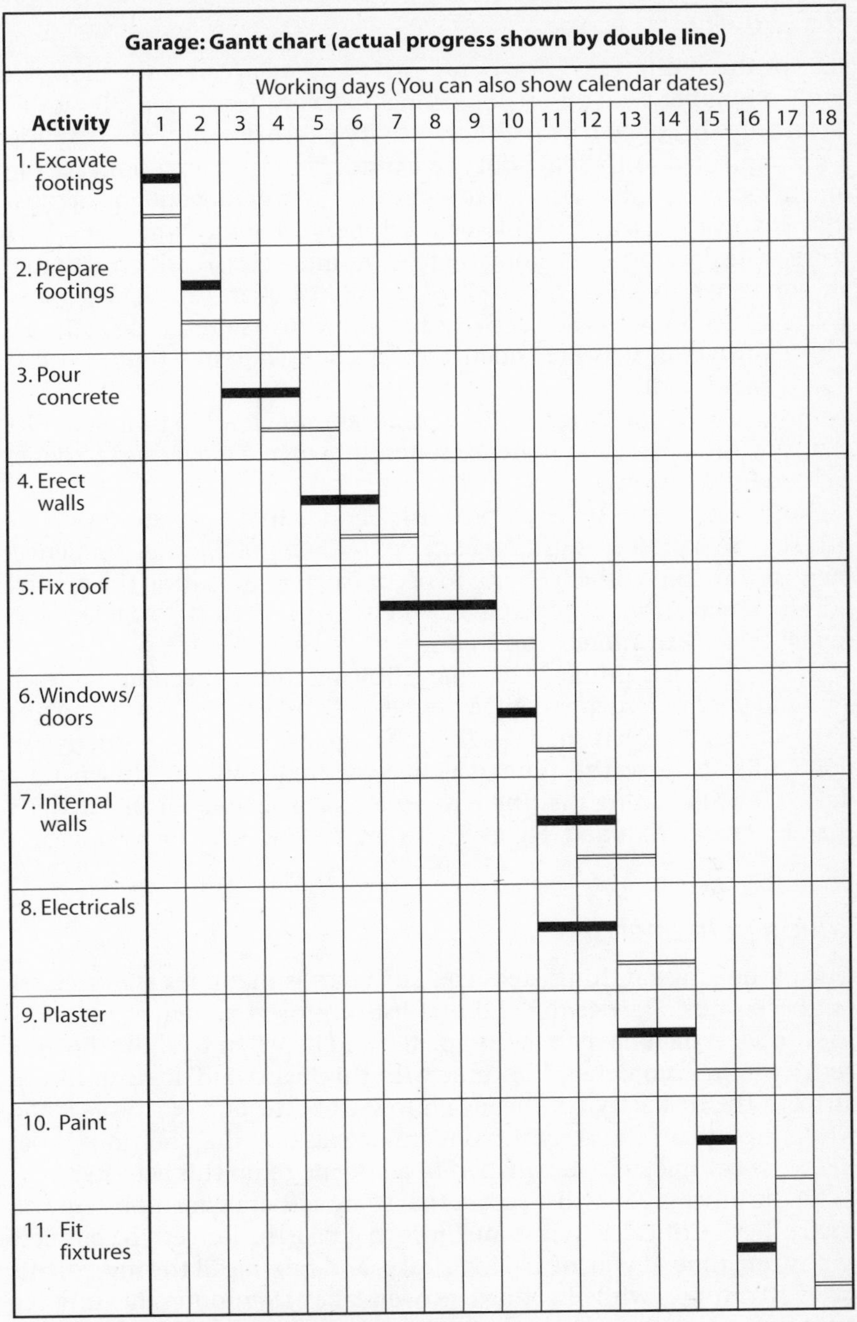

Garage: Gantt chart (actual progress shown by double line)																		
	Working days (You can also show calendar dates)																	
Activity	1	2	3	4	5	6	7	8	9	10	11	12	13	14	15	16	17	18
1. Excavate footings	▬																	
2. Prepare footings		▬																
3. Pour concrete			▬															
4. Erect walls				▬														
5. Fix roof							▬											
6. Windows/ doors									▬									
7. Internal walls											▬							
8. Electricals											▬							
9. Plaster													▬					
10. Paint															▬			
11. Fit fixtures																▬		

Figure 15.1 Gantt chart for building a garage

Notice how one delay during preparation of footings and a second delay with the electricals throws the timeline out by two days.

PERT charting

One of the limitations of a Gantt chart is that it can only show the connections between different activities in a very limited way. Basically, it can only show when a preceding activity has to be completed to allow a subsequent one to start. But sometimes activities are connected in much more complex ways. Activities can be interdependent because they involve the same people or machinery or something else. *PERT charts* were developed to allow you to show more clearly which activities are connected to which other activities. A PERT chart can be thought of as a Gantt chart with each activity also showing its preceding activities (those on which it is dependent) and its subsequent activities (those that depend on it).

PERT stands for Program Evaluation and Review Technique. PERT charts consist of two components: states (shown by a circle) and activities (shown by an arrowed timeline).

States are simply the start or finish of an activity. For example, the first state in a project is usually *State no. 1: Commencement*. Commencement allows some other activity to occur (such as preparing the ground for the excavation of footings), which in turn leads to *State no. 2: Completion of excavation*. And so on.

Figure 15.2 is a simple PERT chart showing the connections between a number of interdependent activities, all of which add up to the project of cooking a dish of spaghetti bolognaise. Some of the activities don't fully occupy the time available for them; this is shown by a dotted line indicating that there is more time available for that activity than is actually required. Figure 15.3 shows a PERT chart for our garage project.

Critical path analysis

One of the unusual things about a PERT chart is that it is easier to work out backwards! Start at the end of a list of project activities and work back to see which have to be completed and by when to allow the final activity to be completed. Continue with this 'backward' logic until you arrive at the first activity. The idea is to start at the end of a project and work through all the activities one by one, asking the question: What has to be completed and by when to allow me to do this activity?

In the process you will discover that some activities are more 'critical' than others. Critical activities are those that take the longest to complete at any one time. If you are baking a cake, and mixing all the ingredients takes 10 minutes while heating the oven takes 15 minutes, heating the oven is the critical activity since it takes longer and cannot be shortened. If you string together all the critical activities in a project (those which take the longest at any one time in the life of the project) then you have the *critical path* of the project.

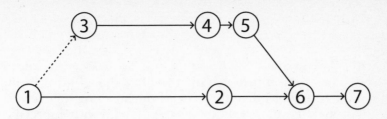

	Activity list	Time
A	Make sauce	25 min
B	Boil water	11 min
C	Cook spaghetti	8 min
D	Drain and serve spaghetti	30 s
E	Add sauce	1 min
F	Serve dish	30 s
	Total time	26.5 min

States	
1	Start making the sauce
2	Sauce made
3	Water boiled
4	Spaghetti cooked
5	Spaghetti drained and served
6	Sauce added
7	Dish served

Figure 15.2 PERT chart for cooking spaghetti bolognaise
Note: We delay the start of activity B (boiling the water) in order to make sure that we finish boiling the water and therefore cooking the spaghetti just in time to coincide with the making of the sauce.

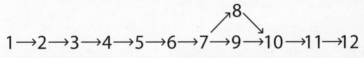

States	
1	Commence project
2	Footings excavated
3	Footings prepared
4	Footings poured
5	Walls erected
6	Roof fixed
7	Windows/doors installed
8	Internal walls erected
9	Electrical work completed
10	Walls/ceiling plastered
11	Walls/ceiling painted
12	Fixtures fitted

Figure 15.3 PERT chart for building a garage
Note: A time scale can be added by indicating start and finish dates or times for each state.

This kind of calculation (*critical path analysis*) is useful to determine which activities you have to pay most attention to when implementing the project. If it takes you a little longer to mix the cake ingredients, then it doesn't affect the finishing time for baking the cake. But if it takes longer to heat the oven than you had thought (for example, you forgot to turn it on) then it will delay the finishing time for the cake.

It is often useful to indicate the critical path with a special coloured line. Delays in critical activities will cause delays in the overall project. Delays in non-critical activities you can live with as long as such delays don't transform those activities into critical ones.

Resource control

It is important to plan the use of resources on a project because few projects receive unlimited resources. Controlling resources means controlling the cost of your project. Cost overruns may eat away your profit, or lead to a project not being completed because you are unable to get the extra funds to do so. All this can be avoided by planning the use of resources in the same way as planning the quality and time control of the project.

Each activity should have a cost estimate attached to it. For example, if every activity was to be contracted out, then it is simply a matter of asking the subcontractors to give quotes for completing their particular activities. Usually, however, things are a little more difficult in that you may have to work out the costs yourself, component by component. This means breaking down each activity into its components and attaching a dollar value to them. Common cost components include:

- labour (including provision for overheads)
- materials
- equipment and plant
- project administration
- using borrowed capital
- profit.

The next task is to construct a matrix of these cost categories against every activity that is a part of your project. This can easily be done on paper, although the computerised version of such sheets (spreadsheets) makes doing recalculations a lot easier.

Table 15.3 shows a project cost worksheet for the garage project.

Pulling it all together

The final step in the control process is to allocate responsibility for each activity to some person. This is simple enough if you are accountable for everything. But in a large project with many people involved it is essential that everyone knows who is responsible for which activities.

Table 15.3 Project cost worksheet for building a garage

Garage: Project costs

Activity	Labour	Materials	Equipment & plant	Project admin*	Working capital**	Profit***
Excavate footings	2 @ $100/day	0	Excavator $200	.25		
Prepare footings	1 @ $200/day	$600	0	.25		
Pour concrete	2 @ $100/day	$800	0	.5		
Erect walls	2 @ $200/day	$700	0	.25		
Fix roof	3 @ $200/day	$900	0	.25		
Install external windows/doors	1 @ $200/day	$2000	0	.25		
Erect internal walls	2 @ $200/day	$800	0	0		
Carry out electrical work	2 @ $250/day	$600	0	0		
Plaster walls/ceiling	2 @ $200/day	$1500	0	0		
Paint walls/ceiling	1 @ $150/day	$400	0	0		
Fit fixtures	1 @ $200/day	$900	0	.25		
TOTAL	$3450	$9200	$200	$600	$65	$6485

*Project administration calculated in fractions of a day at $300 per day.
**Cost of working capital calculated on $15 000 reserved for this project for 20 days; opportunity cost at 9% equals $65.
***Profit calculated on total project costs of $13 515 and assessed value of completed project of $20 000.

The easiest way to record accountabilities is to add another column to your Gantt chart or PERT chart (activity list) with the heading 'Responsibility'. Then, for every row indicating an activity, add the initials of the person who is responsible for ensuring that the activity is completed on time, within budget and to standard.

The real problem is not how or what you track, but what you do with the information that this tracking process generates. As you monitor progress on each activity, variations will arise. Some activities will go over or under budget. Some will take longer or shorter than planned. As mentioned before, one way to log all these is to superimpose them over the PERT chart that shows what was supposed to happen. Simply overlay, perhaps in a different colour, what actually happens as events unfold.

Another technique is to use a *control point chart*. This enables you to indicate where you predict trouble is likely to occur. You can then make a special effort to monitor those trouble points, even preparing what you will do if your predictions come true. The technique itself is very simple. Use highlighters or coloured pencils to mark on your PERT chart those activities which may create problems.

Clearly, as you become more experienced with an activity or project, you quickly learn the likely trouble spots. Over time, you end up doing the control point charts in your head, without thinking about it much. That's why you often see experienced project managers turning up in the right place at the right time just in time to avoid a problem about to happen.

One of the oldest techniques is to use a simple list of all the 'milestones' for a project—key events that give you a broad picture of whether the project is on target or not. Milestones (no-one seems to use kilometre stones!) are most commonly used to monitor time rather than cost, but you can certainly tie in a cost schedule to each milestone. Another useful feature of a milestone chart is that it can prompt the seeking of authorisation or approval to proceed to the next phase of a project. For example, progress on building projects revolves around certain key events such as the inspection of footings, the inspection of supporting walls before they are clad, the inspection of roof structures before they are enclosed, and so on. Milestones can relate to any stage in the project; control points relate specifically to potential problem areas.

Even major projects should have no more than six or seven milestones or they lose their value as broad control mechanisms.

Observations

Project management techniques essentially enable us to complete tasks in a disciplined way. They earn their keep when a project or a set of tasks becomes sufficiently complex or too large for memory alone to be an inadequate control mechanism. These days, the managerial job is more and more about managing complexity. That complexity comes from the increasingly dynamic and turbulent environment in which organisations operate.

As a result, many managers have effectively become project managers rather than process managers. Clearly, project management skills and techniques can help managers cope with this role change. However, too much of project management has been captured by specialists who use technical 'patois' to protect their turf. In reality, project management is built on a handful of simple techniques that work just as well on paper as they do through computer software.

As with most management tools, it is not about the technical complexity of the tools but about the discipline of applying them when it is appropriate to do so. In project management, there is probably no greater sin than 'making it up as you go along', because that approach is virtually inviting failure. For most managers, the better approach is to 'plan it as you go along', using the simple techniques on which project management is founded.

User's guide

The discipline of project management is useful in a wide range of applications, from simply managing an array of discrete tasks to managing complete projects. As is so often the case, the power of the techniques lies in the fact that they force the user to plan. Time to plan is sometimes a luxury for managers but the pay-off from doing it is indisputable. The following simple approach to planning will lead to better outcomes. If these planning steps are completed, all the techniques described will work far more effectively.

Instructions

How to plan projects and tasks

1. *Analyse the task or project.*

   It is absolutely critical to take the time to study and analyse the task you have been given.

   If it involves a group of people, some will have different understandings of what is involved in the project. All these points of view are valuable and need to be taken into account. You have to be sure that in reality all of you are tackling the *same* project and not just hoping for the best.

   • Start to research the project by looking at similar projects that have been carried out previously or by talking to people who know a lot about the task that you have been asked to undertake. You should welcome any and all information.

2. *Write the project definition.*

- When you have a good grasp of the problem, start to define the project by writing a description of it.
- Polish and refine the description by consulting others who have a stake in the project. This may take only a short time. However, don't be surprised if it takes a while for everyone to agree on the words. Once people start to get a feel for the project by seeing it expressed in words, often the real disagreements start. This is normal.
- Talk it through until everyone agrees on the words. There is no point in starting the project until this stage is fully completed.

3. *Write the project objectives.*

- Drawing on the definitions you have written in the previous step, list all the objectives you hope to achieve. These are the end results that your project will produce.

The objectives should refer to the project parameters such as cost, time and quality. This broad description will inform all the subsequent stages in the project.

4. *Write the project outcomes.*

- Make a list of all the outcomes that must be achieved for the project to be considered a success; these are the 'must-have' outcomes.
- Also list any outcomes that you may be able to achieve but that are not a critical part of the project; these are the 'nice-to-have' outcomes.

5. *Consider all options and alternatives.*

- Consider all the options that are open to you to achieve the objective of your project. Generally, there are many alternative paths you can travel to reach a particular goal. If there are many different options (all of which seem acceptable or possible), you should pick the most likely one.

To help select the best approach (especially with larger projects), you may have to do a feasibility study.

There are several different ways of testing the feasibility of a project. Much depends on the nature and type of your particular project. For example, if you are designing a new ocean-going yacht, it is usual to build a scale model and test it for its special characteristics in a flotation tank. Computer simulations are another way to test designs that involve a lot of technical specifications such as bridges, buildings or aeroplanes. You can test consumer reaction to a new product that you want to manufacture by asking a selection of your potential customers what they think of the idea.

All of these are different forms of pilot testing. How much time and effort you spend on pilot testing depends on the cost of the project. If it is a multimillion-dollar project, then it is wise to spend some of that money on a pilot project to determine the feasibility of the overall project. If the investment or the risk is small, then you need to do much less pilot testing.

6. *Select a course of action or approach.*

   • Decide on a course of action that looks as if it will meet your project objective. Use your best judgment. The feasibility testing process will confirm your judgment or make you reconsider.

   If you have completed the first five steps in the project planning process, then by now you will have a 'feel' for the right way to proceed. In making this decision, you are moving beyond the information you have collected (analysis) towards the decision-making part (synthesis). It is a bit of a leap into the unknown but that is part of the fun!

Further reading

- P Williams, *Getting a project done on time: Managing people, time, and results*, AMACOM, New York, 1996.

  This book is easy to understand, with a logical structure. It uses acronyms and other mnemonics to help the reader remember the sequence of tasks involved in project management. The book has a special focus on people skills, with many suggestions on how to gain the cooperation of stakeholders.

- J Frame, *Managing projects in organizations*, Jossey-Bass, San Francisco, 1995.

  This book has become 'the thinking manager's guide to project management', providing a review of the full range of project management issues. It focuses on a wide range of organisational issues, beyond the normal narrow range of project management texts.

- G Reiss, *Project management demystified: Today's tools and techniques*, Routledge, London, 1995.

  As well as explaining the techniques for managing projects, this book covers examples drawn from construction, civil engineering, product launches, publishing, computer hardware and software, scientific projects and aerospace. It offers a sound framework for understanding the concepts of project management.

Note

1. S Cicmil, 'Critical factors of effective project management', *The TQM Magazine*, vol. 9, no. 6, 1997, pp. 390–6.

CHAPTER 16

Leading people
Situational leadership

Situational leadership is effectively the dominant theory behind supervisory-level leadership training around the world. Since its launch by Paul Hersey and Ken Blanchard in 1969, it has rapidly become the de facto standard for supervisory training programs. Whether it is the franchised proprietary version provided by the Blanchard Training juggernaut or one of the many generic versions provided by hundreds of trainers around the world, if you have attended a supervisory training program in the last 20 years, it is highly likely that you will have been trained in the concepts of situational leadership.

The basic idea behind situational leadership is not complicated—adapt your style of leadership to the needs of the person you are supervising. If they are enthusiastic beginners (willing but unable), be highly directive; if, at the other extreme, they are capable and experienced people (willing and able), delegate as much as you can. In between, you may have to deal with the unwilling and unable (persuade and coach them) and the willing but unable (support them). Supervision, therefore, becomes a challenge of understanding the developmental level of those being supervised and then matching the appropriate style of leadership to that developmental level.

There is a sharp contrast between situational leadership theory and the leadership theories that preceded it. Until the launch of situational leadership in 1969 in the *Training and Development Journal*[1], research in leadership theories was mostly about finding the 'one best way' to manage people. For example, one major theory was exemplified by the *Managerial Grid*, a tool invented by Robert Blake and Jane Mouton.[2] The theory was that management style is driven by a trade-off between concern for people and concern for productiveness. Managers who could juggle both of these concerns equally well (a '9–9' style manager in the jargon of the grid) were considered the most effective. This theory was all about the supervisor.

By contrast, situational leadership placed the focus on the person being supervised and made leadership style contingent on the development stage of that person. It clearly made sense to a lot of people and today situational leadership pretty well has the field of supervisory leadership to itself. Situational leadership's claims to being a management powertool seem, therefore, incontrovertible. However, nothing is that simple. We have one very big outstanding question about situational leadership: Does it work? The answer is, at best, 'maybe'. There is actually more research to suggest that it is not effective than there is to suggest that it is. Even after 30 years of research, the jury is still out. Part of the problem is that it is very difficult to study leadership style, either in the field or in the laboratory. There are simply too many variables to control and virtually every study done so far has limitations.

To some extent, none of this matters. Situational leadership theory has such strong 'face validity' (that is, it makes sense to supervisors) that its place as the dominant theory is unlikely to be threatened for a long time. So it is included in this collection of management tools on the basis of its all-pervasiveness, rather than its proven effectiveness.

Background

Most management tools are grounded in at least some theory, however vague and untested. Situational leadership theory (the theory behind the situational leadership tool) was first advocated to an audience of training professionals and this may well be suggestive of its focus. Situational leadership (SL) provided trainers with a seemingly superior basis for training supervisors in leadership skills. For this group of professionals, it had several key advantages:

- SL suggests that effective leadership is a matter of style, not personality. This is important to trainers because style can be taught, whereas personality cannot.
- SL advocates a contingency approach to leadership. That is, the leadership style is adapted to the needs of the situation. This makes sense to trainers because they know from their own experiences that different learners need different approaches. Being a leader is, therefore, not dissimilar to being a trainer.
- Few people are born with the natural ability to modify their supervisory style to meet the needs of the person being supervised. This is important to trainers because it makes trainers necessary. SL has to be learned, which naturally implies that training is required.

So the interests of trainers were more closely matched by SL theory than by any other approach to leadership that had been proposed to that point. Since trainers make all the decisions about what to include in their training programs, it was only a matter of time before SL progressively conquered most supervisory training programs. There may have been a little resistance to paying the fees of trainers franchised by Ken Blanchard. But eventually trainers discovered that SL theory is actually in the public domain and anyone is free to deliver training programs based on it. Most took the opportunity to build the approach into their training programs. (Just don't call it 'Situational Leadership II'—that's a registered trademark belonging to Mr Blanchard.)

Much of the theoretical foundation of SL was provided by Paul Hersey, whose research identified the limitations of the various approaches to leadership development that predominated at the time. Typically, various aspects of leadership behaviour were plotted along a single continuum; for example, from autocratic behaviour to consultative behaviour. The idea was that leaders could have their style plotted along this one dimension. Researchers such as Blake and Mouton (as well as Hersey) soon realised that this was a gross oversimplification. Leadership style involves at least two quite different behavioural aspects: those that relate to the tasks required of the person being supervised and those that relate to the behaviour of the supervisor.

Blake and Mouton were the first to develop a leadership model based on the two axes idea, hence the previously mentioned Managerial Grid. One axis focused on the relationship between the supervisor and the supervised ('concern for people') and the other focused on getting tasks done ('concern for production'). This grid model created five distinct types of leadership:

1. low concern for people/low concern for production
2. low concern for people/high concern for production
3. high concern for people/low concern for production
4. high concern for people/high concern for production
5. middle concern for people/middle concern for production.

Most managers were middling (the fifth type). Blake and Mouton argued that the best leadership style is to have high concern for both. However, further research at the time suggested that it was unlikely that the one leadership style would always bring the best results.[3] For example, most managers can nominate situations in which they have had to be highly directive in relation to tasks in order to get things done. In other situations, they needed to adopt a style that was more considerate of the relationship between themselves and the people they supervise.

On top of this research came the realisation that the Managerial Grid approach focused on the attitudes of the supervisors ('concern'). Attitudes do not always generate behaviours that are aligned with those attitudes. Managers may believe one thing but do something that is entirely unrelated to those beliefs, even though they often don't appreciate the gap (see Chapter 13, Developing self-awareness: Multi-rater (360-degree) feedback).

Hersey and Blanchard pulled all this into focus with the publication of their 'life-cycle' theory of leadership in 1969[4] (they later changed the name of their approach to 'situational leadership'[5]). Their notion that the behaviour of the leader towards the followers should change as the follower 'matures' was drawn from their personal experiences in watching children grow into adults.[6] As the child matures, so it achieves independence. Likewise, as the novice employee matures, so he or she will gain independence. The parent/leader is there to assist the maturing process by providing direction and support. The exact combination of the two should be varied as the child/employee matures. Hersey and Blanchard identified four major stages of the maturing process, with each requiring a different combination of direction and support.

One of the key elements of SL's success and ready acceptance by practitioners is the change of focus from leader attitude to leader behaviour. The earlier models had largely focused on attitudinal dimensions. By focusing on behaviour instead, the task of becoming a situational manager moved from psychotherapy to behavioural training. This behavioural focus is probably the greatest contribution that the theory has made to the practice of management. The leadership debate (at least as it applies to the supervisory level) shifted from personality to action, and it has stayed there ever since. Supervising employees becomes a matter of technique: learn the model ... apply it ... and you will be a more effective supervisor.

Another development was defining the four stages or styles of leadership behaviour more in terms of what the leader does and less in terms of the 'maturity' of the employee (where maturity was meant to indicate the development stage that the employee had reached). The two researchers coined the expressions *telling*, *selling*, *participating* and *delegating* to describe these four styles. They also eventually moved away from the expression 'maturity' because, they suggested, the expression seemed offensive as management began to move away from command-and-control type language.

This change, however, also coincided with the appearance of critical reviews that questioned the substance behind situational leadership theory.[7] These reviews pointed out that the notion of employee maturity is rather vague and possibly contradictory. Hersey and Blanchard never really defined it but it seems to be a combination of motivation and ability. Their four-stage model is not completely convincing in combining the two aspects of motivation and ability. For example, it suggests that the person who is 'motivated but unable' is *less* mature that the person who is 'unmotivated but able'. This seems illogical to many managers.

Hersey and Blanchard went their separate ways in 1979, with each developing a slightly different version of the situational leadership model. Hersey's model is called 'Situational Leadership®' and Blanchard's model is called 'Situational Leadership II®'. Hersey continues to run the Centre for Leadership Studies while Blanchard runs The Ken Blanchard Companies, one of the largest training providers in the world, backed by more than 30 popular business books co-authored by Blanchard. One of these, *The one minute manager*, is possibly the biggest business best-seller of all time.[8]

Both models share the idea of placing focus on the state of readiness of the follower. Both are similar to a learner model where the teacher takes into account the capability of the learners (what they can do) and the motivation of the learners (how willing they are to learn). As such, these models of management and leadership are as sound as any pedagogic strategy. The art lies in making them work in practice.

The tool

The core idea of situational leadership is that supervisors should adapt the style of their leadership to the needs of the employee. This idea fundamentally moved the leadership debate away from attempts to identify a single best leadership style. As a result, it made leadership an interactive process between the leader and the follower. Situational leadership puts the focus as much on the follower as it does on the leader.

The overview that follows draws on both the original Hersey/Blanchard model and the two separate models developed subsequently by each of them.

SL theory proposes that there are two variables that leaders can work with in the supervision process:

- *directive behaviour*—telling people what to do and closely supervising their performance
- *supportive behaviour*—providing support through listening, offering encouragement and facilitating their involvement.

By applying these two variables, four distinct leadership styles emerge:

1. *Directing*—high directive and low supportive behaviour
2. *Coaching*—high directive and high supportive behaviour
3. *Supporting*—low directive and high supportive behaviour
4. *Delegating*—low directive and low supportive behaviour.

The four styles are applied to employees who are in different stages or levels of development. Each development stage derives from the combination of the employee's *competence* and *commitment*. Competence is a function of knowledge and skills, which in turn derive from training and experience. Commitment is a function of confidence and motivation.

The four development stages are *enthusiastic beginner; disillusioned learner; cautious contributor;* and *self-reliant achiever.* These development stages are also referred to, respectively, as D1, D2, D3 and D4. Typically, employees move through these stages in the above order, although it is quite possible for an employee to move backwards. Each of these four stages needs to be matched with the leadership style that is most effective for managing an employee's progress through that stage to the next. The aim is to create as many D4 (self-reliant achiever) employees as possible, thereby enabling the manager to concentrate on delegating.

- D1: *enthusiastic beginner* (low competence and high commitment)

  - Highly motivated but probably not very competent. This is why they need a high level of direction. They need to learn to do their job and gain competence.
  - The manager plays a critical role in directing and if necessary redirecting the employee in order to increase the level of competence.

- D2: *disillusioned learner* (some competence and low commitment)

  - The employee who has started to realise the frustrations of the job and is coming up against its difficulties and complexities.
  - The manager needs to provide additional coaching, but also needs to provide encouragement and to support the employee's efforts to succeed.

- D3: *cautious contributor* (high competence and variable commitment)

  - The employee who has acquired a high degree of competence but is not fully confident to succeed on their own.
  - Such employees need to be supported extensively by being encouraged to make their own decisions but in consultation with the manager. The manager needs to provide encouragement and facilitate courses of action.

- D4: *self-reliant achiever* (high competence and high commitment)

  - The employee who is fully competent and committed. They can work on their own with very little supervision.
  - The manager can delegate tasks with full confidence, knowing that they will be completed well.[9]

The situational leader gives to the employee that which the employee cannot supply themselves at that time, so:

- if *competence* is lacking, then the manager provides direction and guidance, coupled with close follow-up
- if *commitment* is lacking, then the manager provides support and advice to increase the level of commitment

- if both *competence and commitment* are lacking, then the manager provides direction, guidance, support and advice
- if both *competence and commitment* are present, then the manager provides less and less direction, guidance, support and advice.

The process of developing competence and commitment involves five steps:

1. Tell the employee what the task is.
2. Show the employee how to do the task.
3. Let the employee try the task.
4. Observe the employee's performance.
5. Praise the employee's progress.

This approach may need to be taken for each type of task that the employee is required to carry out. Employees may well be a D2 or D3 in some tasks but a D4 in others. The 'situationality' applies to tasks, not to jobs. And for all sorts of reasons, employees may regress to a lower development level for a given task or even all tasks. In that case, the manager adapts their leadership style to match the development level.

Situational leadership emphasises that the process of adapting leadership style to development levels is a collaborative process between the manager and the employee. You can't do situational leadership in secret! Employees need to be aware that they will be managed in accordance with the SL framework. Failure to tell them will most likely lead to confusion and suspicion as to the reasons behind a sudden change in management behaviour. The collaborative approach also creates the opportunity to do formal contracting with the employee about performance goals (see Chapter 11, Managing performance: Goal-setting).

Observations

The conundrum for situational leadership theory is that there is very little research evidence that supports it and quite a bit that does not. And yet it has strong 'face validity' for managers; it simply makes sense as a way to manage people. As one group of researchers put it, 'SLT remains intuitively appealing and empirically contradictory'.[10]

Personally, I find this a bit disturbing. What do we make of a theory (and the tools that it offers) that has little corroborating evidence for its effectiveness? One response from advocates of SL is to ignore the research. Whatever the right response may be, that is not it. So, here is a small sample of recent research into situational leadership theory so that you can judge for yourselves.

- Vecchio, 1987—one of the first major studies of SL theory. It found that: 'SLT was supported most strongly in the condition of low-maturity, where followers require more structuring from their supervisors. Results were less clear with moderately mature subordinates. With high maturity employees, the theory appears to be unable to predict the appropriate leadership style.'[11]

- Goodson and McGee, 1989—found that 'the interaction between leader behavior (initiating structure and consideration) and follower readiness hypothesized by the SLT is not supported by the results'.[12]
- Blank et al., 1990—found that their results 'reveal a lack of support for the basic assumptions that underlie SLT'.[13]
- Norris and Vecchio, 1992—found 'the present study provided little support for predicted mean differences in outcome variables as a function of "matching" on leadership style and subordinate maturity'.[14]
- Cairns et al., 1998—found that their study 'provided very little support for SLT'.[15]

I am hard pressed to nominate any supportive research. In an early study (1982) encouraged by the founders of SL, Hambleton and Gumpert provided supportive findings although their research methodology has been questioned.[16] Hambleton was a colleague of Blanchard and Hersey. Clearly, the research is at best lukewarm in supporting SL.

Admittedly, SL is hard to research. Testing the effectiveness of matching supervisor style to subordinate maturity or readiness will be fraught with methodological difficulties. But the most recent research has found ways around this and has moved out of the laboratory and into the field. As the calibre of research has improved, the findings for SL have become progressively less supportive, except possibly at the lowest level of subordinate readiness. And Blanchard has admitted that few employees these days fall into the category of 'willing but completely unable'. It's a bit of a no-brainer that such employees need lots of direction and lots of support.

One way forward is provided by Reinout de Vries and his colleagues, who have come up with a different way of conceptualising the problem.[17] They suggest that the critical issue is the employee's *need for supervision*; that is:

- Any given employee at any given time has a particular need for supervision.
- The level of this need will be driven by a range of factors including individual characteristics (derived from their personality or personal circumstances), task characteristics (derived from the nature of the task) and organisational characteristics (derived from the nature of the organisation).
- Each of these factors can comprise many distinct characteristics.
- It is the interplay between all these characteristics that determines what an employee requires from their supervisor.

De Vries and colleagues tested this concept by examining five specific characteristics that contribute to the need for supervision: years of service; expertise; hours of contact with the supervisor; level of autonomy; and the skill variety required for the job. Effective leaders seem to be those who vary the 'task directiveness' of their style on the basis of characteristics such as the five tested (although not all were equally strongly related to the need for supervision).

Interestingly, the level of need for supervision did not affect the need for a supportive relationship between the supervisor and the employee. The study found a direct link between a highly supportive relationship between supervisor and employee and job satisfaction. In other words, for effective supervision, a supportive relationship is important at all times. However, the extent of directiveness in relation to the tasks to be carried out by employees should vary with the need for supervision, as judged on individual, task and organisational characteristics that apply in a particular situation. In slogan form, *support them at all times but direct them as needed.*

User's guide

Situational leadership is employee and task specific. It requires that, for any given employee and for any type of task to be carried out by that employee, the manager needs to go through a planning procedure with that employee that will generate a behavioural management strategy. The process is explicit and open, seeking to reach agreement on how the management process will be conducted.

Instructions

How to lead employees situationally

There are four major steps in a 'situational' approach to managing an employee.

1. *Performance planning*

   This step involves a performance conversation between the manager and the employee that focuses on an area of work for which the employee is accountable.

   It primarily involves goal-setting (see Chapter 11, Managing performance: Goal-setting) with a particular emphasis on reaching a common understanding of the standard of performance that is required or expected. This requires clarity about the measures that will be used to evaluate performance and the level of performance that constitutes a satisfactory result.

   The manager's task here is mainly to establish and clarify expectations.

2. *Development diagnosis*

This step also involves a conversation between the manager and the employee, this time focusing on the current development level of the employee.

The aim is to reach agreement on the development level of the employee in relation to the task or area of accountability under consideration. Agreement needs to be reached as to which of the following four categories applies to the employee in relation to the task:

- D1—low competence and high commitment.
- D2—some competence and low commitment.
- D3—high competence and variable commitment.
- D4—high competence and high commitment.

It is likely that agreement can readily be reached on the level of competence. Past performance data can help with this. In addition, the manager can clarify what constitutes high performance by providing examples, or the employee can demonstrate their actual knowledge or skill level. Commitment is a bit more difficult. Many employees are unwilling to indicate the true level of their commitment to a task. Commitment comes from a combination of motivation and confidence. The lack of either can indicate less commitment than is needed for successful task completion.

The manager needs to ask probing questions to determine the actual level of commitment. Past performance data (especially if unsatisfactory levels of performance were achieved) can be used to explore reasons for under-performance. Employees are more likely to admit to a lack of confidence than they are to a lack of motivation. Managers may have to make a judgment based on limited data and ask the employee to confirm their diagnosis. The conversational approach can be helpful in reaching agreement on the employee's attitude toward a particular task.

3. *Matching leadership style*

This appears to work most successfully when conducted as part of a performance conversation.

The employee must understand the range of leadership styles that are available for the manager to adopt.

The manager must facilitate the conversation so that the employee's perception of what is required in the mix of directing and supporting behaviours matches that of the manager.

This presumes a high degree of self-perception on the part of the employee. If this is not present, then the manager may need to take some time to reconcile any differing points of view. In most cases, the leadership style simply derives from the previous step, so it is that earlier part of the conversation that demands a high degree of consensus.

4. *Executing leadership style*

This step is contingent on the performance of the employee. The manager needs to evaluate and monitor performance on a continuous basis.

If performance is acceptable, then the manager can progressively negotiate a less directional role, and eventually less of a supportive role as well.

If performance is not acceptable then, depending on the development stage, the manager increases the level of support and direction. For example, if an employee is not succeeding at development level D3, then the manager needs to adopt a leadership style that is appropriate for D2 (coaching) by providing more direction and maintaining high levels of support.

In the extreme, if the employee regresses to lower developmental levels, the manager may need to commence the contracting process again from the start.

Further reading

Kenneth Blanchard's material is the most readily accessible material on situational leadership. His books, videos and accredited training programs dominate the situational leadership landscape.

* K Blanchard, *Leadership and the one minute manager*, Harper Collins, London, 1986.

Of all Blanchard's books, this is the most directly descriptive of SL. It is a short 'industrial novel', a format which Blanchard made famous. It presents the situational leadership framework very clearly. It also includes Blanchard's *One minute manager* framework for managing people for performance. This is essentially a three-step process of goal setting, praising and reprimanding. In combination, the two frameworks have become the staple of most supervisory training programs around the world.

Notes

1. P Hersey & . Blanchard, 'Life-cycle theory of leadership', *Training and Development Journal*, June 1979 (reprint of 1969 article of the same title).
2. R Blake & J Mouton, *The managerial grid: key orientation for achieving production through people*, Gulf, Houston, 1964.
3. A Korman, 'Consideration, initiating structure, and organizational criteria—a review', *Personnel Psychology*, vol. 19, 1966, pp. 349–61; F Fiedler, *A theory of leadership effectiveness*, McGraw-Hill, New York, 1967.
4. See also P Hersey & K Blanchard, *Management of organizational behavior: Utilizing human resources*, Prentice-Hall, Englewood Cliffs, 1969.

5. See the second edition of P Hersey & K Blanchard, *Management of organizational behavior: Utilizing human resources*, Prentice-Hall, Englewood Cliffs, 1972.
6. P Hersey & K Blanchard, 'Revisiting the life-cycle theory of leadership', *Training and Development*, Jan 1996.
7. Possibly the single most influential review that questioned SL theory was Claude Graeff's 'The situational leadership theory: A critical view', *Academy of Management Review*, vol. 8, no 2, 1983, pp. 285–91.
8. K Blanchard & S Johnson, *The one minute manager*, Fontana, London, 1984.
9. These descriptions are from K Blanchard, 'Recognition and Situational Leadership II', *Emergency Librarian*, vol. 24, issue 4, 1997, p. 38.
10. T Cairns, J Hollenback, R Preziosi & W Snow, 'Technical note: a study of Hersey and Blanchard's situational leadership theory', *Leadership and Organizational Development Journal*, vol. 19, issue 2, 1998, pp. 113–16.
11. R Vecchio, 'Situational leadership theory: An examination of a prescriptive theory,' *Journal of Applied Psychology*, vol. 72, issue 3, 1987, pp. 444–51.
12. J Goodson & G McGee, 'Situational leadership theory: A test of leadership prescriptions', *Group & Organization Management*, vol. 14, issue 4, 1989, pp. 446–61.
13. W Blank, J Weitzel & S Green, 'A test of the situational leadership theory', *Personnel Psychology*, vol. 43, issue 3, 1990, pp. 579–97.
14. W Norris & R Vecchio, 'Situational leadership theory', *Group & Organization Management*, vol. 17, no. 3, 1992, pp. 331–42.
15. Cairns et al., op. cit.
16. R Hambleton & R Gumpert, 'The validity of Hersey and Blanchard's theory of leader effectiveness', *Group & Organization Management*, vol. 7, issue 2, 1982, pp. 225–42.
17. R De Vries, R Roe & T Taillieu, 'Need for supervision—its impact on leadership effectiveness', *The Journal of Applied Behavioral Science*, vol. 34, no 4, 1998, pp. 486–501.

CHAPTER 17

Involving employees
Problem-solving teams

Smart organisations involve their employees in running the business. The idea that staff turn up for work, hang their brains up near the front door, do a day's work and then pick their brains up on the way out, was abandoned long ago by most organisations. But getting the involvement of your people in running and improving the business beyond their normal day-to-day tasks is not always easy. One proven way of getting employee involvement is to ask for their help in solving problems. And employees work most effectively in solving problems when they pool their brainpower in the form of teams.

The practice of using teams to solve problems in organisations has been around for a long time. I doubt if it's possible to identify its exact starting point. Certainly, there have been times when the idea became a little more prominent, such as when these teams were called Quality Circles in the 1980s. The concept reappeared under the title of 'cross-functional teams' a decade later.

Whatever their incarnation, the idea of dedicating a small group of employees to the task of fixing a specific problem seems so obvious that it hardly needs explanation as a management tool. Unfortunately, most organisations have mixed feelings about the mechanism, and many managers find teams to be an unpredictable and unreliable resource. Most managers will readily admit that they have no way of knowing whether a given team will succeed in their task. It's a bit like having a tool that works sometimes, but not always; few managers know what to do to make the tool more reliable.

Initially it seemed that the major benefit from all the attention paid to teams in the late twentieth century was the boost it gave to a host of researchers who focused their attention on what makes teams work. Teams became as well researched as any idea in management could be, and all that research has paid off. We do know what makes some teams effective and others dysfunctional. What is missing is a way to apply this knowledge.

Part of the problem is that the word 'team' means different things to different people. For a start, there are huge differences between permanent function-based teams and temporary problem-solving teams. These differences are significant because what works with one kind of team will not necessarily work with the other kind. For example, short-term problem-solving teams need strong and focused leadership; permanent work teams will work just as well with other models of leadership (for example, where the leadership role is distributed between, or rotated around, the team members).

So it is important to be clear about what kind of team we mean when we talk teams. In this chapter, what is meant by a team is *a temporary group brought together solely for the purpose of solving a particular problem*. Typically, the group is cross-functional—it draws its membership from various functions within the organisation—and it disbands when it has concluded its work. This description excludes permanent teams, project teams, management teams and certainly sports teams of all kinds!

Background

Teams became fashionable again late last century. It wasn't the first time and it probably won't be the last that the team concept was recycled as a management fad. Historically, the team concept (especially as it related to permanent work teams) came from the Work Design/Redesign movement spawned in the UK and Scandinavia in the 1950s.[1]

During the 1940s and 1950s, the ideas of Frederick Taylor[2] were taken to the extreme in factories, offices and mines. As a result, jobs were reduced to their mind-numbingly simplest parts, creating mind-numbed employees. This form of work design often prevented even the simplest forms of human cooperation and interaction. The introduction of team-based forms of work was a backlash against these 'unsocial' forms.

Japanese industry had always used groups as a work structure and this approach evolved to include the formation of formal teams with a problem-resolution or improvement focus. Such teams were known as *Quality Circles*.[3] Along with many other elements that comprised the Japanese way of creating high quality products (such as TQM, kanban and kaizen) Quality Circles were introduced into Anglo-American companies. Unfortunately, the workforce was not very receptive to this highly formalised approach to teamwork and so the concept usually failed. Superimposing ways of working derived from one culture on to other cultures is rarely effective. And so we taught a generation of managers that Quality Circles don't work.

However, the persistence of some organisations with the concept of team-based ways of working (and their successes in terms of business outcomes) ensured that from time to time the idea re-emerged. For example, in 1993 Katzenbach and Smith's influential book, *The Wisdom of Teams*, re-ignited significant management interest in the idea of teams.[4]

Of course, it is difficult *not* to be in favor of teams. Teams (and their close cousin, 'teamwork') sound like the kind of thing you ought to support. But just because it sounds good is not enough reason to support a management concept.

Part of the problem with the team concept is that it is closely associated with success and winning in sport. Again, the logic is unclear because in every sporting competition there are inevitably more losers than winners! And yet managers keep drawing on sporting analogies to explain or justify their support for the concept of teams. But sporting teams are very different from the teams found in organisations. A sporting team spend most of their time practising, not performing; the members are all volunteers (they want to be there) and they typically bring exceptional levels of skill—at least when compared to the spectators. Further, they perform a very limited range of tasks very repetitively (although often superbly) and they are involved in activities that are very exciting for both the players and spectators. None of this applies to most teams in organisations, although occasionally some of these characteristics may relate to work teams. What sporting teams do rely on is tremendous motivation and drive.

This comparison with sporting teams steers management thinking towards motivation, desire to succeed, and highly practised forms of cooperation and teamwork. In fact, these are not the most critical aspects of team functioning in organisations. To be precise, they are largely irrelevant. Teams in organisations can be very successful without being highly motivated, without having a burning desire to succeed and without extensive teamwork.

All of this gets even more confusing when we forget to define what type of team we're talking about. As stated earlier, in this chapter we're talking about problem-solving teams. Their key characteristics are that they:

- are temporary and short-term
- are focused on a problem
- meet occasionally for short periods of time
- are (typically) cross-functional
- comprise only a few members with relevant skills.

To be effective, problem-solving teams need to be able to:

- work cooperatively almost immediately (because they have a short lifespan)

- understand what the problem is (because they don't have time to work out what the problem is)
- work fast in short bursts (because they only meet occasionally)
- recognise the expertise within the team (because they need to work with each other straight away).

All of this is difficult to put in place quickly. There is no time for exercises or practice that will take such teams from the 'forming' stage to the 'performing' stage of team development.[5] There is no time to put together a comprehensive 'team mission'. There is no time to sort out interpersonal relationships. Problem-solving teams are expected to get on with things and fix the problem.

For this reason, much of the team formation stuff that is relevant to permanent work teams or management teams is not relevant to problem-solving teams. What is needed is strong leadership that focuses on team processes, access to problem-solving expertise on a just-in-time basis, and rigorous adherence to a working discipline. The approach outlined below will deliver these requirements. In turn, teams constructed in this way will deliver results.

The tool

The use of problem-solving teams seems to work best if the setting-up process is considered as a series of steps, some undertaken by management, some by the team and some together:

- *Step 1:* Define the problem and clarify expectations.
- *Step 2:* Establish the team.
- *Step 3:* Support the team.
- *Step 4:* Review and celebrate.

Define the problem and clarify expectations

Problem-solving teams are set up to do just that; solve problems. Although this is stating the obvious, it does in fact point to the first common failure in setting up such teams—lack of clarity about the problem to be solved. This occurs mainly because no-one bothers to *write* down the problem. Teams are often given only verbal instructions about the issue they are to deal with. And this leads to confusion, which leads to teams that fail, which leads to managers losing confidence in the team mechanism.

So, the first step in setting-up teams for success is to provide the team with a written problem statement. This will achieve two quite separate things: it will describe a situation or an issue; and it will tell the team what is expected of them in relation to that situation.

- The *issue statement* describes the situation or issue. I prefer this language because statements about the 'problem' (as opposed to the 'issue') often contain assumptions about what the solution is. For example, one team I know were asked by their manager to 'solve the problem with inferior lacquer that is causing peeling' when in reality the peeling was not caused by the lacquer but by something else altogether. The language misled the team for some time before they started to look at the real issue: a peeling problem, not a lacquer quality problem.

   Statements about an issue or a situation identify what the team have to look at. The more descriptive the statements, the more useful they are in guiding a team's actions. The aim is to describe the state of affairs and then let the team do the rest. In the example above, the team should have been asked to 'investigate the cause of peeling and recommend solutions'.

- The *target statement* tells the team what is expected of them. This defines what management is expecting from the team. The most common confusion here is between a target that involves *investigation and reporting* back to management, and a target that involves *fixing the problem*. Confusing the two can lead to conflict about what the team have done. ('What do you mean, you've changed the operating procedures; I just wanted you to report on how we could improve them!')

Table 17.1 describes what is required for these statements to be effective.

Table 17.1 Issue and target statements

Issue statement	Target statement
• is descriptive	• clarifies the direction for action
• clarifies what the issue is about	• includes data to explain the extent of the issue
• should not make assumptions about the solution	• is realistic about what is to be achieved
• is short and simple	• includes any constraints and timelines
	• clarifies whether the team are to 'fix' or 'recommend'

For example, if a team is set up to look at how to improve the reliability of delivery times of a product or a service to a customer, then the issue statement might say something like:

Almost 24% of all our deliveries to customers in the last six months have been late. We have received a number of complaints from customers about this and we need to improve our delivery performance.

The target statement might then say something like:

Investigate the causes of delays in delivery and recommend (within 30 days) options for action that will eliminate 80% of these delays.

Establish the team

Getting a team going involves a whole series of small but important decisions. These decisions don't necessarily take a long time but, because there are quite a few, it is easy to overlook some. This can create problems because it is the small things that matter with teams (it's a bit similar to families).

Here are some of the mini-steps that need to be taken to get a team off to a flying start:

1. Select members for balance and effectiveness:

   - decide the number of members needed
   - decide criteria for membership
   - check availability of proposed members
   - ensure people selected can work together
   - check that the skills represented are appropriate to the project.

2. Ensure the team understand what they are being asked to do:

   - use the issue and target statements to clarify what the team are being asked to do
   - ask the team to discuss the statements and check for common understanding
   - ensure that constraints, boundaries and limits are understood (for example, time limits and authorities to act)
   - check the resources that the team will need to do their work
   - identify and involve stakeholders who have an interest
   - reach agreement on the first steps.

3. Secure adequate resources for the team:

   - define the resources needed (budget, training, time, access to expertise, etc.)
   - sell the work of the team to key stakeholders
   - ensure the resources are made available.

If you attend to the items in this checklist, the team is much more likely to be successful. Omit these steps, and you can expect the team to run into problems.

Support the team

Once it has been established, some managers expect the team just to get on with it. Unfortunately, this approach tends not to work. It is precisely when the team are ready to get going that they need the most support, which should come in two forms—guidance on how to proceed and support when required.

Guidance on how to proceed

A team won't necessarily know how to proceed in solving a problem. Further, there may be different views within the team on the best way to proceed. There is a risk with both of these possibilities that the team won't get going at all! This can be avoided by giving the team some simple guidelines:

1. Decide how the team will do their work.
2. Gather data and analyse it.
3. Keep all meetings short (no longer than 90 minutes).
4. Always set an agenda for meetings and take minutes.
5. Keep checking the target statement to make sure you stay on track.
6. If you get stuck, ask for help.
7. If you're not getting anywhere after three or four meetings, ask for more help.

There are many different versions of this set of rules. The exact detail does not matter and it can be changed and added to over time. The important thing is that there is a set of rules and that the team stick to them.

Possibly the most significant rule is the one relating to gathering and analysing data. It is tempting to suggest that every team should start their problem-solving activities with data gathering and data analysis. Certainly, if the team do not know where to start, always recommend this step (see the User's guide section of this chapter for more detail).

Support when required

Teams will need help, as the rules above predict. When they do, someone needs to step in and help the team with their process, or possibly provide some specialist expertise (for example, in problem-solving techniques). Organisations usually do have people available who have experience in assisting teams in their work. If such facilitation support is not available, train some people in these skills. It's not a full-time job (although some organisations do have full-time specialists available for such roles) and training will give the facilitator valuable skills that will be useful elsewhere.

Not all teams need a facilitator but if they do need an external resource in the form of a facilitator, a manager can play this role and provide support when the team need it. With the best teams, facilitators are never needed. But facilitation support can make the difference between an average team succeeding or failing.

Review and celebrate

Management needs to keep an eye on the teams it sets up. Washing your hands of all responsibilities is simply abandoning the fundamental management responsibility of managing.

Reviewing team progress doesn't necessarily involve a great deal of work. Simply attending the occasional team meeting or asking a team member about progress is enough. Further, such inquiries demonstrate an interest in the work of the team that will help motivate the team to succeed.

When the team do report back on their achievements, the management role becomes one of expressing appreciation for the work done by the team. This is not about rewarding the team (and especially not about financial rewards) but about saying 'thank you'.

One way of emphasising that the work of the team mattered and is appreciated is to arrange a formal opportunity for the team to report back to a senior group of managers. Although many in the team will profess that such a formal presentation is a bit scary, the team actually will appreciate the occasion!

Observations

Problem-solving teams are still under-utilised by organisations and under-managed by managers. On the one hand, teams seem such a simple device for solving problems. On the other, this apparent simplicity leads to complacency about just what management has to do to set teams up for success.

By now, we do know what makes teams tick. The research into team behavior over the last 20 years has been extensive and informative. We know the success factors for teams. The next step is for managers to start applying some of these findings to ensure that the teams they set up are successful.

An analogy can be drawn with the development of assembly-line technology. When this mechanism for getting better performance in the product assembly process was first put in place, performance was dismal. Lines ran slowly and broke down often, workers ran out of components, and the quality of the product was poor. But over a period of 70 years or more, production specialists worked hard to remove as many variables as possible from the assembly line, slowly improving its performance. They used specialist techniques such as Statistical Process Control to bring assembly-line production to the point where we have almost perfect predictability and almost zero variance in the key indicators used to measure assembly-line performance.

Similarly, we currently have a situation where problem-solving teams are a relatively unreliable mechanism for getting a result (a problem solved). We need to apply our understanding of team functioning to progressively remove all the variables in the team process. We know what those variables are and we know how to control most of them. It requires action by managers (assembly lines did not improve themselves!) to bring those variables under control.

Most of the variables that impact on team performance fall into two broad groups. The first group relates to *team formation issues* and includes some of the issues mentioned earlier, such as: unclear or ambiguous problem statements; inappropriate team membership; and lack of a team process. We have solutions to each of these and for managers it is little more than a checklist with items to be ticked off as they are actioned.

The second group of variables relates to *team support*. Teams are fragile entities at the best of times. They involve all the human foibles that appear whenever there is a social setting. We know that one effective way for handling these foibles is to allocate the job of monitoring and supporting the human side of the team to a specialist—the facilitator. Facilitated teams function more effectively. If you want an effective team, give them access when they need it to facilitation support.

Management action in relation to these two groups of issues will remove most of the variables that hold teams back from improved performance. It can be used to turn teams into a reliable and predictable mechanism for solving problems.

User's guide

Once the team have been set up in accordance with the procedures already outlined, they are ready to start their work. There are two key areas where the manager can add value to the team problem-solving process: initial data-gathering and team processes. The first intervention is about getting the team started, and the second is about keeping the team on track.

Teams are often unsure of *where* to start, especially if they are working on a chronic and complex problem. There is a simple answer to this question and it is always the same, no matter what the problem is: *gather data and then analyse it*. In fact, teams that do not start with this step need to have a very good reason for not doing so.

The side benefit of always starting with data-gathering and analysis is that it is a task that is relatively easy to do. Once the team understand the problem and what they are expected to do about it (courtesy of the issue and target statements), it is a straightforward step to gather background information about the issue and examine what's in front of them. Time and again, this step will show that preconceptions about what the problem is, or what the best solution will be, are wrong. Jointly gathering data brings a clear focus on the issue without needing to have lengthy debates. You just do it.

Keeping the team on track involves supporting the team in the same way that a facilitator might do. That is, the manager focuses on the process while the team focus on the content. Although there is a wide variety of issues that can trip up a team, a little facilitation attention will prevent most of these arising.

Instructions

How to gather and analyse data

Data-gathering needs to be kept simple. The emphasis is on data—not on opinions. Usually, with most problem situations, data is already available to a greater or lesser extent. Most problems have a history. Whether the problem relates to machine breakdown, service failures, delivery mistakes, or just about anything else, it is likely that there is some data about that situation somewhere. The challenge will be to find it.

Sometimes, extra data has to be collected. Using the issue statement as a starting point, it is a simple matter to create a data collection sheet. If, for example, the problem is late delivery of products to customers, a data collection sheet can be devised that records every incident of late delivery along with all pertinent facts: customer name; delivery address; delivery method; product or service; date of delivery; rostered and actual time of delivery. This is enough to do a 'first cut' analysis that will suggest where the team have to look for possible causes of the problem.

There is one outstanding technique for doing data analysis and that is *Pareto analysis* (see Chapter 10, Solving problems: Pareto analysis, for more detail). Briefly, the steps involved are:

1. *Create a histogram chart using any two variables.*

   • Order the bars from highest frequency to lowest frequency. For example, for the late delivery of products to customers, the two variables might be customers and late delivery (see the sample in Figure 17.1).

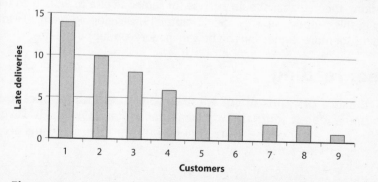

Figure 17.1 Pareto analysis: Customers by late delivery

2. *Using this chart, start to analyse the data.*

For example, where does the problem occur most frequently? With customers 1 and 2, maybe 3? Clearly, a small number of customers represent the bulk of the late deliveries. This is a typical 'Pareto' type result.

3. *Create additional Pareto charts as required.*

For example, do a chart for each of the targeted customers, possibly focusing on other variables such as the time of delivery or the means of delivery as this may provide further valuable information.

Some of the analysis will suggest areas for further investigation. Sometimes, additional and more structured analysis has to be undertaken to uncover the fundamental cause or causes of a problem. Techniques such as *Root cause analysis* (also known as Fishbone or Ishikawa diagrams), *Flowcharting* or *Process mapping* (see Chapter 9, Improving processes: Process mapping and management) may be needed to handle complex situations where the root cause is either difficult to detect or where there are multiple causes interacting with each other to create complexity.[6]

How to keep the team on track

The manager as facilitator can add value to the team in a number of ways:

- teach the team the rules they must follow
- encourage and support the team
- monitor progress and outcomes
- smooth the way for the team (for example, acquire the resources the team will need)
- advise on problem-solving tools and techniques
- keep the team focused on the target
- help develop commitment and buy-in of team members.

It may be appropriate for someone else to take on the role of facilitator. Sometimes, the relationship between the manager and the team is such that having the manager in the facilitator role is simply not feasible. In such situations, the manager should arrange for someone else to work with the team in this support capacity. (See Chapter 19, Developing teams: Team-building, for more suggestions on how managers can support teams.)

Further reading

The aficionados of teams might want to consult erudite publications such as the academic journal *Team Performance Management*. However, for most of us, some of the more general publications on teams are a little more accessible and useful.

- K Fisher, S Rayner & W Belgard, *Tips for teams*, McGraw-Hill, New York, 1995.

This is one of the very best general publications on the subject by Kimball Fisher and his colleagues, from the consulting group Belgard Fisher Rayner. This book is packed with ideas about how to set up teams for success and keep them running. It's like a toolbox for team problems, and it's easy to dip into to solve specific team issues.

- R Weaver & J Farrell, *Managers as facilitator*, Berrett-Koehler, San Francisco, 1999.

For a guide to the role of facilitator in the context of daily organisational life, there is no better book in my view. It's the kind of book that you (well, me anyway!) wish you'd written. The subtitle ('A practical guide to getting work done in a changing workplace') sums up its ambitions and the book goes a long way to achieving what it sets out to do. It should be compulsory reading for every manager who has ever complained that their organisation is not functioning as well as it should.

- M Brassard & D Ritter, *The memory jogger: A pocket guide of tools for continuous improvement and effective planning*, GOAL/QPC, Salem, 1994.

There are many publications on problem-solving techniques. This handy pocket-sized publication by the non-profit organisation, GOAL/QPC, is still one of the best.

Notes

1. For one overview, see M Weisbord, *Productive workplaces*, Jossey-Bass, San Francisco, 1987.
2. See F Taylor, *Principles of scientific management*, Dover Publication, New York, 1998.
3. Quality Circles were first advocated by Dr Kaoro Ishikawa, and written up in many of his books (such as K Ishikawa, *A guide to quality control*, Asian Productivity Organization, Tokyo, 1971). Some have suggested the technique was actually brought to Japan by the US armed forces in the 1940s.
4. J Katzenbach & D Smith, *The wisdom of teams*, Harvard Business School Press, Boston, 1993.
5. Bruce Tuckman developed a well-known model for team development based on four stages, known as forming, storming, norming and performing. See B Tuckman, 'Developmental sequence in small groups', *Psychological Bulletin*, vol. 63, 1995, pp. 384–99.
6. For a handy reference guide to problem-solving tools, try M Brassard & D Ritter, *The memory jogger: A pocket guide of tools for continuous improvement and effective planning*, GOAL/QPC, Salem, 1994.

CHAPTER 18

Developing people
Coaching

Coaching is the technique that managers have turned to in response to the changing nature of the modern workplace. Today, organisations want employees to be capable, flexible and self-managing. Most employees are none of these things when they first join an organisation so it has become imperative that managers acquire the skills that can turn raw potential into valuable human assets. Coaching seems to have become the universally recognised approach for tackling that challenge. However, it does require a shift in management style of seismic proportions—from a directive to a *facilitative* style.

Many organisations are now encouraging this change and for a number of them it is much more than just the latest fad. In fact, the move towards a facilitative style of management may well turn out to be the most significant change in management for many decades. One test of this assertion is to check the management jobs in the 'positions vacant' columns in daily newspapers. The language in the vast majority of these advertisements is the language of coaching. Of course, organisations still want managers who are technically competent in their jobs but they also want managers who can bring out the best in other people. The reality of this change is made apparent by examining the language that was used to describe the requirements for those same jobs 20 or 30 years ago. People management skills then were about control and discipline. Today, the language is about developing and coaching people.

Coaching is the most popular technique for bringing out the best in people. It has easily moved across from the sporting field to the playing fields of business, mainly because the analogies seem so close. Coaches in sport are there to bring out the best in their athletes. Successful coaches are revered almost as much as the individuals or the teams that they coach. Sports performance is easily monitored and widely reported in the media. Some sports coaches have even made the transition from sport to business, and become strong advocates of the coaching role.

However, as is often the case when we borrow from another field of enterprise, few allowances have been made for the differences between sport and business. More worryingly, coaching as a process is still ill-defined and poorly specified. It is easy to be in favour of the coaching approach because it sounds so good and most people think they know what is meant by it. But when it comes to specifying the fine details of what to do and not to do, most managers will admit that they make it up as they go along.

If we are going to rely on coaching as the key technique for growing the next generation that will run our business enterprises, maybe we are obliged to make it a little clearer what the process actually entails.

Background

As coaching has become the preferred technique for managers interested in developing the capabilities of their staff, two separate sources of advice have come to the aid of managers:

- the *prescriptive tradition* of consultants and trainers who develop models based on their own experience and advocate them with considerable passion to their clients
- the *empirical tradition* of academics and researchers who use rigorous research methods to uncover what actually works and formulate theories and models based on their findings.

Coaching has been somewhat overwhelmed by the first tradition and distinctly under-whelmed by the second. Research-based approaches are still catching up with the practices employed extensively in industry. Research is always slow and takes time, whereas consultants can move like greased lightening with a new model when they spot a commercial opportunity. All of which means that, as research findings have started to emerge from those much-maligned ivory towers, it is only now that empirically-based approaches to coaching are coming to the fore. No doubt industry practice will slowly catch up.

Coaching is one of those practices that most people claim to understand without necessarily being able to define it. It is often defined by contrasting it with other managerial practices such as training, counselling and mentoring.

- *Training* is different from coaching in that training starts with a pre-defined input: the training content or curriculum. The task for the trainers is to ensure that this pre-defined content is 'brought across' to the learner so that, on completion of the training, the learner knows things or knows how to do things.

By contrast, coaching is not pre-defined. It is open-ended because it starts with the needs of the learner, not with a prescribed curriculum. Coaching also works over a longer timeframe than training, and many see it as an ongoing process with no 'finish line'. Coaching is almost always one-on-one although training is more often one-on-many.

- *Counselling* (however defined) in the workplace can range from giving advice on performance to admonishing poor performance. It generally has a corrective purpose, and is predominantly directive. It assumes that the learner has somehow strayed from the correct path. Counselling focuses on outcomes such as the behaviours used by the employee and the results achieved.

    By contrast, coaching focuses on the processes used to get those outcomes. Coaching focuses on the capabilities of the employee and how to strengthen those. It assumes that the employee is essentially a learner interested in developing their capabilities.

- *Mentoring* is also different from coaching, although possibly closer to it than either training or counselling. Mentoring typically involves a long-term relationship that is outside the usual boss–employee relationship. It tends to have a career or personal development focus rather than a job focus, although some mentoring relationships go well beyond this. In most mentoring arrangements, the relationship is voluntary, which is not typically the case with coaching. Mentoring implies guidance from an experienced person, often much older than the person being mentored, although peer mentoring also happens.

    By contrast, coaching is more focused on how the person being coached is performing right now. It concentrates on enhancing current capability. Usually, the person being coached does not have a choice about who their coach will be—most often it is their immediate manager.

The type of coaching discussed in this chapter needs to be distinguished from 'business coaching' (also called 'executive coaching'), which is a recent and rather worrying development. Business coaching is a management fad that is currently raging through the business world. (You can tell a management fad by a special marker; it starts to be marketed on a *franchised* basis: 'You too can earn $2000 per day coaching others; only a small investment needed; no qualifications required'.) Business coaching involves an external consultant or adviser working with a manager to improve some aspect of their performance. It is often used as a corrective process in which the flawed manager is somehow 'fixed up'. This type of coaching relationship is, as often as not, imposed on the manager by their own manager, sometimes as a last resort to change undesirable managerial behaviour.

Business coaching is possibly the fastest growing sub-practice of consulting. One estimate suggests that in the US there were 2000 business coaches in 1996, 10 000 in 2002; a figure projected to reach 50 000 in 2007.[1] Already, we are seeing warnings about the negative and even destructive impact of much of this activity.[2] This rapidly growing field is open to anyone who wants to hang out a shingle as 'coach', with many of its practitioners drawn from fields of enterprise other than business and most having few qualifications in any relevant professional areas. In particular, many come from a sports background. Putting senior managers or even whole organisations in the hands of such 'specialists' is a bit like letting the company tea lady design the new computer system—it might work but I doubt it very much. (Apologies to all tea ladies—I do respect that rapidly vanishing breed for their superior motivational and counselling skills.)

Coaching as a managerial practice (and as distinguished from training, mentoring, counselling and business coaching) is a key technique for achieving the level and type of employee capability now demanded by organisations. In many ways, it is an ongoing style of management rather than a technique that is applied intermittently, and it gets results. The approach is related to the situational leadership process (see Chapter 16, Leading people: Situational leadership) but it is less task-focused and works over a longer timeframe.

Some organisations are now relying on coaching to transform them into what are known as 'learning organisations'. Peter Senge in his book, *The fifth discipline*, describes a learning organisation as 'a place where people continually expand their capacity to create results they truly desire, where new and expansive patterns of thinking are nurtured, where collective aspiration is set free and where people are continually learning how to learn'.[3]

Creating a learning organisation is no simple task, but plenty of organisations see sufficient benefit in the concept to devote considerable resources to it. The idea of a learning organisation is almost predicated on managers taking a coaching approach. Although the exact role of the leadership within a learning organisation is still being debated[4], there is little doubt that the coaching role is a key one. It is generally assumed that the role revolves around the facilitation of learning.

Managers can help create a learning culture if they use a facilitative managerial style that encourages employees to learn and to act on their learning. Coaching skills are the closest we have to a skill set that encourages such a facilitative style.

The tool

Although many acknowledge the virtues of coaching, as with many other management tools and techniques, few can provide a working definition or description of it. Coaching is one of those activities that is taken for granted by many. We tend to assume that everyone knows what it involves. It is only when we compare managerial behaviours that we discover that what some describe as coaching behaviour, others describe completely differently. On top of that, we have the common problem of managers believing that they are engaging in one kind of behaviour (for example, coaching) but actually behaving quite differently (for example, directing).[5]

To break through all this vagueness and lack of clarity, we need a clear working description of what is involved when a manager engages in coaching behaviour. This will enable us to evaluate the extent to which managers do actually engage in this type of behaviour and then train them to do it more effectively. Without such a description, we will make little progress on either front.

Recent research is starting to piece together a reasonably accurate picture of what is involved in coaching. This in turn will lead to the development of accurate models that will assist in evaluating and training managers objectively. Some of this research is at odds with the more popular models that have been proposed without the benefit of empirical research.

The research is in its early stages but it provides sufficient detail to build at least a picture of the coaching process. This in turn enables us to operationalise the approach. The description of coaching that is outlined below may be fine-tuned over time with further research, but for now at least it has a basis in fact rather than in mere belief.[6]

Coaching behaviour involves *empowering employees* and *facilitating their learning*. This means managers undertaking specific managerial behaviours that encourage employees to think for themselves and to take action based on that thinking. This behaviour is different from other behaviours that relate to the role of manager.

Coaching behaviours fall into two types: empowering behaviour and facilitating behaviour.

Empowering behaviour involves:

- framing questions in such a way as to encourage employees to think through issues
- being a resource for removing obstacles
- transferring ownership to employees
- holding back from providing answers.

Facilitating learning involves:

- providing feedback to employees
- asking for feedback from employees
- talking issues through collectively
- setting expectations
- promoting a learning approach to issues

- stepping in to others' positions in order to learn
- shifting employees' perspectives and opinions
- offering analogies, scenarios and examples
- engaging with others to encourage learning.

The research shows that managers, employees and observers consider these behaviours to comprise the coaching role. Managers who are considered good coaches do these things often with their employees. Some managers use these behaviours naturally; others have learnt to adopt these behaviours over time.

Empowering behaviour encourages employees to take more personal responsibility for their actions and decisions. The first two empowering behaviours, *question framing* and *removing obstacles,* are the most important ones for achieving this objective. Managers who employ these behaviours are helping employees to become self-reliant and independent.

For *question framing*, managers ask questions of their employees such as:

- What do you think?
- Why would it be different?
- How would this work?
- What would this achieve?
- What are the implications?

To *remove obstacles*, coaching managers provide information and other resources that will enable others to do their jobs. This involves using managerial experience to judge where resource support is needed, and then providing it.

The other two empowering behaviours, although less frequently exercised, are still important:

Transferring ownership means holding others accountable for their work and not accepting accountability back when the going gets tough; the manager can offer to help but doesn't do the job for them.

Holding back involves not providing the answer even when the answer is known or believed to be known by the manager. These empowering behaviours have been observed independently as having a powerful impact on the development of capability in employees.[7]

The facilitative behaviours are more directly associated with learning and growth. These managerial behaviours encourage others to develop new insights, perspectives and understanding. Each of these behaviours involves taking specific action or taking a specific approach to a learning situation. Although some of these behaviours have been built into traditional descriptions of the coaching role in a general way, the research has clarified that there are several different versions of these behaviours that achieve different outcomes.

Feedback traditionally has been considered part of the coaching role. However, the research suggests that there are at least three different types of feedback:

- observational (based on what the coach observed)
- reflective (based on the coach encouraging the other person to make their own assessment)
- third-party (based on the coach obtaining feedback from third parties, which is then provided to the person being coached).

The other behaviours all involve specific coaching actions.

- *soliciting feedback*—asking questions to get feedback from employees on progress with tasks
- *talking issues through*—using discussion to enhance employees' understanding of situations and expanding their knowledge about those situations
- *setting expectations*—ensuring that employees know what is expected of them in terms of performance, but also ensuring understanding as to why those outcomes are important and how they fit into the bigger picture
- *promoting a learning environment*—creating and encouraging opportunities for employees to learn, reflect on that learning, and translate those learnings into systematic ways of doing things
- *stepping in to others' positions in order to learn*—encouraging employees to understand other points of view in order to appreciate different perspectives
- *shifting employees' perspectives and opinions*—arranging new experiences that are designed to create new and multiple perspectives
- *offering analogies, scenarios and examples*—relaying personal events and experiences, as well as the stories of others, in order to encourage insight and understanding
- *engaging with others to encourage learning*—suggesting third parties to communicate with in order to hear and appreciate other views and opinions.

Taken together, these behaviours constitute the most detailed description that has yet been provided to describe the coaching process. It goes far beyond the traditional models that rely on broad principles rather than specific actions.[8] Managers coach when they do these things.

Observations

We do not know how to teach managers to become coaches. Although research is starting to suggest some worthwhile approaches to the coaching process, we seem a long way off any reliable techniques that we can use to turn managers into coaches. This means that we are left with the last resort of management: making it up as we go along.

In fact, this is not as bad as it sounds as long as we don't expect complete reliability and accuracy in selecting and training coaches. For example, many senior managers have a good feel for the management styles of other managers—possibly more so than for their own styles! Exercising that judgment to identify those managers who have the potential to become more of a coach and less of a taskmaster can be a practical way of finding potential coaching talent. Another approach is to ask managers to self-select. That is, encourage managers to volunteer to participate in a coaching program.

Training managers in coaching skills is a bit more complicated. Most coaching skills training programs actually teach training skills. This is probably because trainers know a lot about training so that is what they put into their programs. But changing the language does not turn a training skills program into a coaching skills program. Many of these programs also assume that coaching equates to one-on-one training, which it does not. However, it won't hurt for managers to learn some training skills. It's just that they need to learn a little more about coaching as well. Few programs do that well.

One short description of coaching is *the facilitation of other people's learning*. This means that coaches are really learning facilitators.[9] Employees seem to have an uncanny insight into which managers have the capacity to work in this way with staff. So, one way to select managers with coaching potential is to ask employees. This can be done as part of other surveying techniques, such as 360-degree feedback (see Chapter 13, Developing self-awareness: Multi-rater (360-degree) feedback) or in some other structured way. One organisation I work with simply asks all employees to nominate managers whom they consider to be good coaches; these are then encouraged to become coaches and offered further training in coaching skills.

In identifying managers with high potential for a coaching role, the most critical issue is the beliefs of those managers. Three different sets of beliefs set coaches apart from others:

- their beliefs about the role of the coach
- their beliefs about the learning process
- their beliefs about learners.

Each of these can be assessed by the descriptions that good coaches use about themselves. For example, good coaches describe their role as being about the facilitation of learning and development, and describe their skills as being about how they facilitate learning. They talk about learning being important and that they care about helping others to learn. They describe the learning process as involving trust; that it has to be integrated with work; and that learners need to learn for themselves. They believe that learners want to learn, and that it is important for them to learn.[10] Managers who talk in this way are obvious candidates for coaching roles.

User's guide

Although coaching is a management style rather than a one-off technique, it nevertheless can be approached as a sequence of steps that involves the coach and the person being coached. Repeated iterations of the sequence will encourage the coach to internalise the processes being deployed until they become second nature. Over time, the formalities of the process will become less important and the decisions about how to deal with a particular coaching situation will become more intuitive.[11]

Instructions

Using a coaching sequence

1. *Discuss the job requirements with the employee.*

   - Convey understanding of the context of the job (vision, mission, values, strategies, key results areas, performance objectives).
   - Agree on the performance parameters of the job itself.
   - Discuss the specific development needs of the employee.
   - Set and detail specific performance requirements.
   - Agree on an area of development focus.

2. *Prompt the employee to visualise success in a difficult performance parameter of the job.*

   - Ask the employee to imagine a scenario in which the success has been realised and to describe that scenario in some detail.
   - Ask the employee to detail the actions he or she took to achieve the scenario.
   - Discuss any challenging aspects of the actions suggested by the employee.
   - Agree on first steps that need to be taken by the employee.

3. *Review progress with the employee.*

   - Generate feedback on what has been achieved (what the coach observed; what the employee experienced; what others saw).
   - Talk through issues that arose during the actions taken by the employee.
   - Draw out the learning that the employee has gained from the experience to date.
   - Ask the employee to consider what else needs to happen.
   - If necessary, create specific learning opportunities that will assist the employee to take any action that arises from this process.
   - If necessary (for example, if the employee is not meeting requirements) provide support to the employee by removing obstacles and offering resources.

4. *Review performance upon completion.*

- Agree what happened and what was achieved.
- Provide observational feedback and seek reflective feedback from the employee.
- Seek third-party feedback.
- Discuss how the performance challenge could have been tackled differently.
- Ask the employee to draw out specific learning achieved through the actions taken.
- Ask the employee to nominate the development needs made apparent through the actions taken.

In executing the sequence, coaches should consider the following principles:

- Coaching is always about encouraging learning.
- Learning needs always come from the employee.
- Learning is always best achieved through doing and reflecting on what was done.
- The coach always has to earn the trust and respect of the employee.
- Actions that lead to learning always require a performance focus.
- Learning actions always involve specific behaviours.
- Learning is always invisible and the coach can only find out whether it is happening by hearing the learner reflect on their experiences.
- Learning always happens at the edge of our comfort zone.
- Coaching is never about the coach and always about the employee.
- There are always multiple ways of doing things and there is never one best way.

Further reading

- D Peterson & M Hicks, *Leader as coach: Strategies for coaching & developing others*, Personnel Decisions International, Minneapolis, 1996.

One of the better books on coaching. It is entirely practical but rises above the usual fatuous 'how to coach in one minute' style of book. The book focuses on specific practices which can be deployed by managers in the coaching process. The authors focus on five different coaching strategies, each explained in action steps. It is based on an approach to developing coaches in the workplace that at least has the benefit of many years development in the field. It fits neatly with some of the emerging research and operationalises many of the behaviours described in this chapter.

Notes

1. S Berglas, 'The very real dangers of executive coaching', *Harvard Business Review*, vol. 80, issue 6, June 2002, pp. 86–91.
2. D Noer, 'When it doesn't work: The big three derailment factors in a coaching relationship', Noer Consulting, available at www.noerconsulting.com
3. P Senge, *The fifth discipline*, Doubleday, New York, 1994.
4. Y Altman & P Iles, 'Learning, leadership, teams: corporate learning and organisational change, *The Journal of Management Development*, vol. 17, no. 1, 1998, pp. 44–55.
5. C Argyris & D Schon, *Organizational Learning II*, Addison-Wesley, Reading, 1996.
6. The outline provided here is based on A Ellinger & R Bostrom, 'Managerial coaching behaviors in learning organizations', *The Journal of Management Development*, vol. 18, no. 9, 1999, pp. 752–71.
7. C Orth, H Wilkinson & R Benfari, 'The manager's role as coach and mentor', *Organizational Dynamics*, vol. 15, no. 4, 1987, pp. 56–74.
8. For one typical example see T Barry, 'How to be a good coach', *Management Development Review*, vol. 7, no. 4, 1994, pp. 24–6.
9. A Ellinger & R Bostrom, 'An examination of managers' beliefs about their roles as facilitators of learning', *Management Learning*, vol. 33, no. 2, 2002, pp. 147–79.
10. ibid.
11. Some of this sequence is based on J Burdett, 'Forty things every manager should know about coaching', *Journal of Management Development*, vol. 17, no. 2, 1998, pp. 142–152.

CHAPTER 19

Developing teams
Team-building

Teams have become a staple in many organisations. The language of management now comfortably includes teams, teamwork and team-building. After 20 years of being fashionable, the idea can no longer be called a fad. However, this does not mean that we are much clearer about the process of bringing a group of people together and creating a level of cooperation that produces results over and above what the members of the team could have created individually. And we are even less clear about what it takes to build a team.

This is partially because the team concept has been over-hyped and over-sold. Once it had been launched on to an unsuspecting but trusting business world in the late 1980s, it was rapidly found to have a number of serious drawbacks. Organisations experimenting with the team concept soon discovered that teams take time, teams can fail, not everyone wants to work in teams, not every manager wants to rely on teams, team accountability is a slippery concept, teams vary in effectiveness, and that teams are a slow mechanism for dealing with a crisis. Yet there were enough gains to keep the concept popular. And it helps that it is almost unpatriotic to be against teams!

Today, you are likely to find teams at many levels in an organisation—management teams, project teams, problem-solving teams, work teams and many other forms. Although each of these instances of the team concept involves unique elements, there are also a few core characteristics that make them similar. In one of the better best-selling books on teams, Jon Katzenbach and Douglas Smith define a team as:

> A small group of people with complementary skills who are committed to a common purpose, performance goals, and approach for which they hold themselves accountable.[1]

This often-quoted definition continues to inform much of the discussion about teams and it provides a useful description for recognising a team. It also provides a simple formula for turning a group into a team. If managers work with their teams and ensure that the key elements of that definition are put in place, then there is a good chance that the team will be successful. Each of these elements (membership, skills, purpose, performance goals, approach, accountability) can be put in place by using a specific set of techniques developed by various specialists (consultants, trainers and facilitators and the like) who have worked extensively with teams in a developmental capacity.

This chapter provides a small selection of those techniques, sufficient for any manager wanting to create teams in their workplace. Each mini-technique is designed to obtain a specific outcome and has been included on the basis that it can be applied quickly and effectively. Although teams develop only over time (and some types of teams need a long time to become a real team), putting the foundations in place does not demand a great deal of time or effort.

Background

The process of helping teams to become established and to develop their effectiveness is generally called *team-building*. There is no agreed definition of team-building. Just for once, that probably does not matter because we can use the expression as an umbrella term for all those activities (consultants like to call them 'interventions') that are designed to induce a higher level of 'teamness'. (And, no, I'm not going to try to define that term either!) What really matters is the effectiveness of those activities.

Which activities actually work in helping a team to become a more effective team? This is where things get murky. Despite many decades of research about team-building activities of all sorts, there is little evidence that backs up their effectiveness. We have many claims about effectiveness from all sorts of interested parties, but mainly those with a commercial stake in the question. A legion of team trainers, a host of authors and a plague of consulting organisations claim to know how to improve the effectiveness of teams. But very few can provide evidence to back their claims.[2] What's more, we still have only anecdotal evidence that teams actually can and do perform in a superior manner to a collection of individuals or even just one individual.[3] Personal experience, client references and passionate statements of belief are usually substituted for good research.

It's easy to be critical of the team industry for not being based on good research. In reality, doing research on teams is extremely difficult. Even the most obvious elements of the research present problems when you want to study them seriously. For example, what is high performance in teams? Is it when teams achieve their outcomes? Or is it when team members feel they are part of an effective team? Or is it both? But then how do you compare team task performance to those same tasks being performed by an individual or a group of individuals? Should the tasks be difficult before a team can claim the title of 'high performing'?

What we do have from the research are some bits and pieces that, when replicated, have been shown to have a demonstrable impact on team performance. And we can glean a few other bits from the general observations of researchers who specialise in the field of team research. From another perspective, there is also a fair bit of knowledge about what does not work and why teams fail or fall short of the mark. And although all this may seem hazy, by focusing on these few bits we can at least stay in the land of the probable.

As Richard Hackman (Professor at Harvard University and one of the most experienced researchers in the field) observed:

> The more common reason for substandard group performance is that managers make serious mistakes in designing, supporting, and leading teams. Too often they gather some people together (a lot of people so that the team has plenty of resources and all stakeholders are represented), toss it a task, and hope for the best. That's not good enough! Research evidence is now starting to identify the organizational conditions that must be in place for a team to have a real chance for effectiveness, and these conditions have much to do with structural and contextual features that cannot be implemented through mere exhortations. Creating the conditions for team effectiveness, it turns out, requires that managers know some things and know how to do some things.[4]

In the next section I outline what managers must do. But first, here is a list of what I think managers need to know.[5]

1. *Handle your team carefully.* Teams are fragile entities at the best of time. Use a sensitive approach to the individuals in the team—each member is likely to have particular needs that must be accommodated within the team. To contribute to a team, people have to want to contribute. Your job as team manager is to encourage them to want to contribute. If that seems too big a challenge, don't use the team concept; instead, use the more traditional approach of setting objectives for individuals (see Chapter 11, Managing performance: Goal-setting).
2. *Assume that people want to make things work.* In assembling the team, use those people who will want to contribute and who want the team to succeed. Thereafter, trust them to do their best. If you don't trust them, why put them on the team? Really stupid reasons for putting people on teams include that it will turn conscripts into volunteers,

and that it will turn egomaniacs into team-players. It won't. It will simply wreck the team. So select the best people for the team task and trust them to do the right thing.

3. *When things go wrong, fix problems rather than blame people.* Many things can and do go wrong in teams. When they do, find out what went wrong and then try to fix it. It really doesn't matter who caused the problem. Instead focus on how the problem was caused, and fix the cause. You can do this by asking questions. The more team members believe you are looking for causes and not for someone to blame, the more they will help you find those causes. It is your approach that drives the extent of open communication between you and the team, and also within the team.

4. *Focus on behaviours, not (perceived) attitudes.* People sometimes do the wrong things in teams. Sometimes, they behave inappropriately. When this happens, deal with the behaviour. Don't make assumptions about why the behaviour occurred, for example, by using abstract notions such as personality or attitude. You can't see those things so ignore them. Deal with the actual behaviour. If that relates to a single member of the team, consider dealing with it privately. If it concerns the behaviour of the whole team, then use a team meeting to deal with it. But always make it about the behaviour and never about the person.

5. *Focus on the outcome and on the process.* As the manager, you may have to mandate the outcomes for the team. (It actually works better if you can involve the team in setting the outcomes, but that is not always possible.) At least make sure the team understand why the outcomes are important and satisfy yourself that they do understand what the outcomes are. That means you need to hear them reflect their understanding of the outcomes back to you—they need to do the talking here. You must also focus on the processes the team will use to achieve the outcomes. This is no different from setting objectives with individuals and then monitoring how they go about achieving those objectives.

6. *Pick problems that suit the team approach.* Not every problem is suitable for a team approach. Some are better solved by an individual or divided up amongst a group of individuals. Here are some criteria for judging whether a problem is suitable for a team approach:
   - the task is complex
   - creativity is needed to tackle the task
   - the way forward in tackling the task is unclear
   - a team approach seems an efficient way to tackle the task (for example the task requires many different perspectives to resolve successfully)
   - fast learning is needed to tackle the task
   - a high level of commitment is required
   - implementation requires the involvement of many
   - the task requires cross-functional input.[6]

7. *Teach people how to solve problems.* Teams and team members don't necessarily know how to solve problems. The chances are that you will have more knowledge about problem-solving approaches and tools than they do, so teach them. You can suggest approaches to solving problems that still leave the team in charge. For example, it is always a good first step to do data-gathering and Pareto analysis (see Chapter 10, Solving problems: Pareto analysis). Show them how without doing the task for them.

8. *Be clear about purpose, roles, boundaries and resources.* If you're not clear about the work of the team then the team won't be clear either. Take the trouble to check that you are clear about the purpose of the team. For example, write down the team's purpose and have someone else check whether their understanding is the same as yours. Then make sure that the team understand what their role is. Make sure the team understand the constraints and the boundaries within which they must do their work. Make sure there is complete clarity about the resources that the team can draw on (see Chapter 17, Involving employees: Problem-solving teams, for more detail).

9. *Teams are a mechanism for getting a result, not an end in themselves.* Teams are never the end; they are always a means. Those who argue for teams because teams are 'good' are simply falling under the spell of 'team magic'—and there is nothing magical about teams. The team concept is just a tool that can be used to deal with certain tasks. It is not the answer to every situation or every problem. Use teams judiciously and not indiscriminately. Be highly selective in using this tool.

The tool

Team-building interventions come in all shapes and sizes—from intensive outdoor training exercises where people hang off cliffs on ropes and go white-water rafting, to simple suggestions by management. The handful of interventions outlined below lean towards the latter; I can find no research evidence that the ropes and rafts approach actually works in creating more effective teams (see the 'Observations' section later in the chapter). The modest idea is that managers can set up their teams for success and then provide some assistance to keep the team on track.

It is very difficult to gauge the minimum interventions that a manager must make to ensure team success. There are simply too many variables that impact on team effectiveness to be sure about any one. (One of the leading researchers on team effectiveness suggests that at least 17 distinct variables influence it.[7]) So the issue is how to make this complexity manageable. One way is to concentrate on those variables that are known to have the greatest impact. Although I am not aware of anyone actually carrying out a Pareto analysis to determine this precisely, it seems from the literature that the following six have the greatest impact:

1. membership
2. purpose
3. skills
4. performance goals
5. approach
6. accountability.

Membership

The first step in building a team is to assemble its component parts—the team members. When considering the team's membership you must think about three things: size, background and attitude.

- *Size.* When it comes to teams, size matters. Keep the numbers as small as possible. Err on the side of smaller rather than larger. Fewer works better with almost all teams. The actual number is probably driven by the size of the task that the team will be working on.
- *Background.* This is about the type of individuals that you want to put on the team. Teams need diversity to work well. If you have a team of five people and all of them have similar backgrounds and the same sort of approach to handling tasks, then you risk getting the 'group think' phenomenon where everyone thinks alike.[8] This will hinder the working of the team, especially if the task demands a bit of creativity or innovation. Part of the background is the skills that each member brings to the team (see the 'Skills' section later in the chapter for more detail).
- *Attitude.* This relates to whether people actually want to be on the team or, for that matter, on any team. Some people are not comfortable with the team approach to tackling tasks. Some may well prefer the more traditional approach where their tasks are structured just for them, without the confusion of involving shared responsibility. The point is that there is little point in putting someone on a team who doesn't want to be there. Teamwork requires volunteers, not conscripts.

Purpose

Having assembled the right membership (that is, a small group of different types of people who want to work on a team basis), the next step in building the team is to ensure that they understand what the team's purpose is. This means that first the manager needs to be clear about the purpose.

Managers are notoriously over-confident in estimating the clarity of their own understanding and their capacity to make things clear to others. There is only one relevant criterion here: do the members of the team understand what they have to do? This means that the manager needs to work to that criterion. There is nothing worse than a manager claiming to have explained the purpose repeatedly. What matters is if the purpose is understood, not whether it has been explained several times.

One way to test for clarity of understanding is to have the team members explain the purpose to the manager. The team members need to use their own words to explain what they are being asked to do. If necessary, make this a formal part of the team establishment process. The formality could consist of making the team do a presentation to a management group on their understanding of their purpose. Another approach is for the team to provide the manager with a written version of their understanding of the purpose. For example, if the team is a 'problem-solving team', then the documentation used to scope the work of the team can provide the opportunity to ensure a common understanding of the purpose (see Chapter 17, Involving employees: Problem-solving teams).

One critical aspect of the purpose is that it must require the team to work together in order to achieve it. If this condition is not present, then there is actually very little reason for the team approach to be deployed. Further, a high degree of 'goal interdependence' (the extent to which all team members need to work together to achieve a result) actually drives up the level of teamwork. More interdependence makes teamwork more likely. Much the same applies to the actual tasks performed by the team. If the tasks require close cooperation and sharing of workload ('task interdependence'), this will assist team effectiveness. Teams with high levels of goal and task interdependence are more likely to evolve into effective teams.

Skills

Skills matter because, if the team do not have the capacity to manage either the task itself or the team processes necessary for teamwork, or both, then they are unlikely to be an effective team.

Most managers have a good idea of the technical capabilities of the people they put on to a team. Often, this is a key reason for selecting particular people in the first place. But they are usually less aware of the team skills that are needed to make a team work, and whether those skills are present within the team.

The team skills that are needed to make a team work effectively together will vary according to the membership of the team. If the team members are experienced people who have previously worked in teams, then there may be less need to check the level of team skills. If the team members are unfamiliar with the concept of teamwork, then there may be a need to train members in the required skills.

The exact skills the team need will vary according to their tasks, but some basic skills include:

- managing meetings
- making decisions

- managing participation
- agreeing behaviour rules
- managing disagreement.

Performance goals

As well as understanding their purpose, the team need to understand the meaning of success for them. Success will vary with the task, and success also involves how the task is achieved.

Most teams consider themselves successful only if they achieve the required outcomes *and* if they generate a high degree of satisfaction in achieving those outcomes. This combination—high performance and high satisfaction—is the key to high-performing teams. Therefore, the team need to work to a set of performance goals that derive from the purpose, but are the smaller steps that contribute to achieving the purpose. Each step should represent progress towards team success, whether the milestone relates to the way the team do their work or to what the team have achieved in terms of outcomes.

Performance goals vary dramatically with the type of team:

- Work teams perform best with a scorecard system that reflects the various performance indicators that relate to the work of the team.
- Project teams work best if they can work to a sequence of milestones.
- Management teams work best to performance goals that derive from regular self-assessment by the team as to how they are performing.

Approach

How the team approach the work that they do impacts on their performance. If the workload is shared around the team, this will help team effectiveness. This in turn requires that there is a reasonable level of flexibility within the team. If the team members are highly specialised experts, each working individually to obtain a collective result, do not expect a high degree of teamwork. If, on the other hand, there is considerable sharing of work, with a high degree of backup, overlap and support, then teamwork will be more evident.

Whether or not the team are using the right approach for any given task will become obvious through their style and methods of communication. All members should have a stake in the success of the team. The language used should be that of 'we' not 'I'. The manager only needs to listen to this type of language cue to pick up whether the team are truly taking a collective approach.

Accountability

Accountability in teams is often the greatest concern for management. There is a belief that teams can never be held accountable, and that non-performing team members hide behind those who are pulling their weight. This furphy seems to spring from the fact that managers have to manage more remotely when working with teams.

Micro-management is both pointless and difficult when managing a team of people. Managers who are comfortable with letting teams get on with it once all the other elements have been put in place rarely worry about this kind of accountability issue. What is important is that there is clarity about what the manager is accountable for and what the team are accountable for (see Chapter 12, Enabling others: Empowerment, for some useful techniques for clarifying the grey areas of accountability).

The critical thing about the accountability issue is that it is clarified—problems are caused by lack of understanding more than anything else. The manager may need to 'formalise' who is accountable for what. Potentially difficult areas of accountability can usually be spotted well in advance for any given team task.

Shared accountability is rarely a problem within a team, and if a particular area of team activities presents problems, then the manager can always step in and help clarify matters. Worst-case scenario—the manager negotiates with the team to take back specific accountabilities in areas that are difficult for the team to handle.

Observations

Team-building has a bad name in some quarters. This has a lot to do with the fact that it has attracted a range of advocates who have proceeded to give it a poor reputation through their actions. In particular, two groups stand out.

The first is the outdoor training brigade, whose members advocate a diverse range of adventure-type activities that are supposed to bring out the best in people and turn a motley crew into a high-performing team. There is not a shred of evidence to suggest that any of this works.[9] In fact, there is significant evidence that it does not. It may be a lot of fun but it has little impact on work groups that must return to the workplace to do real work. Following the question posed by the title of one recent article, 'Outdoor training—corporate jolly or valuable development tool', it is safe to bet on 'corporate jolly'.[10]

The other group advocates the use of experiential learning as a team-building technique. Experiential learning is a more complicated bundle of approaches to team-building and development. The basic idea is that groups of people will learn to become teams by going through a series of learning activities that help them figure out what being a team is all about. Some of this stuff works, especially when the learning exercise closely resembles what happens in teams. The problems start when they do not, or when the trainers introduce elements that team members find intrusive or unacceptable. My favourite incident was the football team that indulged in a spot of 'hot coal walking' to inspire them to greater team effort, only to have several members burn their feet so badly they could not play for several weeks!

Some of this team development approach is driven by what the training industry calls the Tuckman model of team development.[11] It is based on research that suggests that teams go through four distinct stages of development, summed up in the phrase 'forming–storming–norming–performing'. The idea is that if managers (or facilitators) can recognise these stages, they can then respond appropriately to help the team work their way through that stage to the 'performing' stage. Although it has been a bit difficult to operationalise the idea, it remains very popular with trainers. From a practical point of view, it is difficult to gauge accurately when a group is in one stage or another. The idea that a facilitator can actively push a group through these stages has not received much empirical support. The Tuckman model is generally accepted as offering a useful insight into group development, but it offers little to the busy manager working with teams on a day-to-day basis.

User's guide

What can managers do to build their teams? The six areas identified are probably a good starting point. If managers attend to the issues that relate to membership, purpose, skills, approach, performance goals and accountability, then at least they are giving their teams a good start. What's more, we know that if these issues are not attended to, then problems will ensue.

Over and above these issues, you can make it up as you go along. If you think the team need to celebrate progress or success, organise something. If you think the team would benefit from some team games that explore issues about team dynamics, there is little risk in arranging some activity. Just make sure you cover the basics.

Instructions

How to build a team

Steps in the team-building process:

1. *Membership*

   - Consider the nature of the team task and select team members on the basis of background (including relevant skills) and attitude.
   - Decide the minimum number of people required to complete the task.

2. *Purpose*

   - Write a purpose statement for the team.

- Check that this purpose can be achieved by the team.
- Check for clarity by:
  - getting a second opinion from another manager
  - seeking feedback from the team.
- Ask the team to reflect back to you their understanding of the team purpose.

3. *Skills*

- Write a list of all the skills (technical and team skills) that need to be represented in the team so that they can undertake the team tasks.
- If not all required skills are represented in the team, decide if training is required (which team members and which skills?).
- Arrange access to supplementary skills (for example, experts who can be consulted on technical issues or team facilitators who can assist with team process issues).

4. *Performance goals*

- Discuss and agree with the team the success measures and the timeline (if required).
- Discuss reporting procedures with the team (for example, frequency and level of detail).
- Give the team feedback on their performance.

5. *Approach*

- Explain your expectations about the way the team will plan and execute its work.
- Observe team planning and execution, and intervene as required.
- Arrange for team facilitators to provide support if required.

6. *Accountability*

- Discuss the issue of accountability, especially shared accountabilities, and explain your expectations.
- Discuss and agree resource implications and explain sources of support.
- Encourage the team to agree on specific roles and accountabilities.
- Decide the follow-up schedule and inform the team of your expectations.

Further reading

If you want a good read on teams that covers almost every type of team, try:

- J Katzenbach & D Smith, *The wisdom of teams: Creating the high performance organization*, McGraw-Hill, New York, 1993.

  This book is very readable and is based on dozens of small case studies that document how teams work or don't work.

If you're looking for more ideas on how to work with a team as a manager (or in some other capacity), try:

- K Fisher, S Rayner & W Belgard, *Tips for teams*, McGraw-Hill, New York, 1995.

This book is exactly what the title suggests—a compendium of hundreds of smart ideas for interventions designed to make teams work more effectively.

Notes

1. J Katzenbach & D Smith, *The wisdom of teams: Creating the high performance organization*, McGraw-Hill, New York, 1993.
2. As long ago as 1981, researchers reviewing the evidence on team-building found that: 'A review of the literature on team building used these criteria for selection: 1. The article described a team-building intervention in an existing organization. 2. Team building was the only intervention. 3. The researchers provided information on the participants and methods of evaluation. Team building was reported effective in an overwhelming majority of cases. However, most studies contained weaknesses in research methods and measurements. Weaknesses included: 1. Use of pre-experimental designs, 2. Use of too few subjects, 3. Exclusive use of perceptual dependent variables, 4. Brief evaluation periods, 5. Use of a change agent as evaluator, 6. Use of team building as one of many interventions, and 7. Lack of an operational definition of team building.' (K De Meuse & L Liebowitz, 'An empirical analysis of team-building research', *Group & Organization Management*, vol. 6, no. 3, 1981, pp. 357–78.) Since that time, according to recent research, little has improved.
3. A Church, 'From both sides now—the power of teamwork', *The Industrial-Organizational Psychologist*, vol. 34, no. 2, 1996, pp. 85–96.
4. ibid., p. 93.
5. Some of these observations derive from K Fisher, S Rayner & W Belgard, *Tips for teams*, McGraw-Hill, New York, 1995.
6. Based on P Castka, C Bamber, J Sharp & P Belohoubek, 'Factors affecting successful implementation of high performance teams', *Team Performance Management*, vol. 7, no. 7/8, 2001, pp. 123–34.
7. M Campion, 'Relations between work team characteristics and effectiveness: A replication and extension', *Personnel Psychology*, vol. 49, no. 2, 1996, pp. 429–52. See also M Campion & C Higgs, 'Design work teams to increase productivity and satisfaction', *HR Magazine*, Oct 1995.
8. J Eaton, 'Management communication: the threat of groupthink', *Corporate Communication*, vol. 6, no. 4, 2001, pp. 183–92.
9. See, for example, S William, S Graham & B Baker, 'Evaluating outdoor experiential training for leadership and team building', *The Journal of Management Development*, vol. 22, no. 1, 2003, pp.45–59; T Keller & W Olson, 'The advisability of outdoor leadership training: caveat emptor', *Review of Business*, vol. 21, no. 1/2, 2000, pp. 4–6.

10. J Payne, 'Outdoor training—corporate jolly or valuable development tool?', *Training & Management Development Methods*, vol. 14, no. 1, 2000, pp. 601–10.
11. B Tuckman, 'Developmental sequence in small groups', *Psychological Bulletin*, vol. 63, no. 6, 1965, pp. 334–99.

CHAPTER 20

Managing time
Time-management techniques

Time management is one of those practical concepts that turns out to be a bit elusive when you try to put it into effect. The idea of improving your personal productivity (that is, getting more things done in the time available) is rather compelling and virtually sells itself to time-poor managers. But the discipline required to put time-management prescriptions into effect can be a bit overwhelming. Anyone reading the standard list of time traps and their solutions is likely to get tired just thinking about all the things you have to do. It sounds like more work, not less!

Like most self-improvement ideas, time management simply demands too much behaviour change. We are creatures of habit and changing the habits of a lifetime is far more difficult than most people imagine; people usually discover this only when they try to do it. The New Year's resolution is traditionally honoured by breaking it within days of making it. The same applies to work situations. Changing managerial behaviour is difficult even if managers know why they should change, how to change and the direction in which to change.

The answer to this conundrum seems to be to keep the change very simple and very small. In behaviour change, modesty and simplicity seem to work best. Adopting new time-saving behaviours should involve very few and very small steps. Grand plans simply do not work. Although hard research is a bit difficult to come by (and is completely overwhelmed by the marketing activities of the prescription sellers), what there is suggests that small first steps are better than grand intentions.

However, this still leaves the question of which small steps actually work best. This is largely a matter of judgment as there is little research into this question. Getting long-term commitment to behavioural change is difficult, but it seems to work best if managers select a technique that suits them. The real test is whether the manager is more likely or less likely to adopt the time-saving behaviour as a habit. Although self-selection is often risky, I don't know what other approach we can use to achieve behaviour change in relation to time management. All of which is a complicated way of saying: 'Dear reader—it's up to you'. If that sounds like a cop-out then please note that one of the few pieces of research in this area suggests that time-management training works only with managers who are committed to making a change before the training takes place.[1] It really is up to you!

Background

Time management invites more prescriptive advice than almost any other aspect of management. For reasons unknown, giving managers advice on how to manage their most valuable resource—their time—has attracted a larger than usual collection of self-appointed experts. Time management has spawned everything from training programs that are thinly disguised sales events for expensive diaries to the ever-longer and ever-more-impressive lists of handy time-management tips in magazines and journals.

Most of this advice is driven by the idea that managers generally feel guilty about not getting enough work done in the normal working day. The pressure to perform is unrelenting and the idea that somehow they might be able to squeeze a little more out of each day is a terribly attractive notion to those under pressure. It has reached the point where it seems some managers spend more time planning their time and worrying about how well they manage it than they do actually getting things done.

What really cranked up the pressure was the publication of Steven Covey's *The seven habits of highly effective people* in 1989.[2] Covey pulled together some of the best ideas around on how to manage yourself. His theme was personal productivity and the habits were a distillation of the best ideas for achieving high levels of it. And, of course, time management is an integral part of personal productivity. Covey's book became a run-away best-seller, with over 20 million copies sold in the last 10 years (which only encouraged him to write another book two years later, *Principle centered leadership*[3], which sold almost as many; closely followed by sequels to the first book, such as *First things first*[4]).

As already noted, research is a bit thin on the ground when it comes to time management. Although much is published, most of it is repetitive material that focuses on time saving ideas. The research that has been done suggests that many approaches to time management simply do not work. For example, it is very popular to tackle the issue of better time management through training. (I confess that such training was the very first that I ever conducted as a trainer, some quarter of a century ago, in the firm belief that it would transform the behaviour of my trainees; it didn't.)

Training people in time-management techniques seems to have little impact on their behaviour. What it does affect is how the participants *think* they manage their time. For example, one piece of research found that a two-day professionally conducted time-management course significantly improved participants' belief that they used their time more effectively. Objective data collected over the duration of the experiment found that their time use was actually similar to what it had been before the course. Commitment surveys taken before the experiment found the same thing (that is, a general belief that time management had improved when in reality it had not) regardless of whether people were strongly committed to the idea of improving their time management or not.[5]

Other research backs up these findings that time-management training is not very effective in changing managerial behaviour.[6] The problem seems to be that we don't have a good understanding of how people deal with tasks. After all, time management is really about task management. Recent research is starting to show that different people deal with tasks in very different ways. For example, some people like to handle tasks in a linear way, with one task being completed before another one is started.[7] Other people prefer to juggle their time between a series of tasks, flitting backwards and forwards from one task to another. In case you need to know, the first type is called a 'monochron' and the second a 'polychron'!

It seems that these two very different approaches to managing tasks and time each have their advantages. The point, however, is that each type of person needs a different strategy for improving their time management. Polychrons easily handle interruptions so they don't need to be trained in how to avoid them; monochrons do benefit from training in how to manage interruptions to their linear ways of working. Most importantly, when the two types work together, they may need to be trained to recognise each other's strengths and weaknesses, and use each other to full advantage. If nothing else, they need to learn how to avoid the conflict that arises from the two different approaches. If you are a polychron working for a monochron manager, you'd better figure out how to manage his linear expectations about the best way to get work done!

The absence of sound research has allowed the management prescription industry to make claim after claim that is unsupported by evidence. For example, it is very popular to suggest that a neat and tidy work area is more productive than a messy one. This idea has been repeated so many times that it has become an apparent fact, simply through repetition.[8] There simply is no evidence to suggest that this is the case. In fact, every time we go down the road of 'one best way', research eventually proves us wrong and we end up having to accept that there is always more than one way to skin a cat. As someone who prefers a messy office (and I know it when someone messes up my mess!), I am irritated by the gratuitous advice of the time-management industry that I should only handle a document once and keep my desk as tidy as possible. I will clean up my desk the day someone can show me the research that proves that it is more productive.

One of the best and most practical pieces of research I have seen focuses on how managers use their time.[9] This is important because, if we know what managers spend their time on, we can work out where the biggest gains can be found in managing time well. The researcher reviewed all the available (empirical) studies on this topic (surprisingly few—only 25 studies between 1963 and 1990). Some of these studies involved managers answering simple surveys, giving estimates of how they spend their time. This is known to generate unreliable data; managers both overestimate and underestimate when they rely on their memories. A more reliable method is to use a diary system where managers complete entries on their activities at set time intervals; this approach is called work sampling. If we take out of the research list all those that are survey-based, and include only those that used the more reliable method of work sampling, we are left with seven studies.

Although there are many interesting observations that arise from the review of the work-sampling studies (for example, managers worked far fewer hours than suggested by the data from studies using self-reporting), the conclusions that are relevant to time management demonstrate that managers spend:

- about 50% of their time in meetings
- more time in scheduled meetings than unscheduled meetings
- between 25% and 30% of their time on desk work
- about 6% of their time on the telephone
- about half their working time in their offices
- about a quarter of their time in other people's offices.

This information is very useful in making decisions about where to spend the time-management effort. If we know where managers spend their time, then we can figure out where an improvement factor will have the greatest impact. Getting more efficient at something you do only rarely is hardly worthwhile. Two criteria are relevant here. Firstly, is the activity under the control of the manager? Secondly, what kind of activity, if managed better from a time point of view, would generate the greatest payback? The following priority areas result from this bit of analysis:

- scheduled and unscheduled meetings
- desk work in own office
- any activity in someone else's office.

To make this clearer, a 10% improvement factor in managing these three activities would generate about 10% more available time overall.

If a manager handles these three activities only a bit more efficiently then she is likely to get a return of about an extra hour a day.

What this also means is that managers should stop focusing on gimmicky time-management tactics, such as only answering the telephone at set times, taking lunch at a time different from everyone else, or sorting the mail while standing up near the rubbish bin.[10] Time management is about managing meetings, managing desk activities and controlling activities that happen in other people's offices. The rest you don't need to worry about.

The tool

Three areas of managerial activity hold the greatest promise of productivity improvement: *meetings*; *desk work*; and *activities that happen in other people's offices*. Time management techniques pay their way when they help managers do these activities more efficiently. Most of the techniques that are likely to impact on these three areas demand a degree of discipline. Basically, the discipline is needed to change habitual behaviour. The following techniques all involve doing something a little (but not a lot) differently.

Managing meetings

Most managers know that meetings consume a significant proportion of their work time. Most also complain that the meetings they attend are less efficient than they could be. Most do nothing about this. That's where the change comes in. To improve the efficiency of meetings somebody needs to do something differently.

There are three broad strategies for improving meeting efficiency: better process, fewer meetings and shorter meetings. Each of these strategies requires a different level of action, but even the strategy requiring most action only asks managers to do a bit more of the things that they already do.

Better process

Most meetings amble along at their own pace because no-one is actually managing the pace. Even with agendas in hand, there is little guarantee that the participants will stick to the agenda, deal with items quickly, or even turn up for the meeting on time or at all. So the challenge is to manage the meeting process. Most organisations have a traditional way of handling meetings. If you want your meetings to be conducted a little more efficiently, you may have to challenge some of these traditions.

For example, what constitutes lateness for a meeting varies from organisation to organisation and even from national culture to national culture. If you think 'late starts' are holding back the efficiency of your meetings, raise the issue and encourage the participants to agree on some principles. This may well be as simple as agreeing that being 10 minutes late is not OK.

If your meetings are hampered by some other aspects of the meeting process, the strategy is exactly the same. Raise the issue and get the participants to agree on some principle that will address that issue. For example, you may decide to agree on time limits for any item under discussion, to set aside any item unless it is supported by a briefing paper, to refuse to discuss items of business that are not on the agenda, and so on. The idea is to focus on the process that is holding back meeting efficiency and then raise the issue in order to make an explicit decision on that process.

This strategy is exactly what is achieved in some meetings when a professional facilitator is engaged to help conduct the meeting. The facilitator focuses on process and makes interventions when necessary to ensure that the meeting is conducted efficiently. By adopting the same strategy, any participant can help improve meeting efficiency at any time.

Fewer meetings

Many meetings are unnecessary. Some meetings occur simply because it is a regular event, regardless of whether there is business to transact or not. If meeting time is available, someone will find a way of filling it. Any 'standing' meeting, whether daily, weekly or monthly, should be reviewed for utility on a regular basis. The question: 'Is this meeting really necessary?' is not asked often enough. It may take a bit of courage to ask the question but the answers are usually illuminating.

If you are responsible for calling the meeting, you have an even greater responsibility to check its usefulness. If a meeting is cancelled for any reason (for example, illness on the part of critical participants), use this as a reason to review the need for the meeting in the first place. In the extreme, cancel some meetings just to see what happens; in many cases, that will be nothing very much.

If people insist on having meetings, ask them to write a purpose statement for the meeting. As often as not, those insistent on having the meeting lose interest when asked to complete this minor formality.

Shorter meetings

Many meetings are actually excuses for something else. Common excuses include the failure to delegate effectively and the failure to accept individual accountability for decisions. Some people use the meeting process to 'spread the blame' for decisions.

One way of dealing with this is to suggest that only items that truly need group decisions should be put on the agenda. The need to make a group decision should be based on explicit criteria. Simply by asking those who supply agenda items to state the reasons for a group decision on the matter will reduce the number of items proposed. People will find it easier not to raise the issue than to explain why a group decision is needed.

Many meetings are simply communication sessions. That is, they are used to disseminate information and, sometimes, to discuss that information. Often, the meeting replicates some other mechanism, such as discussion papers, memos and corporate announcements, that is supposed to perform that function. Again, use the strategy of raising the inappropriate use of meeting time by asking the question: 'Can we handle this in a more effective way?'

Managing desk work

Many managers are inundated with desk work. Their in-trays bulge with paperwork to be dealt with. Briefcases are filled with piles of files that are taken home in the forlorn hope that some private time will be found to deal with them, only to be lugged back to the office the following day, still unread.

Although there are many suggestions made by time-management 'experts' on how to manage this daily grind, there are really only a few techniques that stand out. Probably the most useful technique is the *urgent vs. important grid* that is the backbone of the work of many time-management strategists, such as Merrill Douglass and Stephen Covey (see 'Further reading' at the end of the chapter). The idea is fairly simple. All those activities that take management time can be plotted into one of four quadrants, as shown in Figure 20.1.

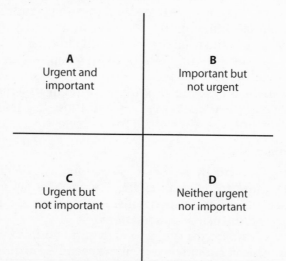

Figure 20.1 Productivity quadrants

Most managers are overwhelmed by the urgent (whether important or not) and end up paying less attention than they should to the important. Consequently, most of their activities end up in the two quadrants that involve urgency (A and C), crowding out some important stuff (B).

The challenge is to reduce the time spent on urgent stuff and make room for the important stuff that is sometimes overlooked. Essentially, this involves prioritisation of tasks. The simplest way is to make task lists and add an indicator of priority. The indicator should take note of importance as much as it does of urgency. This sort of approach at least ensures that there is a degree of balance in the time allocation.

Of course, other techniques can help as well, such as reducing the amount of time spent on the tasks (especially paperwork) and eliminating double-handling of paperwork. The technique of prioritisation may not reduce the workload, but at least it will ensure that the work that is done is the most value-adding work that the manager can do.

Managing activities in other people's offices

Managers are least productive when they are in other people's offices. This covers a host of activities that range from the completely counter-productive, such as interrupting a colleague to get some information that could be obtained by other means, to the completely productive, such as coaching someone in how to do their job more effectively. The trick is to know which activities lean towards one end of the scale and which towards the other.

First, it helps to know that the scale exists and that it provides a means of assessing whether a given activity is productive or not. Second, build in a bias towards productive activities by going out of your way to do them. Because you only have limited time for any type of activity (such as the type that involves going into other people's work spaces), you will inevitably end up doing more productive stuff. It will crowd out the non-productive stuff. If necessary, list all the productive things you do when you work with others in their work spaces. Keep the list in front of you. If something has to be done that is not on the list, reconsider it or at least delay it. Often enough, the need goes away!

Observations

Time management will probably never go away as a topic of interest for managers. Every now and again some new idea comes to the fore and makes an impression on the managerial mind. For example, the introduction of time-management diaries had a huge initial impact as it seemed like a good way to provide discipline in managing time. Those who were already inclined towards such discipline readily adopted the use of diaries. Those who were otherwise inclined did not bother.

Similarly, time-management training seems to have come and gone. It provided some people with ideas that helped their personal productivity. For others, it amounted to no more than an irritation that had to be tolerated because the boss made everyone attend. Much the same happens with the endless lists of time-management 'tips' that are still published on a regular basis in most professional magazines. The ad hoc nature of these lists is easily exposed when you compare a bunch of them and discover that what is listed as the number one time trap on one is not even listed on another. Most of these lists simply contain the personal preferences of the authors. And it does take a certain type of person to make lists of time saving ideas.

Nevertheless, you will find the occasional idea that strikes a chord in the sense that it seems to fit into your ways of doing things and, therefore, could easily be adopted. To that extent, the time-management industry will always have an audience, even if it is only those few who constantly seek ways to do things smarter.

User's guide

If time management is indeed about behaviour change, then you need to do something different. The real question is what will work for you—which is obviously a highly personal decision. The idea of placing a lock on the meeting room door to exclude anyone who arrives late for meetings will not appeal equally to all managers. The idea of having meetings standing up is acceptable in some workplaces but not in others. The idea that telephones should go unanswered for a set period each day would horrify some organisations while others would proclaim it a great step forward.

What can be said with some confidence is that, whichever ideas you decide to apply, it is worth focusing on the three areas already identified as having the greatest payback. If you do go through all the hassle of changing some aspect of your time-management behaviour, it might as well be in those areas that will have the greatest impact.

Change something—anything—about the way you manage meetings, manage your paperwork priorities, and manage what you do in other people's work spaces, and you will 'create more time'.

Instructions

How to improve time management

1. *Meetings*

   - Focus on improving meeting processes.
   - Get agreement on how to improve meeting processes.

- Review meeting necessity.
- Make meeting purpose explicit.
- Justify the need for group decisions.
- Look for alternatives to meetings for getting things done.

2. *Desk work*

- Rate all tasks and activities according to the urgent vs. important grid (for example: A—urgent and important; B—important but not urgent; C—urgent but not important; D—not urgent and not important).
- If it helps, use descriptive tags that emphasise the meaning of the rating (for example, A—absolute priority; B—neglected essentials; C—trivial hot potatoes; D—time wasters[11]).
- Review why you are doing anything with a D rating.
- Prioritise first with the ABCD rating, and then prioritise numerically each item within each rating to generate a sequence for tackling tasks.
- Eliminate double-handling of paperwork (for example, use the BARF system of four action options that relate to any piece of paper that comes your way: Bin; Act; Refer; File).
- Deal faster with the paperwork by changing how it is handled (for example, change from letter to memo; from memo to email; from email to phone call).
- Prioritise further as it suits your style:
  - today before tomorrow
  - strategic before operational
  - easy before hard
  - cheap before expensive
  - facts before opinions
  - customers before others
  - permanent fix before temporary fix
  - big impact before small impact.

3. *Activities that happen in other people's offices*

- Stay in your office unless you have a reason to go elsewhere.
- Remember the impact on others of you visiting them.
- List the productive things that require you to go elsewhere; if something crops up that is not on that list, delay it or don't do it or (last resort) add it to the list.
- Make scheduled visits only.
- Put limits on time spent with others.
- Maximise time use with key people by using agendas and checklists.

Further reading

On the assumption that just about every manager in the world has read Stephen Covey's *The seven habits of highly effective people* (how else do we explain sales of 20 million!), I feel obliged to suggest something else. Covey's book is a great book but it is not the only one to tackle the matter of personal productivity, nor was it the first. Many of the ideas in Covey's book can be found in:

- M Douglass & D Douglass, *Manage your time, manage your work, manage yourself*, AMACOM, New York, 1980.

This book appeared about 10 years before *Seven habits*. Meryl and Donna Douglass provide a different take on some of the core personal productivity ideas covered by Covey (such as the 'important vs. urgent' grid). They offer a very practical approach to time-management issues and provide pragmatic and sensible advice; somewhat in contrast to the 'inspirational tone' that is Covey's hallmark.

This book is particularly useful if you want to work with other people on time-management issues; it is truly a handbook of ideas, tactics, techniques and tips for managing yourself, especially in the workplace.

Notes

1. C Orpen, 'Teaching time management skills', *Training and Management Development Methods*, vol. 14, no. 1, 2000, pp. 201–6.
2. S Covey, *The seven habits of highly effective people*, Simon & Schuster, New York, 1989.
3. S Covey, *Principle centered leadership*, Summit Books, New York, 1991.
4. S Covey, *First things first*, Simon & Schuster, New York, 1994.
5. G Slaven & P Totterdell, 'Time management training: does it transfer to the workplace?', *Journal of Managerial Psychology*, vol. 8, no. 1, 1993, pp. 20–8.
6. See T Macan, 'Time-management training: effects on time behaviors, attitudes, and job performance', *The Journal of Psychology*, vol. 130, no. 3, 1996, pp. 229–36.
7. C Kaufman-Scarborough & J Lindquist, 'Time management and polychronicity', *Journal of Managerial Psychology*, vol. 14, no. 34, 1999, pp. 288–312.
8. See, for example, D Knight, 'Secrets of time management', *Office Solutions*, vol. 19, no. 4, 2002, p. 21.
9. T Oshagbemi, 'Management development and managers' use of time', *Journal of Management Development*, vol. 14, no. 8, 1995, pp. 19–34.
10. D Abernathy, 'A get-real guide to time management', *Training & Development*, June 1999, pp. 22–6.
11. J Nicholls, 'The Ti-Mandi Window: a time management tool for managers', *Industrial and Commercial Training*, vol. 33, no. 3, 2001, pp. 104–8.

Index

Page numbers in **bold** print refer to main entries